WOMEN AND GUERRILLA MOVEMENTS

WOMEN & GUERRILLA MOVEMENTS

Nicaragua, El Salvador, Chiapas, Cuba

Karen Kampwirth

The Pennsylvania State University Press | University Park, Pennsylvania

Library of Congress Cataloging-in-Publication Data

Kampwirth, Karen, 1964–
　　Women and guerilla movements : Nicaragua, El Salvador, Chiapas, Cuba / Karen Kampwirth.
　　　　p.　　　cm.
　　Includes bibliographical references and index.
　　ISBN 0-271-02185-3 (cloth : alk. paper)
　　1. Women in politics—Latin America.　2. Women revolutionaries—Latin America—Interviews.　I. Title.

HQ1236.5.L37 K35 2002
305.42′098—dc21　　　　　　　　　　　　　　　　　　　　　　　　　　　　　　2002005322

It is the policy of The Pennsylvania State University Press to use acid-free paper for the first printing of all clothbound books. Publications on uncoated stock satisfy the minimum requirements of American National Standard for Information Sciences—Permanence of Paper for Printed Library Materials, ANSI Z39.48–1992.

Contents

Acknowledgments

A project like this book, which is the result of more than a decade's work, is invariably an example of what Latin Americans call "trabajo de hormigas," or "ants' work." It is unfair for me to take sole credit for something that would have never happened without the cooperation of many individuals, all contributing their parts to the anthill. First and foremost, I am grateful to the hundreds of Latin American women, and scores of Latin American men, who helped me out, generously sharing their time and knowledge, sometimes even taking me into their homes.

To the following citizens or residents of Nicaragua, I owe a great deal: Angela Rosa Acevedo, Agnes (Xochiquetzal), Raquel Aguirre, Humberto Aragón Morales, don Manuel Aragón, doña Teodora Morales de Aragón, and the whole Aragón Morales Fong family, Klemen Altamirano, Danilo Barrios, Maribel Arostegui Bravo, Gladys Baez, Amy Bank, Blanca (CST), María Teresa Blandón, María Lourdes Bolaños, Alan Bolt, Mary Bolt, Berta Inés Cabrales, Elizabeth Castro de Velásquez, doña Elena Cajina de Quiñónez, Lupita Cárdenas, Silvia Carrazco, Amalia Chamorro, Georgina Cordón, Ana Criquillion, Mirna Cunningham, José Dávila, Violeta Delgado, César Escobar, Yolanda Espinoza, Ana Esquivel, Rosa Julia Esquivel, Alan Fajarda, Fatima (ISNIM), Azucena Ferrey, Mario Flores, Hazel Fonseca, Briceyda Fuentes, Idalia García, Luis and Veronica González, Violeta Granera de Sandino, Dora Herrera, doña Laura and Nancy, Patricia Lindo, Carla López, María Isabel López, Rosa Argentina López, Rosalio López, Marvin Marenco, Arle Martínez, Julio Martínez, Tania Mairena, Marcos Membreño, Lesbia Mendieta, Nora Meneses, Donald Méndez, Juan José Montenegro, Sofía Montenegro, Vanexa Moralla Mora, Zoilamérica Narvaez, Reinaldo Núñez, Gloria Ordóñez, Ligia Orozco, Patricia Orozco, Pedro Ortega Méndez, Alba Palacios, Dina Palacios, Andrea Pérez, Paola Pérez Alemán, María Auxiliadora Pérez de

Matus, Elena Quiñónez Cajina and the whole Quiñónez Cajina family, Mario Quintana, Ana Quirós, Carolina Ramírez, doña Esperanza de Ramos, don Joaquín Ramos and the whole Ramos family, Sandra Ramos, Fátima Reyes, Miriam Reyes, Napoleon Rios, Hortensia Rivas, Ninoska Robles de Jarquín, Matilde Rocha, Nubia Rocha, Irene Rojas, Reyna Isabel Rodríguez, Julio Ruiz Morazán, Feliz Ruiz, Liliana Salinas, Rosa Argentina Silva, Judith Silva, Nubia and Maritza Silva Flores, Dora María Téllez, Ursula Thöt, Doris Tijerino, María Auxiliadora Valario, Milú Vargas, Bladimir Varela, Sara Velázquez, Reina Isabel Velázquez, Donna Vukelich, Lois Wessel, Dorotea Wilson, Yolanda Zamora, Fátima Zelaya, Rosa Marina Zelaya, and José Antonio Zepeda.

In El Salvador, the following people generously shared their time and insights with me: Elba Aguilar, Sonia Aguinada, Irma Amaya, Ana Zulema Argueta, Carmen Argueta, Luis Alberto Avilés, Sonia Baires, Lucía Beltrán, Silvia Briseño, Gladys Colato, Cristina (Flor de Piedra), Deysi Cheyne, Sister Nydia Delgadillo, Rosibel Flores, Doris García, Marta Elena García de Rodríguez, Esperanza Gómez, Rebeca de González, members of the Grupo de Identidad 2001 of the UCA, Sonia Gualdamez, Isabel de Guevara, Norma Guevara, Yolanda Guirola, Isabel Hernández, María Julia Hernández, Virginia Hernández, Morena Herrera, Juana Lemus Flores, Zoila de Innocenti, Eva Linares, Rosi Flores, Aracelis López, Ofelia López, Ana Guadalupe Martínez, Omar Martínez and Juanita, Yanira Marroquín, Mirna Medina, Carmen Elisia Mejía, Guadalupe Mejía, Irma Mejía, Lety Méndez, María Trinidad Mejía, Conchita Menjivar, Violeta Menjivar, Urania Morales, Clara Murguialday, Alicia Panameña de García, Lorena Peña (Rebeca Palacios), Marina Peña Flores, Guadalupe Portillo, Isabel Ramírez, Sandra Ramírez, María Consuelo Raymundo, Aura Rivera, Carmen Rodríguez, Mirna Rodríguez, América Romualdo, Marielos Romualdo, Marta Segovia, María Elena Sánchez, Sara Quintanilla, Marta Valladares (Nidia Diaz), Antonia Vichés, Silvia Vidal, and Evelyn Zelaya.

Unfortunately, the ongoing nature of the war in Chiapas, and the fact that many peaceful human rights promotors have been victimized by military and paramilitary violence in recent years, makes me hesitate to publicly thank the many who generously offered me their time and insights. Given the difficult circumstances within which they must work, I am especially grateful to the many who permitted me to interview them.

A number of institutions offered important support over the course of my researching and writing this book. The sociology departments at the Universidad Centroamericana (UCA) in Managua and San Salvador were quite helpful. Special thanks are due to Marcos Membreño in Managua and Zoila de Innocente in San Salvador. The staff and volunteers with the Boston chapter of the Committee in Solidarity with the People of El Salvador (CISPES) and its San Salvador affiliate, the Centro Internacional de Solidaridad (CIS), especially Sarah Clarke, Mike Prokosch, and Marceline White, played a big role in my initiation into the world of Salvadoran politics. Special thanks are due to David Amdur of the national CISPES office for sharing his insights, along with the photo for the front cover of this book. The staff at CIESAS-Sureste (Centro de Investigaciones y Estudios Superiores en Antropología Social) in San Cristóbal de las Casas, Chiapas, especially Gabriela Vargas, Aida Hernández, Xochitl Leyva, and Guadalupe Salazar were tremendously helpful during 1995, when I was an affiliated guest researcher, and during my later visits to the region. I am grateful to the staff at the Center for U.S.–Mexican Studies (at the University of California, San Diego) for helping make that institute a wonderful place to be when I was a visiting research fellow in the winter of 1997–98. Finally, I'd like to thank the staff at Global Exchange for organizing a women's tour of Cuba in October 1998, with special thanks to Teresa Walsh and Diana Russell.

For its moral and economic support, I thank the gender studies section of the Latin American Studies Association (LASA) for awarding me first place in the Elsa Chaney Competition in 1998 for an earlier version of Chapter 3. I also would like to thank the staff at the Carrie Chapman Catt Center for the Study of Women and Politics for awarding me the Carrie Chapman Catt Prize in 1999 in support of the ongoing research project that has become this book.

The final critical source of economic support for this project was Larry Breitborde and the rest of the administration at Knox College. Because the many requests I made for faculty research grants were never denied, it was possible to make the repeated trips to Latin America that were necessary in researching this book. Very special thanks go to many people at Knox College for interest in my work, especially Brenda Fineberg. Few people ever have the privilege of returning to teach at the very place where they spent their college years. Thanks to all current and former faculty whose courses influenced my thinking on an array of topics. Special thanks to the two faculty members who had the greatest influence on my college years and to what I was to become (for better or worse): Bob Seibert and Isabel Livosky. Thanks also to students who were kind enough to take my courses and engage me in years of interesting conversations, especially to those students who directly supported the project through their own research: Alicia Stephens, James Mutti, Liz Rice, and Monica Novak.

I am particularly grateful to those who were willing to take the time to read and comment upon earlier versions of this book, in part or in whole. They include María Dolores Alvarez, David Amdur, Florence Babb, Cynthia Enloe, John Foran, Victoria González, Ilja Luciak, Laura Macdonald, Enrico Marcelli, Vince McElhinny, Duane Oldfield, Mercedes Olivera, Eric Selbin, Millie Thayer, Julie Shayne, and Jack Spence. Thanks to Sandy Thatcher and the rest of the staff at Penn State Press for their help in transforming a manuscript into a book.

Finally, special thanks are due to my parents, Kathleen Burch and Richard Kampwirth, for their support during many years of research; to Silvia Carrazco for being such a good friend and inspiration; to Duane Oldfield for his unwaivering support and intelligent feedback in all phases of this project; and to Sophia Ah-Hei Oldfield, for providing the sort of help that only a toddler could provide.

Introduction

If the twentieth century was the age of revolution, then surely Latin America was the region of revolution. Over the course of that century, new revolutionary movements emerged every few years across the region, movements that promoted goals such as overturning dictatorships, confronting economic inequalities, and creating what Cuban revolutionary hero Che Guevara called the "new man."[1] But in fact, many of those new men were not men. Thousands of them, especially in the second half of the century, were women. This book is about the women who joined revolutionary movements in Nicaragua, El Salvador, and the Mexican state of Chiapas; how they came to become guerrilla activists; and how that experience changed their lives.

I hope to show that our understanding of revolutionary movements is inevitably poorer if we try to understand those movements in gender-free terms; revolution in the real world has never been gender-free. Further, I will show how, in the cases of Nicaragua, El Salvador, and Chiapas, a series of political, structural, ideological, and personal factors allowed many women to escape the constraints of their traditional roles. Once those constraints were loosened, some of them chose, or were pushed into choosing, to participate in guerrilla movements and other sorts of revolutionary activism.[2]

---

1. Che Guevara's "new man" was to be more egalitarian, more altruistic, and more socially conscious, in short, more revolutionary, than the men of the old regime. On the one hand, the new man was a product of revolutionary struggle. On the other hand, he and others like him would consolidate the revolution (Leiner 1994, 10, 26–27, 34; for feminist interpretations of Che and the new man, see Rodríguez 1996a, 1996b; Vázquez, Ibáñez, and Murguialday 1996, 61–65).

2. I use the term *revolutionary activism* to describe a collection of radical social movement activities that included participation in student groups, radical Catholic groups, labor unions, human rights groups, and economic cooperatives. Some might object that these activities are more appropriately labeled *social movements*, since the tendency to use the word *revolution* for any

REVOLUTIONARY THEORY: WHERE ARE THE WOMEN?

Strangely, theories of revolution have largely ignored the impact of gender relations on revolutionary organizations, despite the fact that women were active participants in late twentieth-century guerrilla movements in Latin America. Within the FSLN (Frente Sandinista de Liberación Nacional) of Nicaragua, many have estimated, 30 percent of the combatants, and many of the top guerrilla leaders, were women (Collinson 1990, 154; Flynn 1983, 416; Reif 1986, 158), though a study of the records of the Sandinista Social Security Institute found that only 6.6 percent of those who were killed in the war against Somoza were female (Vilas 1986, 108).

In the southern Mexican state of Chiapas, women are well integrated into the ongoing movement of the EZLN (Ejército Zapatista de Liberación Nacional), constituting about one-third of the combatants (Marcos 1995; Olivera 1996, 49; Stephen 1994b, 2). Women's participation in the FMLN (Frente Farabundo Martí para la Liberación Nacional) of El Salvador was also quite significant; and the data are more reliable than in either Nicaragua or Chiapas, because at the end of the war in 1992, the United Nations oversaw the demobilization of the FMLN, collecting basic data regarding the guerrillas.[3] Approximately 40 percent of the FMLN membership, 30 percent of the combatants, and 20 percent of the military leadership were women (Luciak 1995, 3; Mason 1992, 65; Montgomery 1995, 123; Mujeres por la Dignidad y la Vida 1993, 35; Vázquez, Ibáñez, and Murguialday 1996, 21).

In discussing similar data, Timothy Wickham-Crowley notes a number of instances in which visitors to guerrilla camps did not see many female combatants. As he rightly observes, this discrepancy "should alert our critical facilities" (1992, 216). I too have reason to doubt the figure of 30 per-

---

sort of social change (e.g., Kaltefleiter 1995; Mintz and Kellogg 1988; Raleigh 1994; Rust 1995; Sargent 1981) runs the risk of trivializing the concept.

But I think the word is justified in this case. Participants in the groups I identify as part of loose revolutionary coalitions were fighting for the end of dictatorships and for the structural transformation of their societies. They shared these goals with the guerrillas, and many of their groups were organically linked with the guerrilla movements. Local elites responded with death threats and sometimes murder, indicating that they were genuinely threatened by revolutionary activism.

3. In Nicaragua, there was no demobilization data, since the Sandinistas did not have to demobilize, having successfully overthrown the Somoza dictatorship in 1979, and governing from that point until they were defeated electorally in 1990. As of this writing in the year 2001, there is no demobilization data for the Zapatistas of Chiapas either, since they remain mobilized in the jungles of the eastern third of the state.

cent armed female participation, if for no other reason than that nearly the same percentage is claimed in all three cases. Nonetheless, years of qualitative research, along with data uncovered by Luciak (2001; 1995) from the demobilization processes in El Salvador and Guatemala, has led me to conclude, like Wickham-Crowley, that even if the percentage of female combatants was not exactly 30 percent, "a quantum leap occurred in women's participation in Latin American revolutionary movements, roughly between 1965 and 1975" (Wickham-Crowley 1992, 216–17). Debates over numbers should not blind us to this leap.

That women were such active participants is somewhat surprising, since in earlier guerrilla movements, such as that of Cuba, their numbers seem to have been considerably lower.[4] Why did women play such an active role in these three cases? Answering that question will require paying close attention to the roles that women play (or do not play) in revolutionary politics. To do so I will use a feminist approach, a method in which gender is a central category of analysis.

Using a feminist approach can help theorists of revolution more easily reach their own goals of explaining the causes and implications of guerrilla struggle. Such a method can improve revolutionary theory by helping theorists to better address the central question of the literature: why do some groups succeed in overthrowing dictatorships while others fail? It simply is not enough to do what theorists of revolution have traditionally done: to look for the support or lack of support of social sectors, with a particular focus on class divisions. Even apparently simple questions regarding class—did the peasantry support the guerrillas?—are complicated, and illuminated, by a feminist approach.[5]

---

4. It has been estimated that only 5 percent of the Cuban guerrillas were women (Wickham-Crowley 1992, 21). Foran, Klouzal, and Rivera argue that women played a wide variety of roles during the guerrilla phase of the Cuban Revolution, providing valuable data on those roles, though they also cited the estimate that one in twenty combatants was female (1997, 32–33).

5. The problem is that "the peasantry" does not exist. Classes, in the abstract, are constructions that do not perfectly mirror reality. In real life, there are only male peasants and female peasants. Theorists sometimes assume that a guerrilla movement that wins the support of 100 percent of male peasants is supported by "the peasantry," but that is faulty math. The guerrilla group with the support of 100 percent of male peasants actually is supported by 50 percent of the peasantry.

It could be argued that, given the power that most male peasants have over their female relatives, the active support of 100 percent of the male peasants will result in the acquiescence of 100 percent of the female peasants. In effect, the support of the male peasants is the equivalent of the support of the peasantry. Indeed, that may be the case at times. But female submission is not a constant factor. It cannot be assumed into a theory of revolution. Instead, the relative autonomy or submission of female peasants must be demonstrated with historical evidence. In cases in which female peasants attain a degree of autonomy from male peasants, they may or may not be incorporated into a peasant coalition.

Timothy Wickham-Crowley has taken steps toward incorporating gender as a factor in revolutionary theory by acknowledging change in the gender composition of recent guerrilla movements in Latin America. He notes that while in the 1960s, the percentage of women who led Latin American guerrilla groups ranged "from zero to 20 percent," by the 1970s and 1980s, women constituted between a quarter and a third of the combatants in Nicaragua and El Salvador (1992, 21). Unfortunately, after uncovering this interesting shift in gender roles, he fails to speculate on the causes of this change in the composition of guerrilla movements.

Instead, his main explanation for the relative underrepresentation of women within guerrilla coalitions is that "men, on average, are more aggressive than women" and that some research suggests that this has "a biological basis" (1992, 23). But if this explanation were the most significant one, the expected outcome would have been no change in women's participation in guerrilla movements since the 1960s. After all, the biology of Latin American women and men has not changed. It is worth asking why women are still underrepresented within guerrilla movements (or perhaps why men are overrepresented). But it is even more important to ask why their numbers are increasing, for the answer to that question will also offer clues to the question about their relative underrepresentation.

Despite the limits of his analysis of the role of women in guerrilla movements, Wickham-Crowley is unusual because he even acknowledges that the role has shifted. Why have most theorists of revolution paid so little attention to this shift? The problem is not that there has been any shortage of recent theoretical works on revolutionary change.[6] Nor is there any shortage of research on the role that gender plays within revolutionary politics.[7] Yet with very few exceptions (Foran, Klouzal, and Rivera 1997; Moghadam 1997; Tétreault 1994), these findings on gender

---

6. In the 1990s alone, the following works on guerrillas and revolution were published: Byrne 1996; Castañeda 1994; Castro 1999b; Colburn 1994; Collier 1994; Farhi 1990; Foran 1997a, 1994, 1993, 1992; Grenier 1999; Goldstone, Gurr, and Moshiri 1991; Horton 1998; Kanoussi 1998; Keddie 1995; Legorreta Díaz 1998; T. D. Mason 1992; Paige 1997; Schultz and Slater 1990; Skocpol 1994; Selbin 1999; Wickham-Crowley 1992. Very helpful reviews of earlier generations of revolutionary theory may be found in several of the contributions to Goldstone, Gurr and Moshiri 1991; in Foran 1993 and 1992; and in several of the contributions to Foran 1997b.

7. See, e.g., Afshar 1985; Barrig 1998; Berkin and Lovett 1980; Castro 1999a; Chinchilla 1997, 1994, 1990; Cock 1994; DIGNAS 1996; Flynn 1983; Foran, Klouzal, and Rivera 1997; Goldman 1993; Hunt 1992; Jaquette 1973; Kampwirth 2001; Kirk 1997; Kruks, Rapp, and Young 1989; Lancaster 1992; Lapidus 1978; Lázaro 1990; Luciak 2001, 1998; Macías 1982; Mason 1992; Massell 1974; Moghadam 1997, 1994; Moghissi 1996; Molyneux 2000, 1988, 1986, 1984; Murguialday 1990; Nashat 1983; Randall 1992; Reif 1986; Reséndez Fuentes 1995;

in revolutionary settings have not been integrated into theories of revolution, except at the level of footnotes.

I suspect that in large part, this inattention to gender is a function of the fact that the vast majority of the work on revolution over the course of the past century has been devoted to some version of a single question. From a movement-centered perspective, this question is the following: Under what circumstances have revolutionary movements succeeded in overthrowing states? Alternatively, from a state-centered perspective, the question becomes, Under what circumstances have states fallen to guerrilla challenges? That question (which I will not address in this book) has informed multiple generations of revolutionary theory and has still not been fully answered to the satisfaction of most participants in the debate. Any question that can generate such lengthy and often heated debate is clearly a good question, but it is not the only question.

Organizing the field of revolutionary studies around this single question has had some negative consequences. Too often, the study of revolution has been reduced to the study of war. This is not to say that the violence of guerrilla struggle may be ignored by revolutionary theorists (for otherwise revolution becomes synonymous with social movements), but overprivileging violence is costly. It has resulted in a body of revolutionary theory in which the overthrow of the old regime is usually the end point, and the period after its overthrow is often incorrectly called the "postrevolution."

In contrast, Latin Americans reserve the term *la revolución* to name the period of political, economic, and social transformation that can only occur after the guerrillas succeed in seizing the state. So the guerrilla struggle and the revolution are distinct periods, separated by the moment in which the old regime is overthrown. At the same time, they are intellectually linked, for the guerrilla struggle makes little sense without the hope of a later period of revolutionary transformation. While many excellent case studies of particular revolutions have been published, few theoretically focused works have analyzed what happens during revolutions (Colburn 1994; Fagen, Deere, and Carragio 1986; Fagen 1969; and Selbin 1999 are notable exceptions).

This book fits into the tradition of the single question in that it too focuses on the period of the guerrilla struggles (a manuscript in progress

---

Saadatmand 1995; Salas 1990; Stacey 1983; Tétreault 1994; Vázquez, Ibáñez, and Murguialday 1996. Reif (1986) and Tétreault's introduction (1994) provide useful reviews of the literature related to women and revolutionary movements.

analyzes the effect of those struggles on gender relations and feminist organizing during the revolution and postrevolution in Nicaragua and during the periods following the guerrilla wars in El Salvador and Chiapas). But it diverts from that tradition by asking some new questions about guerrilla movements, questions that were not asked largely because of the predominance of the old question. Focusing most of our intellectual energy on a single question has meant that questions that do not fit very well into the parameters of the dominant question—including why women have participated in guerrilla movements, and what impact that participation has on them and their societies—have been typically addressed only as asides. This book is an attempt to save a few of those questions from the footnotes.

WHY SO MANY WOMEN IN THE GUERRILLA WARS?

The reasons women have given for participating in the guerrilla struggle are similar to those given by men: to end the dictatorship, to end the exploitation of the poor and the indigenous, to create more just countries for their children. Over the course of my more than two hundred interviews with female activists, only one woman, a Nicaraguan, told me that a desire for gender justice played a role in her initial decision to tie her fate to the revolutionaries. The vast majority joined the revolutionary coalitions so as to live in freer countries and to have more options in life, as did their male counterparts. So I do not argue that women chose to become guerrillas for reasons that were fundamentally different from those that motivated men. Instead, in this book I focus on the circumstances of Latin American women's lives, to understand how those circumstances changed in the final quarter of the twentieth century, making it possible for increasing numbers of women to join guerrilla organizations and other revolutionary groups.

Recent upheavals in Nicaragua, El Salvador, and Chiapas were all made possible, in part, by previous shifts in gender relations. Political-economic changes, including the growth of agroexports, had a notable impact on class structures from the middle of the twentieth century onward, an impact that often included increased inequality and insecurity for many of the rural poor.[8] Those changes, in turn, had a number of gen-

---

8. Many have evaluated the political-economic roots of the guerrilla wars in Nicaragua, El Salvador, and Chiapas (on Nicaragua, see Enríquez 1991; Everingham 1996; Mason 1992; Midlarsky and Roberts 1985; Vilas 1986, 1995; Wickham-Crowley 1992; on El Salvador, see Byrne 1996; Everingham 1996; Mason 1992; McClintock 1998; Midlarsky and Roberts 1985; Mont-

dered effects, including changes in family structures and shifts in migration patterns.

One indirect result of the expansion of export-oriented agriculture starting in the 1950s (especially in Nicaragua and El Salvador), was increased abandonment of wives.[9] As peasant men got pushed off their plots of land, they were forced to leave their communities in search of work. Many never returned. The wives they left behind were more economically desperate than they had been when their husbands were around, but they also had more personal autonomy. The sorts of solutions they found reflected both their desperation and their autonomy.

Many women dealt with the crisis by migrating to the cities. Individual decisions to migrate had unexpected political consequences, because migration tends to facilitate social organizing for a series of reasons. First, the opportunity to compare tends to radicalize by giving migrants the opportunity to compare, to observe that social inequality is patterned and socially constructed rather than random and natural. The second reason that migration sometimes sets the stage for revolution relates to organizing: it is often easier to organize in densely populated and relatively anonymous urban areas than in sparsely populated rural areas. Moreover, migrants typically retain their ties to family and friends in the countryside, facilitating the formation of a guerrilla force with a base in both the city and the countryside.

A third reason that migration facilitates revolutionary organizing is related to grievances. To the extent that social inequality is a factor motivating people to join guerrilla movements, what matters is how they perceive that inequality more than whether inequality is objectively rising or falling as measured by economic indicators. Migrants are more likely to be struck by the appearance of social inequality than are those who stay in

---

gomery 1995; Vilas 1995; Wickham-Crowley 1992; on Chiapas, see Collier 1994; Benjamin 1996; Hidalgo and Monroy 1994; Rus 1995; Tejera Gaona 1996; Villafuerte Solís and García Aguilar 1994).

Some of these scholars have engaged in debates over the impact that the transformation of the rural economy has had on class structure, the sorts of rural poor who were most likely to join the revolutionary coalitions, and whether there were clear correlations between levels of misery and guerrilla support. I will not be directly addressing these debates, but merely drawing two findings out of this literature: first, that the economy of these regions was in transition during the decades leading up to the guerrilla wars, and second, that many of the poor experienced that transition as a crisis. On the basis of those two findings, I will examine the influence of the economic transition on gender relations, an issue that is directly relevant to explaining how and why some women became guerrillas.

9. Data on family structures in Nicaragua and El Salvador are presented in Chapters 1 and 2, respectively.

the countryside, since inequality is typically more visible in the cities than in the countryside: the wealthiest members of society almost always live in the cities, not the rural areas, even when their wealth is based on ownership of farmland. Finally, movements to overthrow the state typically have some urban component because the relationship between the state and society is often more intense (in either a good or a bad way) in the city than in the countryside.[10]

Arguably, the role of women in these new social organizations was facilitated by the two factors previously mentioned (changes in family structures and migration) combined with a third factor: changes in the Catholic Church starting in the late 1960s. A new movement within the church, liberation theology, promoted social organizing in general and women's organizing in particular.[11]

Initially, women formed organizations that were not particularly radical and certainly not feminist; early organizations included a variety of popular cooperatives, such as soup kitchens, child-care centers, clinics, literacy programs, and neighborhood-improvement associations. But for many women, their experience as political activists only started in the soup kitchens. It might have ended there, but did not, because of the knee-jerk authoritarianism of the dictatorships. Severe repression in response to very moderate oppositional activities caused many women to support or join the guerrillas as a means of self-defense (T. D. Mason 1992, 66, 79). The experience of organizing in an unarmed capacity both pushed and pulled women into guerrilla struggle; they were pushed by the government's escalated violence, and they were pulled by their own growing political skills and consciousness.

An important factor that is not directly addressed in T. David Mason's otherwise excellent analysis is the fact that many women joined the armed insurgency at a very young age. Moreover, the factors that motivated young women were not identical to those that motivated slightly older women. The economically oriented organizing that tended to attract single mothers was not the only sort of organizational experience that preceded the decision to join the guerrillas. Large numbers of women who would become guerrillas began their activism within various student groups, at the university level and, more often, at the high school or even

10. On migration, guerrilla movements, and consciousness of injustice, see Farhi 1990, 65–79; Mason 1992, 76–83; Vilas 1995, 20–27, 56–59.

11. On liberation theology and politics in Latin America, see Alvarez 1990; Boff 1985; Booth 1985; Crahan 1987; Collier 1994; Guillén 1997, 1995; Lancaster 1988; Legorreta Díaz 1998; Montgomery 1995, 1983; Peterson 1997; Smith 1991; Williams 1989; Vilas 1995.

grade school level. Sonia explained her reasons for joining the FSLN guerrillas of Nicaragua at the age of seventeen. "I did not go off with the FSLN because of any great consciousness. No, I think I went off with the FSLN because of rebelliousness. . . . I always criticized the fact that [in my Catholic high school] people were treated differently depending on their social standing. . . . The FSLN was like the possibility of changing my life. And yes, I changed it definitively (interview, January 19, 1997).

The motivations of the teenage girls who joined the guerrillas seem to have differed somewhat from those that drove female heads of families. While, according to Mason, the household heads were pushed into the guerrillas more than they were pulled, accounts such as that of Sonia suggest that the teenage girls were pulled more than they were pushed.

Angry about the multiple inequalities that they had to confront on a daily basis, they tended to see participation in the guerrilla forces as an opportunity as much as an obligation. For students, both female and male, who saw multiple opportunities closed to them because of the dictatorship, the way to force those opportunities open was to get rid of the dictatorship. Joining the revolutionary coalition was also a way for many of them to create opportunities in an immediate sense, for the guerrillas allowed many of them to escape the tedium of their homes, to join another sort of family, to start life anew. In the most literal sense, becoming a guerrilla or a clandestine member of the revolutionary coalition meant taking on new identities through pseudonyms, which some would continue to use long after the wars were over.

Finally, the guerrillas themselves had a strong incentive for trying to mobilize women as a result of changes in guerrilla strategies since the 1950s, when the largely masculine 26th of July Movement overthrew the dictatorship of Fulgencio Batista in Cuba. The increased numbers of women may be partially due to the shift from a *foco* strategy, which depends on a small band of guerrillas, to a mass mobilization strategy, which requires much larger numbers of supporters (Wickham-Crowley 1992, 215). Given the need of recent Latin American guerrillas for as many supporters as possible, they could hardly afford to reject the potential participation of 50 percent of the population just because those people were women.

The result of this mix of social change—the growth of agroexports, changes in family structures, increased female migration, the transformation of the church and of guerrilla politics—combined with long-standing political authoritarianism, was the growth of guerrilla movements in which women were significant participants.

But which women? Addressing this question requires filling in one of the gaps in the literature on revolutionary movements: the personal dimension.[12] Paying attention to structural factors (like changes in the distribution of land) or to ideological factors (like the rise of liberation theology) or to political factors (like state violence) is critical to explaining why there were so many women guerrillas in these three cases. But even when added together, those factors still leave the question partially unanswered. The trouble is that many, perhaps most, of the women who were touched by those structural, ideological, and political changes did not choose to become guerrillas or revolutionary activists of any sort. The personal dimension can explain why these macrosocial changes created activists out of certain women.[13]

There were at least four personal factors that shaped the lives of the women who would join the guerrilla movements and related resistance groups. First, the roots of activism would often be set by accidents of birth.

12. Timothy Wickham-Crowley (1992, 10–12) does a nice job of analyzing the costs and benefits of examining revolutions at different levels (those of the international system, nation, regions, or communities). He rightly cautions that it is a mistake to take the nation as the single unit of analysis simply because revolutions happen to nations. Yet while his points are well taken, he fails to mention the possibility of analyzing social change at the level of families and individuals within those families. But given that subjective factors shape revolutionary outcomes (people don't rebel because of rising poverty, but because of rising poverty that they perceive as unjust [e.g., Vilas 1995, 13–15, 20–27]), it is crucial to consider the personal ways in which people experience those changes at the level of the international system, the nation, their region, and their community.

13. Two personal factors that I will not address in this book could be fruitful areas for future research. The first of these is the impact of birth order. One of the first factors that shapes a girl's early political values is her experience of family politics, that is, her interactions with caretakers and siblings; those interactions will vary considerably depending on her position in the birth order. Frank Sulloway analyzed the relationship between birth order and political values, arguing that older siblings tend to be conservative as adults, since they try to emulate their parents when they are children, while younger, especially youngest, siblings are born to rebel as a result of survival strategies developed in childhood (1996, 69). I have reason to question Sulloway's claim that typical first-child strategies always lead to political conservatism, because many of the revolutionaries in my study had been firstborns or the first girls to be born, and because many of the traits that he identifies as inherently conservative (such as a sense of responsibility to care for others) could have easily informed radical political activism (1996, 69, 70, 75). Nonetheless, his hypothesis—that the political strategies learned by a child in interactions with family members will shape their political choices as adults—is quite compelling.

Carlos Vilas identified a second personal factor—family structure—that would be worth further investigation. In Nicaragua 54 percent of those who were killed in the war against Somoza were born out of wedlock and 47 percent of them were raised by a single parent (usually their mother) during their first twelve years (figures that are unusually high even in Nicaragua). As Vilas notes, one explanation for this finding could be the class background of the guerrillas, but he suggests that another explanation may be psychological, that the early experience of living relatively free from adult control might have predisposed them to rebel against arbitrary authority of all sorts, including that of Somoza (Vilas 1986, 109–13).

As the first arena in which power dynamics were played out, the family played a critical role in shaping children's perception of political values such as fairness, justice, and responsibility.

Some women were set on the path toward revolutionary activism by an early childhood experience of resistance to authority. Those experiences ranged from a mother's activism in a union, or a father's membership in an opposition political party, or an uncle's visiting in the middle of the night and talking about the guerrillas when the children were thought to be asleep. That resistance to authority was sometimes as immediate as a girl's battle with her parents for the right to attend school. All those experiences, which I call family traditions of resistance, planted seeds that would germinate many years later, when the structural, ideological, and political conditions were right.[14]

Second, women who eventually joined politically radical organizations did not drop into those groups out of the blue. Rather, the movement to those groups was a slow transition over the course of years. Usually, these women first belonged to social networks, including their families, along with churches, schools, and less often labor unions.[15] Those networks were composed of groups that existed for nonpolitical reasons but that, under certain circumstances, could become politicized. The groups provided safe spaces for recruiting, as well as opportunities for girls to acquire basic organizing skills. One of those women, Katrina, would go on to become a midlevel guerrilla leader in the Fuerzas Populares de Liberación (FPL), one of the five parties that made up the FMLN of El Salvador. Katrina explained how membership in one preexisting network gradually led her to participate in ever more radical groups, a transition that took her from a church youth group to an armed movement in just two years.

14. Family traditions of resistance is similar to the concept of "political cultures of opposition" that is developed by Foran (1997, 1993, 1992; see also Wickham-Crowley 1992, 246). It also draws on Eric Selbin's work on the relationship between culture and agency in revolutionary politics (1997, 123–33, 1999). But "family traditions of resistance" is a more precise concept than "political cultures of opposition" in that it can explain why a particular person picked up on a tradition of resistance whereas another (raised in the same culture but in a different family) did not. Clearly, other socializing networks, such as schools or churches, help to explain why some seize the cultures of opposition that are available to them. But families are probably the most important socializing networks because of their universality and intimacy. They are also almost always ignored by revolutionary theorists.

15. Some might object to considering families as preexisting networks that led some women to revolutionary activism, since, obviously, all women came from families of some sort. Yet many women did not come from families that inculcated rebel values in their daughters. In addition to the political socialization that relatives sometimes engaged in, people who were already involved in revolutionary politics were more likely to try to recruit their relatives, because they could generally trust their relatives more than other people.

At the age of fourteen I began to work with the Christian communities. A year later, I heard talk of FECAS [Federación de Campesinos]. Within that organization there were people who I knew. Because of the affection I felt toward them, I began to identify with FECAS. At the age of sixteen I began to feel persecuted, seriously persecuted. I had two options: I could either renounce the organization and flee or I could become more involved. I thought that it was better to become more involved. And that is how I began to work in the popular militias. That was the first stage of the FPL. (Interview, July 4, 1996)

While Katrina's initial decision to work with the Catholic Church certainly did not make it inevitable that she would become a guerrilla, given the high levels of state violence in El Salvador, that decision did make her eventual recruitment by the guerrillas more likely. A girl who was excluded from the social networks of the schools and the church was less likely to be recruited for radical political activity than a girl who was integrated into the preexisting networks of her community.[16]

In both Nicaragua and El Salvador, more of the women I interviewed had been channeled into the revolutionary coalition through a student group than through any other preexisting network. Even for women who had left school long before they became revolutionaries, having attended school for longer than the average girl seemed to have increased the likelihood of becoming a radical activist, since greater number of years in school meant greater literacy (which in turn meant easier access to oppositional newspapers and political pamphlets, and greater personal self-confidence). Educational level is also an indicator of class background—the poorest of the poor are the least likely rebels.[17]

The final factor, year of birth, may have been the single most important personal factor. A person's age at the time of major societal turning points greatly shaped how these events were interpreted and how, or if, the person took action. For example, the emergence of liberation theology, which offered a framework for understanding historic injustice and gave meaning to the struggle against inequality and authoritarianism, may have had some impact on most people. But the people on whom it had a life-transforming influence were those who were directly involved in the

16. On preexisting networks and social movement theory, see Alvarez, Dagnino, and Escobar 1998, 14–16; Alvarez 1990, 57–82; Freeman 1975, 48–70; McAdam 1982, 43–47; Wickham-Crowley 1992, 37–42; 226–27.

17. On the role of students in revolutionary movements, see Arjomand 1986, 398–402; Colburn 1994, 27–28, 44–45; Farhi 1990, 67; Grenier 1999, 97–128; McClintock 1998, 250; Parsa 2000, 94–129; Pizarro Leongómez 1996, 24–25; Wickham-Crowley 1992, 33–37, 42–43.

movement. And few were as directly involved as students in Catholic schools.

Although older people might participate in base communities, forty-year-olds, as a rule, are not as impressionable as fourteen-year-olds. Forty-year-olds are also less likely to be willing to invest great time and risk in organizing, because they have greater family and work responsibilities and because older people tend to be more cautious than younger people. Struggle against dictatorship could—and did—get activists killed. Young people tended to be more willing to assume such risks.[18]

The chart on page 14 is a summary of the factors that, in combination, explain why so many females were mobilized into oppositional organizations during the civil wars in Nicaragua, El Salvador, and Chiapas.

WHAT I DID

In the discussion of my methodology, it is important that I explain what I did and, perhaps more important, what I did not do. Fundamentally, this is a study of activists. Although their activism took many different forms, and the meaning of that activism for the participants differed widely, there is a significant difference between women who participate in groups that aim toward social change and those who are too overwhelmed or (more rarely) too content with their lot to organize. In no sense should this book be read as the story of how the civil wars affected "women"; many women experienced the upheavals of the civil wars in different, and less empowering, ways.

But though this study, like most studies of revolutionary movements, focuses on those who participated in such movements, it differs from the majority of studies in an important way. In general, the women I interviewed were not former guerrillas who had held the positions of most prestige such as commanders (as is typical in studies of guerrilla movements), nor were they the women who held positions of least prestige such as cooks or caretakers of safe houses.[19] Instead, those I interviewed

18. On the young age of most members of revolutionary coalitions, see Jaquette 1973, 344; Luciak 1995, 4–5, 15; Wickham-Crowley 1992, 42–43; Vilas 1986, 108–16.

19. By calling such support workers low-prestige, I am referring to the way they often experienced their work, and the way they were perceived, in other words, as women who carried out women's work. Of course, with regard to the viability of the guerrilla forces, providers of food were at least as critical as combatants.

Ilja Luciak found that women in low-prestige categories were sometimes thought of as combatants by other members of the Salvadoran FMLN. Of the 8,506 combatants demobilized by the United Nations in 1992, 2,494, or 29.2 percent, were women. Of the 4,090 FMLN political personnel (also considered guerrillas), 1,453, or 35.5 percent, were women. The demobilized

---

FACTORS THAT LED TO MOBILIZATION
OF WOMEN AS GUERRILLAS

STRUCTURAL CHANGES

Land concentration, increasing insecurity for rural poor
  (due to economic globalization and population growth)
  → male migration and often abandonment of families
  → rise in number of single-female-headed households
  → female migration (to cities or Lacandón jungle), which broke traditional ties,
    made organizing more possible

IDEOLOGICAL AND ORGANIZATIONAL CHANGES

Rise of liberation theology
  → growth of religious and secular self-help groups

Change in guerrilla methods
  → from foco organizing to mass mobilization
  → from military strategy to political-military strategy

POLITICAL FACTORS

State response to those self-help groups was often repression
  → repression pushed many women into more-radical activities in self-defense

Ineffectual state efforts to co-opt (especially in Chiapas) gave women new
  skills and new resentment

PERSONAL FACTORS

Family traditions of resistance
Membership in preexisting social networks (student groups, church groups,
  labor unions)
Year of birth

COMBINATION OF ALL FACTORS

  → mobilization of women in guerrilla movements and other revolutionary organizations

---

included 60 people who were under 13 years of age (including 2 one-year-old babies, a 5-year-old girl and a 6-year-old girl). Just as surprising was the fact that 170 of the demobilized combatants were over the age of 60 (including 5 women in their 90s). "[I]n the eyes of the guerrillas themselves, the category of 'combatant' is not limited to the arms-bearing fighter"; after years of traveling and working with the guerrillas (work that was hardly free from danger), some women in traditionally female support roles insisted that their participation be acknowledged in the demobilization process (Luciak 1995, 3–4).

Further evidence of the breadth of the category of guerrilla was provided by another study of 1,100 Salvadoran women who had been demobilized by the United Nations. Of those demobilized guerrillas, 28.8 percent reported that they had worked as cooks, 15 percent had been health workers, 15.2 percent were combatants, 10.7 percent had been part of the base of support, and 40.3 percent had carried out some other sort of work (Fundación 16 de Enero were mostly midprestige women. My category of midprestige women includes what other scholars have called members of the rank and file, or the base, since any woman who served in combat automatically enjoyed some prestige, given the glorification of violence that played a not so insignificant role in guerrilla culture.[20]

In addition to the combatants, the midprestige members of the revolutionary coalition were women who either had some authority in carrying out traditional women's work (such as the heads of nursing brigades) or did work that created opportunities for them to make decisions (such as student activism or human rights activism or political-education work). Such work was much more likely to be personally empowering than cooking tortillas. Moreover, their position in the middle meant that, on the one hand, they were not shielded from the brunt of machismo within guerrilla ranks, as were female commanders, but, on the other hand, they had the opportunity to develop political skills and consciousness that might not have been available to very low-ranking female participants.

Because of this combination of grievances and organizing skills—both legacies of their guerrilla experiences—the vast majority of the women I interviewed continued to be active in social movements long after the guerrilla wars had concluded. The social-movement activists I spoke to lived and worked, with a few exceptions, in the capitals of their countries or state: in Managua, San Salvador, and San Cristóbal de las Casas.[21] Choosing to focus my interviews on specific cities rather than trying to get an overview of each country had a cost, but also a benefit. The cost was that my view of women's activism was limited to that of groups that do at least some of their work in urban areas. Nonetheless, that limitation was mitigated in at least two ways: first, many of these groups also work in rural areas; and second, many of today's urban activists trace their roots to

---

1993, 10). Yet another study, based on in-depth interviews with 60 women of the FMLN, included the following within the category of guerrillas: combatants, radio operators, doctors, nurses, rural outreach workers, and financial workers (Vázquez, Ibáñez, and Murguialday 1996, 114). But while they all went under the category of guerrilla, they did not all enjoy the same status. "While being a radio operator was less prestigious than being a combatant, the radio operators felt more important than the nurses and the outreach workers, and they in turn felt more important than the cooks. . . . But even though only a minority of those interviewed were combatants, they were all armed" (Vázquez, Ibáñez, and Murguialday 1996, 115–16).

20. To an extent, men also gained a degree of prestige by using arms, but this was more the case for women, who stepped further away from their traditional roles by becoming combatants.

21. I consider San Cristóbal de las Casas to be the cultural capital of indigenous Chiapas and thus the more logical site for a study of Zapatismo than the heavily mestizo city of Tuxtla Gutiérrez, which is the political capital of the state.

small towns and rural areas. Indeed, as I argue, migration itself plays an important role in explaining the rise of revolutionary women's organizing.

The benefit of this focus on three cities was that it allowed me to gain a more comprehensive view of civil society in those sites than would have been possible had I attempted a more superficial overview of several countries. Over the course of ten years (1990–2000), I conducted a total of 205 open-ended interviews with female political activists (76 in Nicaragua, 69 in El Salvador, 57 in Chiapas, and 3 in Cuba).[22] These interviews ranged in length from fifteen minutes to three hours, with the average interview taking about an hour. In addition, I participated in workshops and conferences and followed the press.

The method I used to find the women I interviewed is sometimes called "snowballing." I began by approaching an organization that worked on women's issues (either on such issues exclusively or as a special project within a mixed-gender organization), described my project, and interviewed one or more activists in that organization. Then, at the end of the interviews, I asked for suggestions of other women or organizations I should include in the study, thus building a sample of major participants in the women's movement, as identified by movement activists themselves. The majority of women I interviewed were activists in women's organizations or women's programs within mixed organizations; a few were former women's movement activists; a number were congresswomen (all of whom were former guerrillas); and a few were officials in government women's offices.

In effect, I moved backward in time, from the present to the past. I started by identifying women who were involved with the women's movements in Nicaragua, El Salvador, or Chiapas in the 1990s. A significant subset of my sample of activists in Nicaragua and El Salvador were former guerrillas. This was not the case for the women I interviewed in Chiapas, for I conducted the two Central American studies in the postwar period, whereas the study of Chiapas was carried out while the war was ongoing, at a time when the Mexican military made it difficult for foreigners to spend time in guerrilla territory.

---

22. In October 1998, I participated in a weeklong women's delegation to Cuba sponsored by Global Exchange. During the course of that week, I interviewed three women who worked in a regional office of the Federation of Cuban Women and heard talks by more than a dozen women from different walks of life (including an economist, college professors, writers, journalists, health care workers, and lesbian feminist artists). My fieldwork in Cuba, obviously, did not compare with that in the other three countries, and so my discussion of the Cuban Revolution in Chapter 4 is mostly based on secondary sources.

The women I interviewed in Chiapas worked with women in various organizations; many had years of experience in the indigenous communities that were the base of support of the EZLN, and some were born in those communities and continued to live there. Although, to my knowledge, none of them were part of the EZLN, they could accurately be called participants in what I have called the revolutionary coalition (see note 2 for an explanation of this concept) or in what Xochitl Leyva Solano (1998) has called "the new Zapatista Movement."

In all three countries, many of those who were social-movement activists in the 1990s were former or (in Chiapas) current revolutionary coalition activists. So my sample of former and current revolutionaries is skewed in that it does not include those women who were mobilized in the decades of the 1960s, 1970s, and 1980s, but who had chosen to withdraw from political life by the 1990s, returning to lives as private citizens, workers, and, nearly always, mothers.

Yet while many Central American revolutionaries did not stay politically active after the wars, those who did were drawn from a wide cross section of Nicaraguan and Salvadoran society: they were of both rural and urban origin, from peasant, working-class, middle-class, and (rarely) upper-class backgrounds. Many had been involved in student opposition groups; many more, especially in Nicaragua, would continue their education after the war against the old regime had ended. In the Appendix to this book, I review the literature on the social backgrounds of the participants in the Nicaraguan FSLN and the Salvadoran FMLN, challenging many of the common assumptions in that literature. Rereading the available data leads me to suggest that many earlier studies have underestimated the urban component of these movements; oversimplified the class backgrounds of the participants in those movements; and incorrectly assumed that women and men who participated in the guerrilla movements and revolutionary coalitions came from the same sort of backgrounds and had undergone the same sort of experiences prior to becoming revolutionaries. In fact, there is evidence to suggest that the thousands of women who chose to link their fate to guerrillas were more likely to have been of urban origin and to have attended high school or college than were their male counterparts.

AN OVERVIEW OF REVOLUTION IN THE REAL WORLD

In this Introduction, I have outlined my arguments, setting them in the context of the literature on revolutionary movements, and have summarized in the chart my hypothesis regarding how and why, in the last quarter of the twentieth century, women were mobilized in significant numbers in Latin American guerrilla movements. The rest of this book builds upon these arguments.

In Chapter 1, I evaluate the FSLN (the guerrilla movement that overthrew the Somoza family dictatorship in Nicaragua in 1979) through the lens of gender relations. By following the personal stories of a number of the women I interviewed for this book, I illustrate how a series of political, structural, ideological, and personal factors—in combination—pushed some Nicaraguan women, and pulled others, into revolutionary politics in the 1960s and, especially, in the 1970s. The answer to the question of why the FSLN was the first guerrilla movement in Latin America that was truly a dual-gender coalition can be found in these combined factors.

In Chapter 2, I consider the role of women in the FMLN of El Salvador, both detailing the factors that led thousands of women to join the guerrilla coalition and analyzing gender relations within the guerrilla coalition. The factors that led to women's massive participation in revolutionary politics in El Salvador were similar, in many ways, to those that led to women's participation in Nicaragua, despite the significant differences in the histories of the two countries: the Nicaraguan guerrillas succeeded in overthrowing a dictatorship in 1979, while more than a decade of civil war in El Salvador would end in 1992 through a negotiated settlement between the guerrillas and the state they had tried to overthrow. This similarity in the two cases of guerrilla warfare from the perspective of gender relations, despite their great differences from the perspective of the state, points to the value of approaching the study of revolutionary movements from new perspectives. Whether or not movements are fundamentally similar or different and what lessons one movement may offer students of another movement are very much a function of the questions that scholars choose to ask.

In Chapter 3, I shift from an analysis of guerrilla movements that emerged during the cold war era, and that were influenced by Marxist-Leninism, to a guerrilla movement of the post–cold war era, the EZLN of Chiapas, Mexico. In this chapter I analyze the EZLN's roots in the indigenous communities of Chiapas, considering the influence of factors such as the church, migration, tourism, and party politics on women's decisions to join the revolutionary coalition. The case of the EZLN is a particularly important one for the field of revolutionary studies, for it points to the future of revolution in the post–cold war era. It is a movement that largely rejects the vanguardism of Marxist-Leninist theory, at the same time as it integrates gender justice into the revolutionary agenda in a way that is much more explicit than was the case for its Central American predecessors.

Finally, in Chapter 4, I compare Nicaragua, El Salvador, and Chiapas with Cuba, a comparison that allows me to refine my arguments by introducing variation into my analysis. Cuba is a good test case since relatively few women participated as combatants in the guerrilla phase of the Cuban Revolution. By revisiting Cuba in the 1950s and viewing it through the framework of the theory explaining the role of women guerrillas that I have developed through the cases of Nicaragua, El Salvador, and Chiapas, I am able both to shed light on the reasons for the limited role of women in the guerrilla phase of the Cuban Revolution and to sharpen the theory I have developed throughout this book.

1 New Roles for Sandino's Daughters

Extreme inequality and authoritarianism are all too common in the world. Yet the collapse of authoritarian regimes, and the transformation of a guerrilla group into a revolutionary government, are terribly uncommon. If only for that reason, the many analyses of the Sandinista guerrilla struggle that have already been written are welcome.[1]

But there is at least one other reason for reviewing this remarkable history again. The Sandinista guerrilla struggle was unlike that of Sandino in the 1930s (an ultimately unsuccessful movement against an earlier Somoza) and unlike guerrilla struggles throughout the Americas up until that time, in that thousands of women participated as both armed and unarmed members of the guerrilla forces and revolutionary groups that together formed the Sandinista coalition.

Why were so many Nicaraguan women able to break the constraints of their traditional roles so as to enter the armed struggle in the 1960s and 1970s? Why did the massive entry of women into the guerrilla struggle first happen where it did? Why did it happen when it did? Rethinking the fall of the Somoza regime through the framework laid out in the Introduction can help answer those questions.

But first, what was the Somoza dictatorship like, and why did it fall? The dictatorship can be seen as a logical outcome, intended or not, of the U.S. Marines' three-decade-long occupation of Nicaragua in the beginning of the twentieth century. The founder of the family dictatorship, Anastasio Somoza García, was an officer in the Marines-created National Guard, and the intellectual author, in 1934, of the assassination of Augusto Cesár Sandino. His victim, Sandino, the leader of a band of

---

1. The many studies of the guerrilla phase of the Sandinista revolution include Booth 1985; Everingham 1996; Farhi 1990; Horton 1998; Selbin 1999; Vilas 1986; Walker 1981.

nationalist guerrillas who sought to end U.S. occupation of Nicaragua, was ambushed and killed as he was leaving peace talks. Shortly afterward, Somoza would seize power, initiating more than four decades of family dictatorship.

So from the very beginning of the Somoza dynasty, the opposition was nationalistic and anti-imperialist. When the dictatorship fell more than forty years later, the Sandinista coalition (named after Sandino, of course) would also be nationalistic and anti-imperialist. It would be a cross-class coalition, and also a dual-gender one.

Personalistic, exclusionary dictatorships, such as that of the Somoza family, have historically been more vulnerable to revolutionary overthrow than any other sort of dictatorship (see, for example, Farhi 1990, 32–36; Foran 1992, 19; Goodwin 1997, 17–21; Skocpol 1994; Vilas 1986, 91; Wickham-Crowley 1992, 263–301). Because they try to maintain power and privilege for a very restricted group of people (in this case the Somoza family and some members of the National Guard), they often alienate the very groups of people who have been critical in supporting nondemocratic rule elsewhere.

In countries that are highly unequal, the upper and middle-upper classes, especially the landed elite, have the most to lose in a transition to an effective system of one-person, one-vote. But while members of those classes will tend to support dictatorship, they will not do so under any circumstances. They will not do so if they are excluded from the economic and political power that they consider to be rightfully theirs. This is what happened in Nicaragua: the upper and middle classes, especially the youngest members of those classes, the students, were to turn against the dictatorship that had turned against them.

A combination of Somoza's violent and exclusionary policies, along with a guerrilla agenda that was more explicitly nationalistic than Marxist, allowed for the formation of a multiclass revolutionary coalition. But what allowed for the formation of a dual-gender coalition? While the full answer to that question will take up the rest of this chapter, a preliminary answer may be found in the nature of Somocismo itself.

Women are often believed, in Latin America at least, to be more likely than men to support conservative politicians.[2] The reasons for this are

2. Because of "the widespread belief that women would vote for the status quo rather than for change, and that the female vote would be under the thumb of the conservative Catholic Church" Latin American leftists usually opposed giving women the right to vote. Instead

akin to the causes of peasant conservatism. Women, like peasants, tend to be especially vulnerable. They are less likely to be literate, less likely to have access to good jobs, and more likely to be hurt by political or economic change than are men. For these reasons, both peasants and women (and especially peasant women) are often more likely to support a stable dictatorship than to take a risk on an unstable democracy. This is especially the case if the national or local dictator makes even minimal efforts to give them something for their loyalty, a phenomenon known as clientelism.

The Somoza family hoped that clientelistic appeals to women would help to bolster the dictatorship, playing on images of familial benevolence (especially through the figures of the female members of that family) in an ultimately unsuccessful attempt to bolster the family's legitimacy. It was under the Somozas, in 1955, that Nicaraguan women finally got the vote, and members of the family, especially Luis and Anastasio Somoza Debayle, repeatedly claimed to be defenders of women's rights. For instance, women's rights were a theme in almost all of Anastasio Somoza Debayle's presidential campaign speeches in 1966. He would assert that his family and the Liberal Nationalist Party were to be credited with "having undertaken the job of incorporating into political life our most beloved one . . . the Nicaraguan woman" (quoted in González 1996, 8; also Kampwirth 1993, 65–67; González 2001).

The contradiction between the discourses of governmental benevolence and empowerment of female citizens, on the one hand, and the reality of violent exclusion of both women and men, on the other, may have been one reason for women's mobilization against the dictatorship. The reason the Somozas' female mobilization strategy did not work terribly well (and perhaps backfired) was that while vulnerable people, such as women and peasants, may be more conservative than others under some circumstances, they also may be more radical than others under other circumstances. Halfway through the dictatorship, Nicaragua began to change in ways that allowed many women to choose the latter option.

"women were enfranchised by conservatives in Chile, Brazil, and Peru with the explicit intention of using the women's vote to counter the growing political radicalism of an increasingly mobilized male electorate" (Jaquette 1989, 3; also see González and Kampwirth 2001; González 2001; Miller 1991, 97). Valentine Moghadam made a similar observation regarding French leftists' resistance to enfranchising women because of their belief that women were inherently conservative and would be controlled by the priests (1997, 144–45).

THE STRUCTURAL CRISIS

Starting in the mid-twentieth century, a series of socioeconomic changes occurred as Nicaragua, like other countries in the region, became more tightly linked to the global economy. These changes meant that by the 1970s, at the end of more than four decades of dictatorial rule by the Somoza family, Nicaragua was even more unequal than it had been in the 1930s. As agroexport crops (principally coffee, cotton, and beef; but also tobacco, sugar, and bananas) became more important economically, one effect was that many peasants were pushed off their land.[3]

The Somoza family encouraged this trend and was one of its chief beneficiaries. Only eight years into the Somoza dictatorship, the family had already acquired forty-six coffee plantations and fifty-one cattle ranches (Enríquez 1991, 33–46). During the course of the Somoza regime, Nicaragua was characterized by a progressively more unequal distribution of resources; the process of land concentration became particularly pronounced in the 1950s and 1960s. In 1963, 51 percent of all farms were smaller than seven hectares, though altogether they constituted only 3.6 percent of Nicaragua's farmland. In less than a decade, many small farmers had lost part or all of their land. By 1971 small farms made up only 43.8 percent of all farms and only 2.2 percent of all farmland (T. D. Mason 1992, 68).

During that same eight-year period, owners of large plantations of more than 350 hectares gained control of more land: in 1963 their plantations constituted 41 percent of all farms, rising to 46.8 percent of all farms by 1971. So many poor farmers were pushed off their land that by 1978, shortly before the overthrow of Somoza, more than "three quarters of the economically active population engaged in agriculture could be classified as landless or land poor" (T. D. Mason 1992, 68).

Increased landlessness had the effect of putting downward pressure on wages, especially as the main cash crops—cotton and coffee—were not very labor intensive, except during the harvest. Many who had formerly worked as subsistence farmers on small plots of land found themselves competing for a relatively small number of jobs on the plantations of large landowners. A fixed demand for workers combined with a rising supply meant that wages tended to fall. To make things worse, food prices rose as

---

3. Many scholars have documented and debated the impact of the expansion of agro-exports on the rural economy in Nicaragua, these include Enríquez 1997, 1991; Everingham 1996; Mason 1992; Midlarsky and Roberts 1985; Vilas 1986, 1995; Wickham-Crowley 1992.

land was concentrated and converted to cash crop production and less land was utilized for food production, ending Nicaragua's self-sufficiency in food (Enríquez 1991, 46). Squeezed between rising food prices and diminishing opportunities to earn income, most rural dwellers did not have enough income to cover even minimal nutritional requirements (Enríquez 1997, 62–63). Understandably, they were increasingly desperate to find solutions to the growing agrarian crisis.

PERSONAL SOLUTIONS TO THE NATIONAL CRISIS

One solution to the rural crisis was migration, to other rural areas, to urban areas, or less often, abroad, in search of work. Temporary migration in search of rural work was a predominantly male phenomenon, since men had greater opportunities to earn money in agriculture than did women. Moreover, men had far fewer child-care duties than women did, making temporary migration easier for them.

Yet far too often, men temporarily migrated to earn money for their families but ended up permanently abandoning those families instead, as they became demoralized in the face of growing poverty or met new women. This was especially common in the case of landless men. While it is true that male disloyalty to their wives and children was not a new phenomenon in Nicaragua, many believe that it became aggravated in the mid-twentieth century for reasons that, at least in part, were socioeconomic.[4] "Men are like marines: a woman in every port. Here there is a

4. Good data on family structures is difficult to come by in Nicaragua, particularly if one is interested in tracing change over time. Three of five studies that were conducted between 1950 and 1975 found that about a quarter of all households were headed by single females. The other two studies reached different conclusions: Reynaldo Antonio Tefel's 1972 study of poor urban households found that 48 percent were headed by single women and the Banco de Vivienda de Nicaragua's 1975 study found that only 10.4 percent of households in the study were headed by single women (reviewed in Diebold de Cruz and Pasos de Rappacioli 1975, 12). Another compilation of three sources, estimated that one-third to one-half of households were headed by single females by 1978 (Mason 1992, 76). A third review of two later studies found similar figures: 24.3 percent of households were headed by women according to a 1987 study, and 28 percent according to a 1993 study. Both the 1987 and 1993 studies found that rates of single-female-headed households was higher in urban areas: 30.3 percent and 37 percent respectively (Fauné 1995, 92). A fourth review of studies that were not cited in the first three reviews also found high rates of single-female-headed households nationwide, and even higher rates in Managua: about 50 percent according to a 1970 study, and 60 percent according to a 1984 source (Stephens 1988, 139).

All these studies found that rates of female-headed households in Nicaragua were high nationwide and even higher in the urban areas, and they seem to have shown an increase over time, though some of the variation was probably due to class and regional differences in the samples.

woman in every harvest. In the coffee harvest, a woman; in the cotton harvest, another woman" (interview, July 17, 1991).

Single-female-headed households were especially vulnerable economically. Since there were fewer economic opportunities for women than for men in the countryside, women made up a significant proportion of the hundreds of thousands who migrated to the cities during the second half of the twentieth century.[5] Migrating to the cities in search of work was so common that between 1950 and 1980 the population of the capital, Managua, grew from 110,000 to 662,000, an increase of 507 percent (Vilas 1995, 59). During this thirty-year period, Nicaragua converted itself from a predominantly rural country into a predominantly urban one. Only 15 percent of the population lived in cities in 1950; 54 percent were city dwellers by 1980 (Enríquez 1997, 182).

The women who would become active in the revolution were involved in this process of mass migration at least as much as anybody else. Sixty-one percent of the women in my sample, all of whom lived in Managua or neighboring Ciudad Sandino when I interviewed them, were born and raised somewhere else.[6] In an effort to fend off the agrarian crisis, many of those women moved (or were moved) multiple times before settling down in Managua.

Alejandra was born in 1960 in the rural town of Achuapa in the department of León. Like many poor children, she rarely lived in one household or in one place for very long.

[At first] I lived with my maternal grandmother. My grandmother worked in the countryside. I helped my grandfather as well. [My cousins and I] would go out with him to carry firewood, water, to sell cookies and pudding in town. I also did housework. . . . When I was about six years old I went to Chichigalpa, which is more urban, with my other grandmother. There I had the chance to go to school. I started grade school with my younger brother. . . . I went to Managua, when I was eight or

---

5. This inequality in employment opportunities—men having greater opportunities to work in rural agriculture, and women having greater opportunities to find work in urban domestic service—was a long-term trend in Nicaragua, a trend that helps explain the sexual imbalance between urban and rural dwellers. That imbalance became less acute over time, though it did not cease to exist during the second half of the Somoza dictatorship. In 1950, 44.2 percent of urban dwellers were men, while 55.8 percent were women; in 1960, 46 percent were men, whereas 54 percent were women; in 1970, 47.1 percent were men, and 52.9 percent were women; and in 1980, the year after Anastasio Somoza was overthrown, 47.9 percent were men, while 52.1 percent were women (figures from García and Gomáriz 1989, 360; see also Mason 1992, 76)

6. Of the thirty-six women who told me about their life histories, fourteen were from Managua, and twenty-two grew up elsewhere.

nine years old, where my mom worked as a maid. After that I went to León with a sister of my grandmother. That was a family with a lot of money, Sandinista. They put me in school and I managed to catch up to the right grade level for my age. Mom later began to work in a drug store; I helped her. It was in the San Judas neighborhood [of Managua], at that time it was wild, now it is a neighborhood but at that time the neighborhood did not exist yet. At that time I was about ten or eleven years old. From that point on [my mother] began to gain more independence. She worked in a hotel, later she bought a piece of land. When the earthquake struck [in 1972] I went to Chichigalpa with my grandmother. My mom went to work in Costa Rica. Later she returned and we were reunited again. . . . That was until 1977 when I began to associate with the Sandinista Front. (Interview, February 2, 1997)

All that traveling helped develop skills that Alejandra would draw upon when she joined the Sandinistas at the age of seventeen. Travel allowed her to develop more independence and a clearer understanding of the class and regional divisions of her country than would have been possible had she stayed in one place. The opportunity to compare is a radicalizing experience that Alejandra, like thousands of others, gained as an unintended consequence of her family's attempts to survive the crisis of capitalist modernization.

Alejandra's mother, like many Nicaraguans from the countryside, confronted the crisis with two main strategies. The first, as I have just discussed, was to migrate. The second strategy was for more women to enter the labor force. In her aggressive and desperate search for income, Alejandra's mother was not alone. Women made up 14 percent of the economically active population in 1950; they were 29 percent of the labor force by 1977 (Mason 1992, 74).[7]

These structural changes—the concentration of land, the breakup of households, the large-scale entrance of women into the labor force, migration to the cities—had their effect on participation in the guerrilla struggle. Large numbers of the newly landless were open to mobilization

7. These figures are useful for illustrating increases in women's participation in the paid labor force, but they greatly underestimate that trend. Such figures measure women's participation in the formal labor force (that is, in salaried positions where the worker pays taxes and may receive benefits). But women in Latin America are overrepresented in informal-sector jobs, where they pay few or no taxes, receive no benefits, and go unnoticed by government economists, though anyone who has ever been to a Central American city could hardly fail to notice them. Many of the jobs that Alejandra and her mother did, such as carrying wood, selling candy, or cleaning the houses of others, would not have made their way into economic statistics.

by a group, such as the FSLN, that offered political and economic solutions to their problems (Booth 1985, 85; Mason 1992, 72).

Not only do these socioeconomic factors help explain high levels of participation in the guerrilla struggle, they also help account for the high levels of *female* participation. Along with other factors, the disruption of family life and the massive entrance of women into the workforce (both indirectly caused by land concentration), started many women on a path of community involvement that eventually led to participation in the guerrilla struggle.

Emilia, the director of a women's center in Ciudad Sandino (a working-class suburb of Managua) at the time of our interview, discussed how the absence of male authority figures, and the experience of migration from the countryside to the city, allowed both her mother and her to participate in revolutionary organizations in the 1970s.[8] The fifth of eight children, Emilia was born in the rural town of El Sauce in the department of León and lived there with her parents until 1963. "Mom raised me until I was ten years old. She washed, ironed, and took care of chickens and pigs to sell. Then my mom separated from my dad and I had to work as a maid. I lived where I worked. . . . In 1966 I still worked as a maid. My bosses were organized with the guerrilla army. . . . One began to hear about Sandino's guerrillas. They told me that perhaps some day all of you can cease to be maids" (interview, January 27, 1997). For a rural woman, like Emilia's mother, the loss of her husband's support created a economic crisis that could only be resolved at a very high cost. Since she was already working for income, the only way to survive was to send her young children out to work. For Emilia herself, entering the workforce did not create organizing opportunities, at least not immediately, despite the fact that her bosses were themselves organized in the guerrilla struggle. But it did plant the idea of organizing, as she had heard of "Sandino's guerrillas." After migrating, she would act on that thought.

In 1972 we came to live here in Ciudad Sandino. My mom was the first to organize. Later she started to integrate me. At that time Maura Clarke came and with her we started to organize ourselves directly. Maura was a very revolutionary compañera *despite the fact that she was a nun. There were ten women more or less. They*

8. Ciudad Sandino, named after the hero of the rebellion against Somoza and the U.S. Marines in the 1930s, had a different name under Somoza, obviously. Prior to 1979, Ciudad Sandino was OPEN 3 (Operación Permanente de la Emergencia Nacional), a shantytown created for the hundreds of families who lost their homes due to flooding near Lake Managua in 1969 (Williams 1989, 45; Randall 1981, 18–23).

started to put water and light meters. They charged twenty cordobas for water. So we started to go out into the street. We said ten [cordobas] yes, twenty no. Light also: fifteen [cordobas] yes, twenty no. . . . The majority of the women were very timid, they didn't want to leave their houses on account of their husbands . . . [in contrast] the majority of us were single women. I had already been married and I had separated from him; I had a daughter. We lived with my mom and a sister. . . . That was the beginning of the struggle and we already were started to talk more deeply as women, about women's rights. Around 1978 we gave the organization a name: AMPRONAC [Asociación de Mujeres ante la Problemática Nacional]. It was already a national organization. (Interview, January 27, 1997)

The economic crisis that drove Emilia's family to migrate did not disappear with their arrival in Ciudad Sandino. But things were different in some ways: organizing was easier.

In part that was because the church, through the Maryknoll sister Maura Clarke, supported women's organizing. That organizing was not very radical; the call was merely for lowering the price of basic services. And it was hardly feminist, if feminist organizing is that which directly challenges gendered power relations. Nonetheless, it was a threat to many, and men often dealt with that threat by forbidding their women to participate. So the women who organized through the church were not drawn from all sectors: they were mainly single women, those who were most economically desperate, but also most personally free.

At that time I was already a worker. We organized in the factory, we would bring flyers to the factory. They said to me, Emilia, they are going to kill you, they are going to imprison you. But I didn't pay much attention. Around 1978, once in a convention in Carazo, a Sandinista convention, some reporters arrived from La Prensa. *They didn't let them in, but a reporter took a picture of me. . . . When I arrived at work, my boss called me and he showed me the photo and he said, what were you doing there? He said, look, if I see you there again, I will have you arrested. . . . The next day the National Guard arrived at my workplace [but] didn't take anyone. At 3:00 that afternoon we left. Another* compañero *got off his bus and there they were waiting for him. He was in prison for three months. You couldn't recognize him when he got out, he was all swollen. And they kept a watch on my house. (Interview, January 27, 1997)*

Emilia's work was risky, without a doubt, but the same sexism that made it hard for women to organize also gave a certain degree of protection to activist women. While her fellow worker, a man, was captured and tortured for three months, she was not. Her house was watched by the police, but even though she was also heavily involved in revolutionary organizing, she was not seen as equally threatening.[9] The dictatorship's own sexism left women like Emilia relatively free to organize in ways that would bring an end to the dictatorship.

A series of structural or socioeconomic changes created the conditions that allowed many more women to organize than had done so during past crises. Yet by themselves, socioeconomic changes do not create a revolution. Discontent needs to be channeled, and there is nothing preordained about the shape that channel will take. As Carlos Vilas has noted, both radical right-wing and radical left-wing groups seek to mobilize the same kinds of people: the losers in the sorts of socioeconomic transformations I described earlier. "Revolution and counterrevolution compete, sociologically speaking, for the support of the same actors" (1995, 28).

CHANNELING THE CRISIS

Why did the Nicaraguan revolutionaries win the support of so many discontented women? A number of ideological and organizational changes, beginning in the 1960s, channeled the discontent generated by the structural crisis of the 1950s. The most important of these changes, for the purpose of explaining female participation in the guerrilla struggle, were (1) the transformation of the church, and (2) the transformation of guerrilla strategies.

Liberation theology emerged far from Central America, in South America and Europe, but it was to have an explosive effect in Nicaragua. This new theology came out of two events: the Vatican II Council (1962–65) and the Latin American Bishops' Conference at Medellín, Colombia (1968). At Vatican II, as a result of significant rethinking of the church's traditional role in the world, the church was called "to dialogue with the world, to confront it, to live within it, and to influence it" (quoted in Williams 1989, 1). In 1968, the reformist thought of Vatican II was applied to Latin America, and, in the process, extended significantly. It was in Medellín that, as many have claimed, the church changed sides. Part of this process meant that in the years following the Medellín conference,

9. Women certainly were not immune from the Somoza dictatorship's violence, but in comparison with men, they were somewhat less likely to be targeted by the regime. In other countries, the myth of women as inherently apolitical and harmless has also led to women finding themselves somewhat freer than men to join in opposition politics (e.g., Alvarez 1990; Jaquette 1989; Long 1996; Reif 1986; Waylen 1994).

growing numbers of clergy, like Maura Clarke, left the comfort of rectories and convents to work and live with the poor. These experiences deepened their commitment to change, leading, oftentimes, to political action.

And it was not just a few clergy members who sought to practice their religion through struggle against worldly injustice. Through *comunidades eclesiales de base* (Christian base communities, or CEBs), poor people were mobilized to prayer, analysis, and often radical action. While the claim that the church organized the guerrillas is a gross simplification of the re-lationship between consciousness and action, the FSLN did find its most radical and receptive constituents in the areas were the CEBs were al-ready present (Montgomery 1983, 92; on liberation theology in Nica-ragua, see also Booth 1985; Crahan 1987; Lancaster 1988; Vilas 1995).

One of the many women who became politicized through religion was Dorotea Wilson.[10] Although Wilson was unusual in that she would rise far in the guerrilla ranks (in the late 1990s she was one of only three women on the FSLN's National Directorate), her roots in the liberation theology movement were not unusual. The fourth of nine children, Dorotea Wilson was born in 1950 in Puerto Cabezas, on the Atlantic Coast of Nicaragua. When her father, a miner, and her mother, a house-wife, separated in 1961, the family was pulled apart.

The children were divided. My dad took the four boys and me. The rest went with my mom. I ceased to have contact with my mom. I went to live in the mining area, I studied there with the Maryknoll mothers. . . . I studied all of grade school with them. María Laura, who they killed in El Salvador, was my teacher. . . . When I was seventeen or eighteen years old I went to live in a convent, to study. They were Carmelites of the Blessed Heart, they were contemplative. . . . I finished up with other nuns from the Order of Saint Ines, a religious school. (Interview, February 5, 1997)

Such schooling was a logical preparation for a life in the clergy, and in fact, Wilson was to become a missionary. But her religious training was also a form of political training. This is how she answered me when I asked what her first political experience had been:

The contact with the progressive clergy helped me a lot to think about poverty in Nicaragua. And also the experience of living in the mining area. . . . I joined the Sandinista Front while I was a missionary. Four out of the eleven of us joined the

---

10. I identify Wilson by her real name, instead of a pseudonym, because she is a prominent public figure, and thus, this bibliographical information is a contribution to the historic record.

guerrillas. Although the others all knew; they supported us morally and with their silence. And they worked in the rear guard. In 1975 or '76 I joined the Sandinista Front, we had contact with the base communities. In 1976, we started to create cells, on the [Atlantic] Coast and in Managua. (Interview, February 5, 1997)

Dorotea Wilson was only one of many who pointed to their religious education as being critical in initiating them into political life. Silvia, a firstborn who did semiclandestine work with the FSLN in the 1970s, explained that in her school "the nuns taught us another manner to live one's religion, it was a very practical manner . . . that left quite an impression on me" (interview, January 15, 1997).

Perhaps more surprising was the story of Cristiana. Also a firstborn, Cristiana, the daughter of a senator from Somoza's party, would go on to become a student activist against Somoza. She traced that activism to the liberal ideology of her father (who tolerated her activities even when he disagreed), her mother's spirit of service, and her religious training. "I studied in a religious school: La Asunción of León. It was the era of Medellín, there was a very social focus. I participated in community organizations from a very young age. In high school, I participated in fund-raising projects, in lay missionary programs. I spent a year in Guatemala, in an indigenous town. That was very important" (interview, January 30, 1997).

So far, the story I have told about why so many Nicaraguan women involved themselves in the guerrilla struggle has focused on factors that had nothing to do with the guerrillas themselves. Socioeconomic changes increased the numbers of single-female-headed households and the rates of migration from the countryside to the city. The structural changes caused by globalization created greater inequality and discontent than ever. That discontent would then be given meaning by the new liberation theology movement. But neither the structural nor the ideological changes that occurred in Nicaragua were controlled by the guerrillas.

What the Sandinista guerrillas could control was their own strategy: who they would admit to the guerrilla ranks, how they would recruit, and where they would organize. Possibly learning from the defeat of Che Guevara in Bolivia, and definitely learning from their own military defeats over the course of the 1960s, the Sandinistas were the first Latin American guerrillas to drop the small-group orientation of the foco strategy in favor of a strategy of mass mobilization.[11]

11. Tomás Borge, the only one of the three original founders of the FSLN to survive to see Somoza overthrown, identified the 1967 massacre of Sandinistas at Pancasán as the turning

Mass mobilization was different from Cuban foco strategy. It meant that the guerrillas sought to recruit all who would consider joining, in any capacity. If a female missionary was willing to struggle alongside more-traditional guerrillas, she was more than welcome. Male guerrillas had to overcome their sexism, at least to the extent of inviting women into their ranks, if they were to succeed with their mass mobilization strategy. This is not to say that they ceased to be sexist, but rather that it was in their interest to suppress sexist feelings, to increase their numbers.

Once the FSLN admitted women as equals, the traditional gender division of labor often broke down, under the nontraditional conditions of guerrilla life. Dorotea Wilson, the missionary from the Atlantic Coast who became a guerrilla leader, discussed relations between men and women during the guerrilla struggle of the 1960s and 1970s and compared it with the revolution of the 1980s, the time following what many Nicaraguans call the "triumph," or the overthrow of Somoza. "There was more equality in the mountains than after the triumph. We shared what we had. We shared the cooking duties, the gun cleaning, the responsibilities in the cadre. . . . There wasn't gender consciousness in the guerrilla forces, what there was was an incredible solidarity. At any time men as much as women could be killed. Later a machista life began, which is Nicaraguan culture. They returned to what they considered a normal life" (interview, February 5, 1997).[12] Her description of the egalitarianism of the guerrilla struggle, to be followed to a return to "normal" inequality once the dictatorship had been overthrown, was quite common. But her memory of near perfect egalitarianism during the guerrilla struggle was far from universal, as illustrated by María's answer to my question about relations between men and women:

Look, I spent a lot of time being annoyed. . . . There was one compañero *in particular that always wanted the* compañeras *to screw with him. I myself, for exam-*

---

point that marked the end of the Sandinista's use of the foco strategy and the beginning of the mass mobilization strategy (Borge 1984, 49, 55–56).

12. Ilja Luciak offers further evidence that the FSLN's guerrilla-era commitment to gender equality was more instrumental than principled. For instance, while the early goal of movement toward gender equality that appeared in the FSLN's 1969 Historic Program was often attributed to FSLN founder Carlos Fonseca, Luciak reports "well-founded speculation that the section on women was conceived by an 'internationalist' FSLN collaborator" (2000, 17). He also quotes Dora María Tellez, who rose to the rank of commander during the guerrilla struggle, as having no recollection of ever having discussed gender issues during the guerrilla period (2000, 17). Another reason to suspect that the guerrilla-era commitment to mobilizing women was mainly a response to temporary need rather than a permanent commitment to placing women in powerful positions was the fact that, as Luciak documents in detail, women were greatly underrepresented in positions of formal power after the FSLN took power in 1979 (2000, 17–25 and tables 1, 2, and 3).

ple, had relations with him and I didn't want to. Later it didn't seem right to me. I do think that in many things . . . there wasn't the same level of responsibility. One thing is that the experience in the city is different from the experience in the mountains. For the most part people helped us, they gave us food. I never had to serve the compañeros. (Interview, January 23, 1997)

What could explain the differences in María's and Dorotea Wilson's perceptions of guerrilla life? María mentioned one difference between their experiences—she worked in the city whereas Wilson worked in the countryside—though she mentioned that factor to suggest that women were expected to serve *more* in the countryside. It is possible that she was wrong about that; perhaps life was more egalitarian in the mountains, which could explain Wilson's experience. Or perhaps age and status shaped men's treatment of them: Wilson joined when she was already twenty-five or twenty-six years old, and a missionary, while María was only nineteen and a student when she became an activist.

Wilson probably was treated better, whether she started with a greater prestige or merely acquired it quickly.[13] That early experience with the guerrillas may very well have shaped the divergent paths their lives would take: Wilson would go on to make her entire career within the Sandinista party, while María would eventually reject her party membership and become assistant director of an organization that defended the rights of sexual minorities.

In addition to recruiting both women and men for the guerrilla struggle, the Sandinistas produced a second strategic innovation, a shift from a purely military strategy to a political-military one. Part of this latter strategy involved efforts to incorporate a wide variety of social organizations into the Sandinista coalition, either by actively founding new groups or by incorporating preexisting opposition groups into the fold.

Of all these groups, probably most vital to the success of the Sandinistas were the student organizations. Student groups were an integral part of the great web that was Sandinismo; in fact, they were the single most

---

13. I say that she "probably" was treated better, for one explanation of the discrepancy between their memories would be that their experiences in the 1980s and 1990s have colored their memories of the 1970s, leading Wilson to remember gender relations as more equal than they were, or leading María to remember them as more unequal than they were. But although that possibility should not be discounted, I think their memories are probably reliable. First, Dorotea Wilson was quite willing to criticize Sandinista sexism following the overthrow of Somoza. Second, many other women have given similar accounts to me. In their cases there was also a positive correlation between the level of a woman's prestige within the guerrilla struggle and her recollection of gender relations as having been equal.

important type of revolutionary organization. Of the twenty-two organizations that belonged to the Sandinista-affiliated Movimiento Pueblo Unido (United People's Movement, or MPU), nine were student groups (Booth 1985, 111). Oftentimes, student groups, whether organized by the FSLN or not, served as spaces for recruitment into the guerrilla movement.

Sonia was born in 1957, the older of two girls born to a single woman who briefly made her living as a rural teacher, and later (after she was fired for political reasons) as a washerwoman in the town of Somoto, near the border with Honduras. According to Sonia, an independent "protest theater group" that she helped organize in high school was her first political experience. Her participation in this group was one reason why the local guerrillas identified her as a good candidate. "In 1974 or '75 they looked for me through a *compañero* to carry mail between Honduras and Nicaragua. The group was the GPP [Guerra Prolongada Popular], which was very big into political training. First they gave you a lot of political lessons, a lot of reading, Maoism . . . so many crazy things, this about Mao, Soviet books, Maxim Gorky's *Mother.* And we would get together to talk" (interview, January 19, 1997). Sonia's early experiences in the GPP tendency within the FSLN illustrate the fluid links between revolutionary groups and the armed guerrilla organization. Initially, she was not recruited for battle but for running mail. Nonetheless, she was socialized in the same way as others; that is, into a movement that employed a political-military strategy.

When the Guard cracked down in 1975 or 1976, killing the man who had initially recruited her, she was left without contacts. She could have stayed in Somoto, where her personal relationships protected her. "My best friends were daughters of the Guard—they were hippies—anyone might have said that I was a hippy but not that I was from the Sandinista Front" (interview, January 19, 1997). But Sonia was anxious to reconnect with the Sandinista web, so she left for Managua, where she worked in the student movement at the National Autonomous University.

Within a year, she returned to her home in the North, for a number of reasons. First, she was unemployed and out of money. Second, the National Guard increasingly used violence against college students. And there was a third reason for her decision to leave the university:

The fact is that we were very attached to our tendencies as well. There were people around from the GPP but one didn't know who they were. Until 1978 I spent my time very disconnected in Somoto, in Esteli, until the point when I said to myself, enough is enough. . . . The situation was such that you had to do something. . . . I decided that it doesn't matter, the first tendency that comes looking for me is the one I will join. So then the Terceristas contacted me. I involved myself in organizing refugee camps in the mountains, land seizures, demands for minimum wage, work with peasants. I would go to Honduras. By that time I was already afraid that they might kill me. My work involved moving people around, getting false papers, buying arms, and also detecting people who turned us in to the Guard since I knew the area very well. We would steal vehicles in Honduras, getting a hold of a lot of medicine. It was logistical support. (Interview, January 19, 1997)

What Sonia called logistical support occasionally involved combat, and it always involved the risk of being "disappeared" (tortured and murdered) if one was caught by the National Guard. Her work probably should be located somewhere in the center of the range of activities that lay between combat and support.

Sonia's complicated response in explaining her role in the FSLN was not unusual: within the Sandinista coalition there was a long continuum between unarmed and armed work. The armed guerrillas were very dependent on the unarmed revolutionaries for support, for recruitment, and for the unrelenting pressure that would help to bring down the dictatorship. As with any continuum, the distinction between one position and another was not always clear. A student activist was not armed, but she might be called upon to make and throw Molotov cocktails on occasion. And her work was not necessarily less dangerous: while it would be easier for her to plausibly deny links to the guerrillas if she were caught, it was also easier for the National Guard to catch her, since her work was more public.

Sonia's story is a nice illustration of the importance of the shift to the mass mobilization strategy in enlisting activists and in keeping old activists within the Sandinista fold. Although she temporarily lost her connection with the FSLN as a result of her contact's death, she was to reconnect on multiple occasions. In fact, the main limit to reconnection was a psychological one, that is, her loyalty to one of the three tendencies within the FSLN.[14] Those tendencies would reunite in the year of Somoza's fall.

So far, I have shown how the combination of structural factors (economic globalization, high rates of single-female-headed-households, and mass migration to the cities) and ideological and strategic factors (the rise of liberation theology and the FSLN's shift to the mass mobilization strategy) made it possible for large numbers of women to join the Sandinista

14. On the tendencies, see Booth 1985, 143–46.

coalition. But those public factors do not fully explain why particular women became Sandinistas. I now turn to the personal characteristics—family traditions of resistance, participation in preexisting networks, and year of birth—that help explain why specific women became revolutionary activists.

PERSONAL ROOTS OF REBELLION

Millions of women experienced the structural crisis, organizational opportunities, and dictatorial violence that characterized Nicaragua in the second half of the twentieth century. But most of those women did not join revolutionary organizations. Instead, most women, and most men for that matter, did their best to find personal rather than public solutions to the crisis. In short, most people fled from risk. And this was logical enough, for the chance of successfully overthrowing the dictator was very low and the cost of defeat very high. Why did some women seek out public, or organizational, solutions to their personal and national problems?

One answer can be found in the families into which these women had been born. Accidents of birth helped to create revolutionary activists, long before the revolutionary organizations even existed. Girls born into families with a tradition of resistance to authority (especially if some family members were involved in anti-Somoza activism) were more likely than girls from less political families to become involved with the Sandinista coalition. Moreover, oldest children were more likely than their younger siblings to be confided in by adults and to be socialized into family traditions of resistance. Mónica explained that her first political experience occurred in 1960, when her father asked her to help prepare to seize the barracks of the National Guard. "He was an anti-Somoza fighter. That made a big impression on me. He needed help to make some Molotov cocktails. It was my job to cut the bicycle tires and stick them in the bottle" (interview, January 28, 1997). Mónica was only twelve when she first directly participated in the struggle against the dictatorship. It is doubtful that she would have been chosen for the task of weapon making if there had been older children in the house. But because luck made her the oldest of her five siblings, she was chosen for the task that would start her on her activist path.

Family networks, such as Mónica's, were one of the most important preexisting networks used by the Sandinistas for recruitment. Trust probably was the single most important reason for the reliance on family networks; Sandinistas might pay with their lives for the mistake of trying to recruit a person who turned out to be a Somoza supporter. In fact, family loyalties often overrode political loyalties, and I have heard various stories about how Somoza supporters, even National Guardsmen, knew of a relative's involvement with the Sandinistas but protected him or her with silence. Another reason for the reliance on family networks was that, after decades of mass migration, families were widely dispersed: a contact in one area could lead to a new Sandinista stronghold in another part of the country (Booth 1985, 141).

Family traditions of resistance may have played an especially important role in mobilizing those women who could look to female relatives as role models of resistance. Diana, the ninth of ten children, who was raised in the small town of Matiwás in the department of Matagalpa, explained to me that her own great-grandmother had played a role in an earlier antidictatorial movement:

Women always participated to a certain degree. There was the example of Sandino. While women were not involved in combat [in Sandino's army] the army had an enormous support network of women. My great-grandmother was part of a women's collaboration network. . . . Women joined, above all, because of their level of sensitivity to the most acute problems. That is normal, it is a projection of our traditional roles, which are to save others. The only difference [between the Sandinista rebellions of the 1930s and 1970s] was that young women were involved in combat in the second case. While it wasn't a completely conscious effort, you could say that it was one way to demand women's rights, by participating in a sphere which has traditionally belonged exclusively to men, that is, war. (Interview, January 24, 1997)

Because of its long history of foreign intervention and dictatorship, Nicaragua also has a long history of resistance. These traditions allowed late twentieth-century revolutionary activists to imagine that resistance was possible. But not everyone was caught up in that political culture. Those who were more likely to be so were people, like Diana, who were socialized into that culture through their families, often to be recruited later on through family networks.

Family networks were central to the success of the Sandinistas, but they were not the only preexisting networks that provided recruitment opportunities for the FSLN. Church groups, and especially student groups, that existed prior to the Sandinistas were central to the revolutionary project. Many church and student groups were founded for reasons that originally had nothing to do with Sandinismo. Because of those origins, they were spaces where participants could safely acquire organizing skills without being identified as opponents of the dictatorship. In fact, sometimes the activists themselves did not recognize the full extent of their involvement with the Sandinista coalition. Esperanza, the older of two siblings, discussed her surprise when she realized that she had become a Sandinista activist right within her Catholic school:

At that time I was very ignorant. I didn't understand why the Sandinista Front existed. I would say that they were communists without even knowing what communism was. . . . The Association of High School Students was, let's say, a cell of the Sandinista Front. The Sandinistas tried to mobilize students in high schools like mine because we could support them. When I joined, I joined because I was attracted by their talk of changes. But they never spoke of the Sandinista Front. Then they invited me to a meeting at the UNAN [the National Autonomous University]. What a meeting. It was in 1977. We started to sing the Sandinista anthem and I was scared to death. (Interview, January 25, 1997)

Despite her initial fear, by the next year, when she was eighteen, she was working more directly with the FSLN. "It was my first contact with the writings of Sandino and Che Guevara. That was a complete awakening" (interview, January 25, 1997).

Organizing students was critical for various reasons. Student organizations were preexisting networks that could be mobilized for new purposes. Students, whose job was to read and write, could occupy themselves with the writings of Sandino and Che without attracting too much attention. And participation in student organizations was fairly easily hidden from the eyes of disapproving parents. I asked Esperanza how her parents reacted to her activism. "My parents didn't know anything. My brother was even in a guerrilla cell, of the GPP. I knew his secret and he knew mine. It wasn't until after the revolution that they realized" (interview, January 25, 1997).

The women I interviewed who participated in the anti-Somoza struggle were, on average, far more educated than the average Nicaraguan woman. In my sample, 76 percent had attended at least some college, 12 percent attended at least some high school, and the other 12 percent attended at least some grade school.[15] In sharp contrast, only 3.6 percent of Nicaraguan women have attended college, while a full 27.8 percent of

---

15. Out of the 34 who discussed their educational histories with me, 24 had attended some college (a few had master's degrees), 5 attended some high school, and 5 attended some grade school.

Nicaraguan women have not attended school at all (Acevedo et al. 1996, 103).

These figures are dramatic. But they need to be qualified in several ways. My data were collected in 1997, while the source for the national-level data is 1992. That could make a slight difference in the educational figures, though the period in which access to education made its greatest advances was during the revolution (1979–90), when, in fact, nearly all the women I interviewed continued their formal education.

Comparing the educational levels of the women I interviewed in Nicaragua with the educational levels of the women I interviewed in El Salvador (detailed in Chapter 2) suggests that the opportunities created by the revolution are the most important explanation for why so many Nicaraguan women had gone to college. One might have expected the Salvadorans to have similar educational backgrounds. The difference is that they had not lived through a revolution, since the Salvadoran guerrillas did not succeed in overthrowing the military dictatorship.

Living through a revolution (during which time education was basically free at all levels) seems to have been a great advantage for the Nicaraguans, at least in terms of education. The average educational achievements of the Salvadorans were considerably lower than those of the Nicaraguans: while 76 percent of the Nicaraguans had attended some college, 46.6 percent of the Salvadorans had done so; 12 percent of the Nicaraguans had attended some high school as opposed to 33.3 percent of the Salvadorans; 12 percent of the Nicaraguans had attended some grade school as opposed to 20 percent of the Salvadorans.

Another factor to consider in explaining the high rates of education among the women I interviewed in Nicaragua is that guerrillas, especially guerrilla leaders, have tended to be drawn from the ranks of university students. Timothy Wickham-Crowley found that the emergence of broad-based guerrilla movements in Latin America has been consistently proceeded by an explosion in university enrollments. In the case of Nicaragua, university enrollment increased from 3,042 to 15,579 between 1965 and 1975, an increase of 412 percent (1992, 220).

While the arguments about the educational backgrounds of guerrilla leaders or high-prestige activists would not necessarily apply here (since this is largely a study of midprestige activists), it seems logical that they would apply to many midprestige activists. A woman who had been in school during the last years of the dictatorship was more likely to have participated in anti-Somoza student activities than a woman who had dropped out of school early. The woman who was still in school was more likely to have come from a relatively privileged background, providing her with the resources that facilitate activism. The poorest of the poor are very unlikely revolutionaries, since they are too overwhelmed by the reality of everyday life to be able to organize to change that reality.

The final personal factor that could exceed all the others in importance is year of birth, or age. Obviously, only women who, at the time of the Sandinista struggle against Somoza, were already past early childhood and had not yet reached old age were likely to join the Sandinista coalition. Still, even with those parameters, the majority of the female population was available for mobilization by the Sandinistas, at least in theory. However, activists were drawn from a much narrower band of the age spectrum.

The women in my sample who participated in the struggle against Somoza were born between the years 1935 and 1961. Twenty-five of them were born between 1948 and 1961, while only three were born before 1948. Clearly, women who were born earlier or later might have been just as angered by the dictatorship; they might have been just as socially engaged; and they might have been just as willing to take personal risks to democratize their country. But they had been born at the wrong time.

The average year of birth of a Nicaraguan woman who participated in the struggle against Somoza (in my sample) was 1954. That means the average woman would have been fourteen in 1968, when liberation theology first emerged on the world stage. She would have been eighteen when the devastating earthquake of 1972 hit Managua, causing a national crisis that shook the foundations of the dictatorship. By that point she was old enough to make the decision to join the guerrillas (even if her parents disapproved) and young enough not to be burdened with the responsibility of children, or at least not many.

WHY SO MANY SANDINISTA WOMEN?

A series of political, structural, ideological, and personal factors—in combination—pushed some Nicaraguan women, and pulled others, into revolutionary politics in the 1960s and, especially, the 1970s. The answer to the question of why the FSLN was the first guerrilla movement in Latin America that was truly a dual-gender coalition can be found in these combined factors. The country's personalistic and exclusionary dictatorship, that of the Somoza family, extended certain limited rights to women with one hand at the same time as it stole from those same women with the other. Lifting expectations and then dashing them is one way in which states can bring guerrilla movements upon themselves.

But personalistic and exclusionary dictatorships are hardly a recent phenomenon, and male guerrillas have struggled against them for a long time. What was new about the Sandinistas is that they incorporated large numbers of women into their ranks. This was possible due to a series of structural, ideological, and personal factors that happened to come together at the same time. Land concentration and growing economic inequality, starting in the 1950s, had the effect of leading to increased rates of family abandonment on the part of fathers. Single mothers moved in massive numbers to urban areas, where they desperately sought out ways to support their children.

One of those ways was to act collectively. While collective action was not invented in the 1960s, there was a new global ideology—liberation theology—that gave a distinct meaning to collective action. Through liberation theology, the church changed sides; and, to a large extent, changing sides was a gendered as well as a class shift. If to be truly Christian meant to work for the kingdom of God on earth, nobody was exempt, not females, not even young females. The Latin America of the late 1960s and early 1970s was a very different place from the Latin America of the 1950s in which the Cubans overthrew their dictator. In that pre–Vatican II world the opportunities for women's mobilization were far fewer, as I will discuss in Chapter 4.

Another major ideological shift also clearly contrasts with the Cuban guerrilla struggle. When the Sandinistas emerged in 1961, they employed the same *foquista* strategy that the Cubans had effectively used, but they were not to stick with that strategy. Instead they shifted from the small foco bands to a mass mobilization strategy that required them to reach out to women, like it or not. They were fortunate enough to find women who had already been freed from many of their traditional constraints.

The women they successfully recruited were those who had been touched in very particular ways by the changes of the previous generation. While all Nicaraguan women had been raised in a country in which there were traditions of resistance to illegitimate authority, the women who actually joined the Sandinistas were socialized into those traditions early on, in very powerful and personal ways: through their families or their favorite teachers.

Although the majority were from poor backgrounds, a large minority of them were privileged in class terms relative to their society, one in which to be lower-middle class was, and is, to be privileged.[16] Relative privilege also meant that they were more likely than some to be students, a sector from which the FSLN recruited heavily. I suspect that female rank-and-file Sandinistas were more likely to be of urban origin, and to have traced their political roots to the student movement, than were male rank-and-file Sandinistas. I have no definitive way of confirming my suspicion, since all the people in my sample were women and I know of no study of the backgrounds of Sandinistas that simultaneously breaks down data by sex and social background.[17] Yet studies of other guerrilla movements (the Cuban guerrillas, the guerrilla movements of the 1960s, and Peru's Sendero Luminoso) have found that while women who participated in those movements were mainly of urban origin (or migrants to urban areas) and highly educated, only some of the men fit that description (Barrig 1998, 112–14; Foran, Klouzal, and Rivera 1997, 25–34; Wickham-Crowley 1992, 21).[18]

It seems likely that the average woman of the FSLN was also more urban and more educated than the average man of the FSLN, since urban women and students generally were freer to violate their traditional gender roles than were rural women and nonstudents. As a rule of thumb, I think we should assume that the social origins and motivations of female guerrillas and male guerrillas will differ in most, if not all, cases. To some extent, males and females always see the world differently, and act differently, because their experiences and opportunities differ. The greater the disparity between the way men and women are treated in a given society, the more likely that male political activists (including guerrillas) will differ from female political activists.

Finally, the women who tied their fates to the Sandinista coalition were nearly always young: fairly free from familial duties, and fairly oblivious to the serious risks that participation in the Sandinista coalition entailed. Yet as it turned out, they, and not their more cautious elders, were right. The multiclass, dual-gender coalition that was the FSLN was to triumph over the Somoza dictatorship, ushering in the revolution in July 1979.

---

16. In the cases where I have data on their class backgrounds, 15 were from poor backgrounds (with parents including peasants, bread bakers, construction workers, maids, and market vendors), while 11 were from middle- or upper-class backgrounds (with parents including teachers, landowners, housewives, owner of a public-transportation company, and a senator).

17. An exception is Wickham-Crowley's chart of the social origins of guerrillas, though it only reports the origins of top leaders (1992, 335–36).

18. These studies are discussed in greater detail in the Appendix on the social origins of the guerrillas.

2 Feminine Challenges to Military Rule in El Salvador

Barely a year after the Sandinista guerrillas successfully overthrew the Somoza dictatorship in Nicaragua, another guerrilla coalition declared war on another dictatorial regime, this time in El Salvador. In El Salvador, as in Nicaragua, women constituted a significant proportion of the guerrillas and other revolutionary activists who desperately sought radical solutions to extreme problems, playing prominent roles both in the FMLN (Frente Farabundo Martí para la Liberación Nacional) and in a variety of organizations that formed the revolutionary coalition, including church groups, student groups, and labor unions. In El Salvador, just as in Nicaragua, women chose to take on such risks for reasons that were similar to those that motivated their male counterparts, though their experiences within the revolutionary coalition often differed in important ways from men's experiences.

Despite the significant differences in the stories of Nicaragua and El Salvador from a statecentric perspective (the Nicaraguan FSLN successfully overthrew the dictatorship, whereas, after more than a decade of war, the Salvadoran FMLN was to accept a negotiated settlement with the state it sought to overthrow), the recent histories of those two Central American countries have much in common from the perspective of many of the women who helped make those histories. By focusing on some of the individuals who participated in the revolutionary coalitions, rather than on the state as is common in studies of revolutionary situations, my comparison of the cases of Nicaragua and El Salvador points to the need to ask a variety of questions, using a variety of methodologies, if students of revolution are to avoid flattening what are in reality complicated processes. Before analyzing Salvadoran women's participation in the war of the 1980s, I will briefly review the similarities and differences between

Nicaragua and El Salvador, seen from the perspective of previous studies of the two cases.[1]

EL SALVADOR AND NICARAGUA COMPARED

In discussions of twentieth-century politics in Latin America, the story of the guerrilla struggle in El Salvador is often lumped together with that of Nicaragua. In fact, there are some good reasons for this lumping: in both countries, decades of dictatorship set the stage for guerrilla wars; in both countries, a rural crisis broke family bonds and drove waves of migration to the cities; in both countries, the varied responses to that crisis were informed by the liberation theology movement; and in both countries, the United States played a prominent role in politics. Yet lumping can only be carried to a point. First of all, the nature of the dictatorships in the two countries varied in ways that would shape the fates of those who sought to oppose them. While the personalistic Somoza family dynasty engendered the wrath of the great majority of Nicaraguans, the military dictatorship in El Salvador was impersonal, abstract, collective. Although it was equally long-lived and even more brutal than its Nicaraguan counterpart, it was not associated with any one individual or family who could be blamed for the hardships that most Salvadorans faced. The case of El Salvador—in which guerrillas failed to overthrow the state—shows once again that impersonal military dictatorships are far less likely to fall to guerrillas than are personalistic family dictatorships (see, for example, Goodwin 1997, 20; Midlarsky and Roberts 1985, 183–87; Wickham-Crowley 1992, 158–59, 205–6, 282–88).

A second difference between the two cases lies in the role of the United States. While the United States played an important role in both countries in the second half of the twentieth century, its involvement in the first half of the century was far more prominent in Nicaragua. The Somoza dynasty, after all, was founded immediately upon the final withdrawal of the U.S. Marines in the 1930s; and the Somozas' own police force, the National Guard, had been created by the Marines as part of an effort to construct professional, modern institutions in Nicaragua. So in Nicaragua, defying Somoza was a nationalist act. It was the same as defending Nicaraguan dignity against the government of the United States, a

---

1. The introduction to this chapter was informed by many comparative studies of Nicaragua and El Salvador. These include Booth and Walker 1989; Everingham 1996; Foran 1992; Grenier 1999; Kampwirth 1998a; Luciak 2001, 1998; T. D. Mason 1992; Midlarsky and Roberts 1985; Paige 1997; Selbin 1999; Stephen 1997; Vilas 1995; Wickham-Crowley 1992.

government that, in the eyes of many, was in bed with the Somozas, figuratively and sometimes literally.[2]

The relationship between the military dictatorship in El Salvador, also founded in the 1930s, and the government of the United States was far less direct. It was not until the 1960s that the United States became heavily involved in Salvadoran politics as part of Kennedy's Alliance for Progress (Montgomery 1995, 49, 51). And by that time, U.S. foreign policy toward Latin America had changed dramatically in style and substance. Gone were the days of the nineteenth and early twentieth centuries, when the Marines regularly stepped in to fix politics in disobedient countries. The logic of the Alliance for Progress was more subtle.

Seeking to prevent "another Cuba," the proponents of the Alliance for Progress employed two main strategies. On the one hand, those policy makers recognized that few would support guerrilla movements if they had other options, if they could imagine another way to bring an end to decades of political and economic exclusion. So advocates of the Alliance for Progress encouraged political parties and fair elections, along with a series of economic and social changes, including land reform and greater educational opportunities.[3] On the other hand, in case those reforms were slow or poorly implemented, the Alliance for Progress also supported a counterinsurgency strategy to root out and destroy incipient guerrilla groups and their supporters (Dunkerley 1982, 47–71; Loveman and Davies 1997a, 23–29).

In the 1960s and early 1970s, the Salvadoran military grudgingly implemented a number of reforms while enthusiastically implementing counterinsurgency measures. Ultimately, one of the causes of the civil war that would officially begin in 1980 would be the Alliance for Progress itself, the program that was supposed to prevent future guerrilla wars. The military was happy to open up political spaces to opposition parties in exchange for economic assistance from the United States, as long as those parties had no real chance of winning. But when opposition coalitions

2. In De Mrs. Hanna a la Dinorah, Viktor Morales Henríquez details the first Somoza's affair with the wife of the U.S. ambassador, making explicit comparisons between the fall of Rome and the fall of the Somoza dynasty, both notable for their sexual decadence. "It was a sister, a beautiful and attractive sister from the north, who committed the unforgivable and fatal error whose tragic consequences continued throughout the past 46 years of our history" (1980, 12).

3. Ironically, Alliance for Progress–era promotion of educational opportunities for previously excluded groups, an effort to stave off revolutionary challenges to the Salvadoran government, helped create the space—the urban universities—in which the guerrillas first organized. "The paradoxical outcome of US-sponsored developmentalism was that the Agency for International Development (AID) and the Ford Foundation ended up being the main sponsors of a countercultural industry built around national universities . . . that were notoriously devoted to the denunciation of US imperialism" (Grenier 1999, 52).

headed by the Christian Democrats won national elections in 1972 and 1977, those coalitions were violently crushed. Following the murder of hundreds of their supporters, the winning candidates were forced to flee into exile.

In the end, political and economic reform on a foundation of counterinsurgency was practically no reform at all. In fact, these false reforms were worse than no reform, for they raised people's hopes, only to later crush them, an excellent way for the state to inadvertently foster a guerrilla movement. Many political moderates who had supported the reforms of the 1960s and 1970s would become the revolutionaries of the 1980s.

But not all of them. From 1980 onward, what happened in El Salvador was basically that the center disappeared. This differed dramatically from the situation in Nicaragua a few years earlier, in which support for the Somoza dynasty, or the Right, was what collapsed. In El Salvador, refugees from the stolen electoral victories were split: some joined the guerrillas under the banner of the newly formed FMLN, while others kept the Christian Democratic name as they moved to the right, allying with the military and its death squads.

There were various reasons for differences in the balance of power in the two countries. The contrast in the nature of the dictatorships—personalistic in the Nicaraguan case, collective in the Salvadoran—certainly played a role. It was much harder for any opposition force, either reformist or revolutionary, to mobilize people against an impersonal military target, with neither a name nor a face. Another major difference was in the nature of the guerrilla coalitions: the Sandinistas were, in comparison with the FMLN, both more unified and more nationalist. Throughout the war, the FMLN was always divided into five parties, though it sought to speak with one voice. It was also more explicitly Marxist than the FSLN and so more likely to alienate members of the middle and upper classes, who had supported the Nicaraguan guerrillas. Finally, at least some of the support for the Right was simply a function of realistic political analysis, for the Salvadoran Right was better prepared to defeat an armed opposition than the Nicaraguan Right had been.

Although there was no single person or family around whom opposition could build, the Right in El Salvador was highly unified, compared with that of Nicaragua.[4] Moreover, it enjoyed massive military support

---

4. Of course, to say that the Salvadoran Right was more unified against the guerrillas than was the Nicaraguan Right is not to say that it was completely unified at all points in time. Paige (1997), Williams and Walter (1997), and Stanley (1996) all provide interesting and detailed analyses of divisions within the military, the state, and the economic elite in El Salvador.

from the administration of American president Ronald Reagan (which had not been the case for Somoza when President Jimmy Carter was in power).[5] And it was exceedingly brutal: approximately seventy-five thousand would die in the civil war. More than 95 percent of those human rights abuses were carried out by the armed forces and its death squad allies, as would be documented by the United Nations (cited in Vilas 1995, 135–36 and Montgomery 1995, 242–43). So the risks of supporting the guerrillas in El Salvador were even greater than the risks in Nicaragua had been.

But for many people, despite the extremely high price of supporting the guerrillas, the cost of allowing the military dictatorship to continue was also unbearably high. In the end, the civil war that engulfed the entire decade of the 1980s resulted in a stalemate and the sort of negotiated settlement that the Right would have never conceded to without the war. Without the war, the power of the traditional landed elite might have never been broken; certainly the dense network of organizations that made up civil society in postwar El Salvador would have been far more sparse, and far less capable of promoting the interests of their members.

While the FMLN never succeeded in overthrowing the old regime as had the Nicaraguan FSLN (so El Salvador never had a revolution), by the end of a decade of civil war, El Salvador was a different place from what it had been, and many of its women were different people. In this chapter I will consider how so many women came to tie their fates to the revolutionary coalition, and how their experiences within that coalition transformed them. Much as in neighboring Nicaragua, the transformation of Salvadoran rural life in the mid-twentieth century was one of the first steps in the chain of events that led thousands of Salvadoran women to join the guerrilla coalition.

THE RURAL CRISIS IN EL SALVADOR

Starting in the mid-nineteenth century, and especially in the decades following World War II, world demand for tropical products such as coffee, sugar, and bananas increased dramatically. Responding to those new op-

---

5. During the 1980s, the Salvadoran government received approximately 3.6 billion dollars from the U.S. government. The Reagan administration's support for the Salvadoran government was unprecedented in the history of El Salvador. That the U.S. government would play such a significant economic role in supporting any Latin American government was also unprecedented. In the mid-1980s, the United States alone funded "between 20 percent and 43 percent of the Salvadoran government's budget" (McClintock 1998, 221).

portunities, the political and economic elites of El Salvador used a variety of mechanisms to ensure that ever increasing amounts of land were devoted to meeting that international demand. At one extreme, in the nineteenth century, the state simply decreed that indigenous communities would plant two-thirds of their land in coffee instead of in food crops for their own consumption. If they failed to do so, their land would revert to the state. When, to the surprise of policy makers, many indigenous communities did plant their land in coffee, government officials responded by simply abolishing communal land (Montgomery 1995, 30). Once communal land had been abolished, more-subtle economic mechanisms were employed to shift land from the hands of peasant food farmers to wealthier export-crop farmers: tenant farmers were evicted; permanent workers were replaced with temporary workers; and peasants were forced to sell their plots to pay off their creditors (T. D. Mason 1992, 67–68).

As in Nicaragua, one result of this transformation of the Salvadoran economy was that growing numbers of people found themselves without land. According to the more conservative estimates, the landless and land poor constituted 51 percent of the economically active people who worked in agriculture in 1961; by 1971 they were 60 percent of agricultural workers (McClintock 1998, 168).[6] Arguably, the concentration of land in progressively fewer hands played a role in fueling the discontent that would explode in the guerrilla war. As more people found themselves without land, their already modest standard of living dropped even further.

El Salvador was a spectacular example of the success of neoclassical economic theory, as macroeconomic growth rates soared when Salvadoran elites seized their comparative advantage by moving land out of subsistence production and into agroexport production.[7] But ironically, it was an equally spectacular example of the failure of neoclassical economic theory as misery and inequality also exploded.[8] "In other words, it was

6. Other good sources on the transformation of the Salvadoran economy and its political impact include Byrne 1996, 20; Everingham 1996; T. D. Mason 1992, 68; Midlarsky and Roberts 1985; Montgomery 1995; Vilas 1995, 53, 56; Wickham-Crowley 1992.

7. The annual median rates of gross domestic product (GDP) growth were 4.7 percent in the 1950s, 5.5 percent in the 1960s, and 6.4 percent in the 1970s (figures from the United Nations Economic Commission on Latin America, CEPAL, cited in Vilas 1995, 63)

8. In 1970, the poorest 20 percent of Salvadorans had to share a mere 3.7 percent of the national income while the richest 20 percent shared 50.8 percent. Inequality was even worse by 1980, when the poorest 20 percent shared only 2 percent of the country's income while the richest 20 percent had a full 66 percent (CEPAL and IICA/FLACSO cited in Vilas 1995, 68). As a result, the vast majority of Salvadorans were condemned to live in misery. In the 1990s, El Salvador had the lowest per capita caloric intake of any country in the hemisphere; 73 percent of

not the failure of capitalist development that provided the economic in-
gredient for revolution—it was its success" (Vilas 1995, 66).

In contrast, Cynthia McClintock argues that economics does not explain why the FMLN was formed and supported by many people; she observes that the FMLN guerrillas she interviewed identified political rather
than economic factors as the catalysts for the rebellion (1998, 284).[9] Like
McClintock, I found, through my interviews, that former guerrillas and
revolutionary activists did not generally mention economic factors when
explaining their decision to join the revolutionary struggle. Over and over
again, they explained that their horror in the face of the state's violence
was the catalyst that led them to take the final steps to becoming radical
opposition activists.

But to leave it at that is to make a false distinction between long- and
short-term causes, or between underlying factors and catalysts. Without a

---

all children suffered malnutrition and 77 out of 1,000 children died in infancy (Montgomery
1995, 24; see also Booth and Walker 1989, 74–77).

Neoclassical economists claim that the opposite will happen, that the majority will benefit
whenever a country can focus its production on the area in which it has a comparative advantage. In the Salvadoran case, the comparative advantage was in growing tropical crops, such as
coffee and sugar, which could then be sold at a fairly high price to wealthy northern countries.
While that meant that fewer people would be producing food, the high prices they received for
their coffee were supposed to allow them to buy corn from northern farmers, who could produce corn much more cheaply than Salvadoran farmers, given their comparative advantages in
soil and technology. According to the theory, Salvadoran farmers would sell expensive coffee,
buy cheap corn, and have some surplus to spend or invest otherwise. Salvadorans would then
become progressively more affluent, which is what happened, if the Salvadoran economy is
measured in strictly macroeconomic terms.

But contrary to the predictions of neoclassical economists, the majority was hurt by the pur-
suit of comparative advantage. Why was neoclassical economics such a poor guide? Fundamentally, the problem is that neoclassical economists ignore class structure. It is true that pursuing
comparative advantage will benefit the majority if there is already a fairly high degree of equality in a society. But if the benefits of agroexports are paid mainly to a small elite, and the costs of
shifting into agroexports are paid mainly by the already poor majority, then the effects of pursuing comparative advantage may be catastrophic, as they were in Central America.

9. McClintock also argues that economics did not play a major role in the emergence of
the FMLN because, although there was increased landlessness in the decades leading up to the
formation of the guerrilla movement, there "is no evidence of a sharp overall decline in Salvadoran peasants' living standards or of a threat to peasants' subsistence" (1998, 167). But my
reading of some of the data she presents suggests that a decline in living standards did accompany the increase in landlessness. She reports that annual incomes for landless Salvadoran families were roughly $315 in 1975 and below $225 in the late 1970s (1998, 170). Furthermore,
she cites two sources as suggesting that the incomes of the rural poor declined by about 15 percent in the 1970s (1998, 372 n. 54). The key to understanding our different interpretations of
this data may be her use of the phrase "sharp overall decline," which has a particular meaning
in the context of her study, a comparison of the FMLN of El Salvador with Shining Path of Peru.
She argues quite convincingly that the economic decline in Peru was much sharper and that the
Shining Path's supporters were motivated much more by economic grievances than were the
supporters of the FMLN. Nonetheless, the data she herself presents suggests that economics may
have played some role in setting the stage for the FMLN as well, just a less direct role.

doubt, rejection of state violence was usually the short-term cause that led women to become guerrillas. Yet potential catalysts may have no more than momentary importance in the absence of underlying factors. In El Salvador, those underlying factors were linked in a chain of events from the promotion of agroexports, to increasing landlessness, to the breakup of rural households, to increases in women's participation in paid labor, to migration to Honduras or to cities, and finally to new organizing opportunities in those cities.

The majority of rural dwellers who saw their already precarious conditions worsen as they lost access to land for food production desperately sought some solution. Migration was one way out. Hundreds of thousands went to neighboring Honduras, which has traditionally been less densely populated than El Salvador, in search of land or paid employment on Honduran agroexport plantations. That solution worked fairly well until 1969, when between one hundred thousand and three hundred thousand Salvadorans were forcibly returned to their homeland at the end of the "Soccer War" between Honduras and El Salvador (Byrne 1996, 20).

Another solution was to temporarily migrate within El Salvador in search of work. But, as in Nicaragua, this internal migration seems to have contributed to the number of households headed by single females, as husbands who left in search of work often failed to return.[10] As they lost access to land, along, sometimes, with their husbands' economic cooperation, those women would have been more desperate than ever. One

---

10. Whether the percentage of households headed by Salvadoran women increased during the middle decades of the twentieth century, or whether historically high levels of female-headed households were simply maintained during those decades, is not altogether clear from the existing studies. One observer noted that while a third of all urban households in the 1950s were headed by women, "by 1978 fully 39.5% of urban poor households were female headed" (T. D. Mason 1992, 76). But given that the data cited by Mason compares "urban households" in the 1950s with "urban poor households" in the late 1970s, it is possible that the difference is due to differences in the samples, rather than changes in Salvadoran society. For in El Salvador, as in other places, female-headed households are more likely to be poor than are other sorts of households; one would expect larger numbers of single-female-headed households in poorer neighborhoods.

Other studies are similarly difficult to analyze. One report notes that single-female-headed households have existed for a long time in El Salvador, citing data that suggests that the percentage of female-headed households might have been greater in 1950 than in 1970 (30 percent urban/20 percent rural in 1950 vs. 14.6 percent urban/9.2 percent rural in 1970), only to increase again by the late 1970s: a 1978 study found 39.5 percent of poor urban homes were headed by women, while a 1979 study reported that 20 percent of poor urban homes were headed by women (UNICEF 1988, 23). Finally, while one study reports that the percentage of the single people in the population decreased between 1971 and 1985, from 39.3 percent to 24.9 percent (UNICEF 1988, 24), another study reports that the percentage of women and men who were single increased from 1979 to 1985: 31 percent of women were single in 1979 compared with 38 percent in 1985; 39 percent of men were single in 1979 compared with 42 percent in 1985 (García and Gomáriz 1989, 108–9).

of their responses was to seek paid employment: in the last half of the twentieth century, women's participation in the formal workforce increased. While only 17.8 percent of the economically active population was female in 1961, that percentage increased to 21.6 percent in 1971, 33.5 percent in 1978, and finally 34.8 percent in 1980 as the civil war began (UNICEF 1988, 17).[11]

The breakup of rural households could also help explain the mass migration to the cities, led by women in search of work or other solutions to their problems.[12] One of the reasons that women led the movement to urban areas is that they had a greater incentive than men to leave the countryside, especially if they were the main breadwinners for their families. Rural women had an even harder time than men in providing for their families, since they were not even considered for many agricultural jobs, and in the case of jobs in which they could get hired, they were often not paid as much as men for the same work. Nonetheless, poor women had certain job advantages over poor men in the cities: domestic service, always one of the greatest sources of (poorly paid) employment for urban Latin American women, is a field that has traditionally been closed to men.[13]

While the balance between agriculture and services in the national economy shifted over the course of the second half of the twentieth century, the economic balance between men and women did not change greatly: agriculture was always a field dominated by men and services by women.[14] Because of women's disadvantages in rural employment, com-

---

11. In the case of women's workforce participation, the data cited in different studies are also inconsistent, although, unlike the data on household heads, at least they are not contradictory. García and Gómáriz (1989, 115) report a somewhat lower percentage of women in the workforce in 1978 (30 percent) than UNICEF had reported (33.5 percent). One possible difference in the data may be indicated by the terminology used: the authors of the UNICEF study detail the percentage of women in the Economically Active Population (Población Economicamente Activa or PEA) while García and Gomariz report the percentage of women in the Salvadoran workforce (fuerza de trabajo salvadoreño). The economically active population normally includes unemployed people who are actively seeking work; in contrast, the workforce probably only refers to people with jobs.

12. In 1950, El Salvador was an overwhelmingly rural country: 63.5 percent lived in the countryside and only 36 percent in the cities. There was a steady stream of migration to the cities in the 1950s and 1960s (by 1970, 39.5 percent of Salvadorans were urban dwellers), but the most significant movement occurred in the 1970s and 1980s. By 1980, 44 percent of Salvadorans lived in cities, a rate that increased to 48.2 percent by 1988 (García and Gómáriz 1989, 107; figures cited in Fauné 1995, 30 illustrate the same pattern with some variations).

13. In the introduction to their edited collection on household workers in Latin America, Elsa Chaney and Mary García Castro (1989, 3) estimate that household workers account for no less than 20 percent and up to 33 percent of all Latin American women who are counted in official employment statistics.

14. In 1950, 75.7 percent of men worked in agriculture; at the same time, 12.4 percent of women did so. In 1960, 72.4 percent of men worked in agriculture compared with 7.3 percent

bined with their advantages in urban employment, Salvadoran women have been more likely than men to live in cities at least since 1950.[15]

These national figures are consistent with the data from my study. Of the forty-eight women who told me their life stories, only eleven, or fewer than 23 percent, lived in the same place where they had been born; the vast majority had migrated from the countryside to the capital.[16]

ORGANIZING OPPORTUNITIES AND RISKS

At this point, with the arrival in the cities, my story shifts dramatically. Up until now, the story I have told—of the rise of agroexports leading to greater rural landlessness, which drove migration—has been a very individual one. True, it was an individual story that was repeated thousands of times over, but those involved experienced the process as a series of individual decisions, rather than as collective actions. The choice to migrate to the city was certainly not experienced as a political action, though upon arriving in the cities, people found that new collective and political opportunities would open up. Initially those collective actions were not revolutionary, in the sense of being directed at an overthrow of the regime, though that part of the story would soon follow for some of the women who migrated and especially for their daughters.

Yamilet was one of those daughters of migration. The third of three girls, she was born in San Salvador in 1961 to "a peasant woman who migrated to the city when she was very young to make a living, and a man who was a salesman, who abandoned my mother after she became preg-

---

of women. In 1970, 69 percent of men and 5.2 percent of women were agriculture workers. In 1980, 55.8 percent of Salvadoran men and 5 percent of Salvadoran women worked in agriculture. At the same time, as the percentage of workers in agriculture steadily declined, the percentage in services steadily increased. In 1950, 10.7 percent of men and 62.8 percent of women worked in services. In 1960 those percentages were 12 percent and 67.7 percent; in 1970 they were 17.6 percent and 76.5 percent. Finally, in 1980, 24.4 percent of men and 76.8 percent of women worked in the service sector (Inter-American Development Bank cited in Mason 1992, 73; also see García and Gomáriz 1989, 118).

15. In 1950, 34 percent of men lived in cities, compared with 39 percent of women. In 1960, 35.8 percent of men and 41 percent of women lived in cities. In 1970, 37.7 percent of men lived in cities, compared with 41.3 percent of women. In 1980, 42.3 percent of men and 46.1 percent of women lived in cities. Finally, by 1989, slightly more than half of all women, 50.7 percent, lived in urban areas, compared with 46.8 percent of men (García and Gomáriz 1989, 141).

16. A few of the women I interviewed had migrated to San Salvador from foreign countries. One, a Catholic sister, was from Nicaragua; another was born in the Basque country in Spain and had ended up in El Salvador after nearly a decade in Nicaragua. The other two foreigners were both Mexican, and both had been actively involved in FMLN support work during the war.

nant with me" (interview, June 26, 1996). Although they were poor, Yamilet's mother worked hard to make sure that her daughters could attend high school, working up to four jobs at once to make that happen.

Yamilet was a student at the Young Ladies Central (Central de Señoritas), a public institute, in the second half of the 1970s, the same time that the urban social movements that had characterized opposition politics in El Salvador throughout the twentieth century were on the upswing (Lungo 1989, 93). She was not an activist, at least not initially; however, she could hardly ignore the changes in the world around her.

I think I was a normal girl who studied, had fun, had friends, we would go out together, but there was this special situation, there was a rise in the activism of the student movements. I did not participate directly except for a few demonstrations that I attended. And also there were church movements in my neighborhood, I taught catechism to children. I distributed the church magazine Orientación *and that magazine was persecuted. I belonged to a youth group in my neighborhood: we would get together, we would sing, we held retreats and we would reflect. (Interview, June 26, 1996).*

Yet even though her volunteer work was largely confined to church groups, that did not protect Yamilet from the growing government violence around her.

I remember that one time a man went to a meeting of a group that we belonged to and he was from a group—ORDEN—that was one of the most evil organizations in El Salvador.[17] He was armed and drunk at the meeting. He came into the youth meeting and he started to say incoherent things to us, he showed us his ORDEN membership card that had been authorized by a military officer, he showed us his gun. That is, he did not directly threaten us but just by being there without any reason and talking incoherently . . . it made us afraid. (Interview, June 26, 1996)

Many residents of San Salvador were afraid in the mid-1970s. Yamilet and her friends all knew something was wrong, but nobody spoke of it. Yet the signs were all around them.

---

17. ORDEN (Organización Democrática Nacionalista or Democratic Nationalist Organization) was a right-wing peasant organization that was founded by the military in the 1960s to keep order in the countryside (Montgomery 1995, 106). By the mid-1970s, as Yamilet's story illustrates, the presence of ORDEN was also felt in the cities.

For example, we knew that dead bodies would appear on the street, that our fellow students would disappear, that some demonstrations had been repressed, for example the student demonstration of 1975. I was very close the day of the demonstration and the only reason that I didn't go was because the school closed its doors and did not let anyone leave and that was how we were saved, really, because that was one of the biggest student massacres. . . . So I had no direct tie with any student movement but reality has a way of getting out. (Interview, June 26, 1996)

And in her very physical surroundings, her neighborhood in a poor suburb of San Salvador, there was yet another sign: huge shantytowns had sprung up on the outskirts of the neighborhood, populated by refugees from the violence in the countryside. Reading all these signs, Yamilet decided that, if she wanted to go to college in peace, she would have to leave El Salvador. For despite the hopes of her new neighbors, city dwellers were hardly immune from the government's wrath, and city dwellers who were students were at especially high risk.[18]

So when a friend told her of scholarships for study in the Soviet Union, she rushed to apply. Luckily for Yamilet, applicants did not have to be affiliated with the Communist Party; what mattered was their performance on a series of exams. Because she did well on those exams, she was awarded one of the approximately forty scholarships that were offered that year. Shortly afterward, in September of 1979, Yamilet left for the Soviet Union with the intention of spending the following four years studying psychology. But again, Salvadoran politics would force itself into her life.

18. In the early 1980s, students were much more likely to be killed than were members of the general population. Although college students constituted only three-fifths of one percent of the population of El Salvador in 1980 (27,100 out of 4,525,000), and high school students slightly more than one and a half percent (73,000 out of 4,525,000), students made up a much larger percentage of the victims of state violence: 7.2 percent of those who were killed in the early 1980s and 17.3 percent of those who were disappeared. My impression from the secondary literature on El Salvador as well as my own interviews is that college students were more likely targets than were high school students, although the latter were hardly immune (Booth and Walker 1989, 148, 156; Valdés and Gomáriz 1995, 106).

Jorge Castañeda reports similar findings regarding the vulnerability of intellectuals (especially students) to state violence: 64 percent of the people the Brazilian dictatorship (1964–78) acknowledged killing were "so-called intellectual workers, of which half were students. . . . In the larger universe of those 'officially' tortured by the regime, intellectual workers represented 55 percent of the total." Castañeda claims that those who died "as a result of [state] repression . . . [constitute] a sample more or less identifiable with the guerrilla movement," (1994, 78); however, caution is called for regarding the direction of causality. It is doubtless true that many of those who were tortured were guerrillas, but there were also many who became guerrilla supporters after their detention and torture for a much lesser crime (such as supporting a strike or participating in a human rights group or even fitting the state's profile of a guerrilla) led them to lose hope in the efficacy of peaceful resistance.

Only a month after Yamilet left the country, the military government headed by General Carlos Humberto Romero was thrown out of office through a coup d'état and replaced with a coordinating committee, or junta, composed of reformist military officers and civilian leaders. The idea was to try, one last time, to head off the approaching civil war by addressing socioeconomic inequality through land reform, and by deescalating government violence through dismantling some of the most brutal government agencies. A body was even created to investigate human rights abuses, satisfying many of the concerns of the Carter administration, which had been quite critical of human rights abuses under the ousted Romero regime.

So the Carter administration renewed economic and military assistance to the government, ignoring the fact that none of the reforms had brought the security forces, and their associated death squads, under control. In fact the rate of murders committed by the security forces and OR-DEN actually increased under the rule of the reformers. Ultimately, the centrists had failed in their attempts to save El Salvador from civil war. Most of them would resign in protest in the first days of January 1980, having given up on moderate reform as a way out (Byrne 1996, 53–62; Montgomery 1995, 72, 75–79).

Those would-be reformers were faced with two options, two ways to interpret the failure of reform. Both interpretations were based on the realization that the political center no longer existed in El Salvador. According to one interpretation, if reform was impossible, then better to ally with the regime, better to support the status quo—no matter how bloody—so as to prevent a revolutionary outcome.[19] That was the route chosen by those who stayed in the Christian Democratic Party.

And so the Christian Democrats, those who had been robbed of two electoral victories in the 1970s by the military government, were to ally with that very same military. Days after the breakup of the reformist coup coalition in January 1980, leaders of the Christian Democratic Party entered into a pact with the military, a pact that allowed the military to claim that its government was a civilian one, and that allowed the Christian Democrats some access to power (Montgomery 1995, 129; Vilas 1995, 85).

---

19. There is no word other than "bloody" to describe the status quo in 1980. That year, "more than 8,000 extrajudicial executions for political reasons of civilian noncombatants were recorded," murders committed mainly by state security sources with the help of paramilitary groups and death squads (Vilas 1995, 85). Among the murdered were Mario Zamora, a national leader of the Christian Democratic Party; and Oscar Romero, the archbishop of San Salvador.

The other interpretation of the failure of legal reform was that the only option left was extralegal reform or a revolutionary solution. Many of the moderate reformers from the 1979 coup coalition, including a number of former Christian Democrats, would soon join the revolutionary opposition (Booth and Walker 1989, 83; Montgomery 1995, 110–11). In 1980, that revolutionary option was more organized and cohesive than ever, driven to unite by the escalation of government violence, along with the example of a successful recent revolution in neighboring Nicaragua, success that was attributed in part to the unity of the FSLN.

So in October 1980, the radical opposition formed a five-member guerrilla coalition, the FMLN. With their declaration of war against the government that they thought was already waging war against the reformers of El Salvador, more than a decade of open civil war had begun.

Far away in the Soviet Union, Yamilet was occupied with learning Russian and then studying psychology. Even so, she and her fellow students were hardly indifferent to the war back home. "We worked within an organization of Latin American students and of course we were supporting the liberation movements. We would work and send money through the Communist Party, which was our contact." In 1982, a delegate from the party asked "if I would be willing to return to El Salvador to join the armed struggle." "I told him yes. . . . It was already 1983 when a telegram arrived . . . saying that I had to be in Moscow in a week. . . . [From there] we went to Nicaragua, in Nicaragua we received training for a few months. I was organized within the Communist Party. All five parties [of the FMLN] were in Nicaragua" (interview, June 26, 1996). By the end of 1983, she had finished her training and illegally returned to El Salvador, by way of Guatemala, where she would work on the war front, following the government's radio communications, and later as a political organizer for the Communist Party, one of the five parties of the FMLN, helping to found a women's group that was to serve as support for the war effort.

Yamilet's story is unusual in some of its details: few spent the early years of the war in the Soviet Union. But in a more profound sense, her story is quite common. From being a girl who sought to live a quiet life—to go to college, get a job, and support her single mother—Yamilet ended up involved in some of the least conventional and most dangerous roles available to Salvadoran women. Clearly Yamilet made choices that would eventually lead her to the warfront. But just as clearly, her choices were constrained, severely constrained, by the government's widespread use of violence against even the most moderate reformers, such as Yamilet and the other members of the church group that was threatened by the man from ORDEN. In short, she made radical choices, but she made them within extremely narrow constraints, constraints that had been set by generations of military dictatorship. In the 1980s, Yamilet was not the only Salvadoran woman to make such choices.

PERSONAL ROOTS OF REVOLUTIONARY ACTIVISM

In thinking back over their lives, the women who had chosen to join the guerrilla groups or other organizations within the revolutionary coalition identified a series of factors that they saw as transformative, starting them on the path toward political activism. Those experiences included migrating within the country or from Honduras, hearing family stories of past political violence such as that of the Matanza of 1932, participating with a relative in a strike or with the Christian Democratic party, and joining a preexisting network such as a student or church organization. Those transformative events led them to conclude that there was tremendous social injustice in El Salvador and that by challenging the military regime, they might help mitigate or even end that injustice. While that is a logical conclusion, it is hardly the only possible conclusion.

Women who chose not to join the revolutionary coalition might have had similar experiences that they interpreted differently. For instance, through migration, a hypothetical woman might have also noticed the extreme economic inequality between and within regions in El Salvador. Yet she could have decided that such inequality was inevitable, precisely for being so common. Or hearing family stories of a grandparent who was killed in the Matanza of 1932 might have been enough to convince her that political activism was dangerous and should be avoided. Or joining her mother in Christian Democratic campaign rallies, only to see the military steal away their electoral victories in 1972 and 1977, might have taught the lesson that there was no point in opposing the military dictatorship, which always retained veto power. And when other members of her radical Catholic groups received death threats, she might have simply left those groups: withdrawing into family life, fleeing the country,[20] or converting to evangelical Protestantism.[21]

20. Simply leaving an organization did not completely free a woman from risk, of course, since the leaders of the death squads would not necessarily know or care who had submitted their resignation. The difficulty that people faced in protecting themselves from political violence helps to explain the massive migration out of the region in the 1980s. By the end of that decade, "more than 1.3 million Nicaraguans, Guatemalans, and Salvadorans had migrated, legally or illegally, to the United States" (Vilas 1995, 161).

21. Evangelical Protestantism tends to promote individual as opposed to communal values

All these choices were more common than the decision to go off with the guerrillas. Why did some women make the riskier choice to join the guerrillas or other groups within the revolutionary coalition? Certain aspects of their personal histories, I think, predisposed them to making the choices that they did. These personal factors included being raised in a family with a tradition of resistance, belonging to one or more pre-existing networks, and being young at the time when the guerrillas emerged.

Sonia Aguinada, who rose up through the ranks of the FMLN and would be elected to Congress in 1994, was socialized into a family tradition of resistance by her grandmother, the woman who raised her.[22] "My mother had me when she was sixteen, she got pregnant by the neighbor across the street. My father died before I was born [and so] my mother was left single, pregnant. My grandmother took over child care, basically my grandmother raised me. . . . I was the little one. The youngest of [my aunts and uncles] was thirteen years older than me" (interview, July 15, 1996).

Her grandmother was the first to introduce her to politics. "My grandmother was very political. . . . In 1932 she was a big supporter of the movement, one of her uncles was hung to death. At that time [my grandmother] knew Farabundo Martí, Miguel Marmol. . . . My grandmother always read the newspaper, she discussed everything that was happening. I think she raised her children with those ideals, especially me" (interview, July 15, 1996). With her grandmother—who in 1957 had helped found the Communist-affiliated Women's Fraternity (Fraternidad de Mujeres)—six-year-old Sonia participated in that organization's demonstrations. In keeping with the family tradition of resistance that was taught to her by her grandmother and an uncle who was murdered in 1968 for being a union activist, Sonia Aguinada joined the incipient guerrilla move-

---

(in an otherworldly sense, an individual relationship with Jesus; in a more worldy sense, entrepreneurial activities, gender inequality, and political withdrawal). It is, perhaps, the polar opposite of liberation theology in its political implications, which may explain its appeal in Central America. Generally, the death squads left evangelicals in peace only to attack activists in the liberation theology movement, though the military's murder of all but one of the residents of the evangelical town of El Mozote in El Salvador in 1981 demonstrated that conversion did not offer complete protection from violence (on El Mozote, see Danner 1993; on Evangelicalism in Latin America, see Burdick 1992, 172; Stoll 1990, 6–7, 333–38; Vilas 1995, 141–43).

22. Aguinada's guerrilla group within the five-member FMLN coalition had been the ERP (Ejército Revolucionario de los Pobres). Although she was elected to Congress in 1994 as a representative of the FMLN, by the time of our interview in 1996, she represented the breakaway Democratic Party (Partido Demócrata), a social democratic party that was made up of most of the former members of the ERP along with a faction of the RN (Resistencia Nacional, another of the five groups that made up the FMLN). Because of her national and international prominence, I call her by her real name (as I do other elected officials).

ment in 1972, when she was seventeen years old. By that point she had already been politically active for years: attending demonstrations with her grandmother, supporting the teachers' union through the Association of High School Students (Asociación de Estudiantes de Secondaria), and as a member of the Young Communists (Juventud Comunista) from the age of thirteen.

Membership in groups like the Young Communists was critical in channeling many women into opposition activism.[23] The women who joined the revolutionary coalition of the 1980s did not just wake up one day and decide to try to overthrow the military regime, for isolated individuals rarely make such radical and risky choices. Instead, the people who were already integrated into preexisting networks—formed for non-revolutionary and often nonpolitical purposes—were the ones who were most likely to become revolutionaries.[24]

Thirty-five women who had been guerrillas or otherwise involved in revolutionary politics in the 1980s answered a series of open-ended questions about their life stories. Through those interviews, the importance of preexisting networks—religious organizations, student groups, labor unions and family networks—was clear, since all of them mentioned belonging to such a network before joining the revolutionary coalition. It was in those networks that they developed the political values and skills that would eventually lead them to take radical actions to end the dictatorship. Moreover, belonging to those networks put them at greater risk of becoming victims of governmental violence than might have been true had they not been involved in community work; to some extent, becoming a revolutionary was a means of self-defense.

By far, the single most important preexisting network was the family that girls were born into. Twenty-three out of thirty-five (or 66 percent)

23. In Sonia Aguinada's case, membership in the Young Communists in the late 1960s and early 1970s did not directly lead to her becoming a guerrilla, since the Communist Party did not enter the armed struggle until 1980. For Sonia, joining the ERP meant breaking with her family's party. Until 1972, she had viewed the early guerrilla attempts as had other members of her party. "Up until that point the guerrillas struck me as risk seekers, they seemed very inconsistent to me." But after "the famous electoral fraud" of 1972, she reconsidered the Communist Party's strategy of challenging the military regime through electoral means. Leaving the Communist Youth to join the ERP guerrillas "was not easy at all, my family identified with the traditional opposition" and thought that the only revolutionaries were those who were affiliated with the Communist Party. In fact, they suspected that the guerrillas were actually CIA pawns. She would not fully reconcile with her own family "until 1980 when the revolutionary reconciliation occurred" [in other words, when the five-member FMLN coalition was formed] (interview, July 15, 1996).

24. On preexisting networks, see Alvarez, Dagnino, and Escobar 1998, 14–16; Alvarez 1990, 57–82; Freeman 1975, 48–70; McAdam 1982, 43–47; Wickham-Crowley 1992, 37–42; 226–27.

mentioned the influence of relatives—parents, aunts and uncles, grand-parents, siblings—in the development of their political values or in the decision to join the revolutionary coalition. Sometimes whole families joined the guerrillas, especially in the rural areas, where the government's violence was less selective than in the urban areas.

But just as often, the same parents who had inculcated antidictatorial values in their daughter were terrified when they realized that she was actively involved in opposing the dictatorship. That terror was understandable. When state security or the death squads realized that an individual was involved in revolutionary activities, they sometimes tortured or killed some of that person's relatives as a form of revenge.

So when Bianca's family discovered that their nineteen-year-old daughter was active in the Revolutionary Brigade of High School Students (Brigada Revolucionaria de Estudiantes de Secondaria, or BRES), "they started asking questions. There was a general terror of political persecution. They practically ran me out of the house" (interview, June 25, 1996). Having nowhere else to go but the house of a friend who was also involved in the BRES, she soon joined an urban guerrilla cell, distributing literature, making bombs, and eventually participating in combat.

Sometimes family networks would capture some who did not consciously choose to join the revolutionary coalition, as illustrated by Florencia's story. While Florencia was never a formal member of the revolutionary coalition, she would come to identify with the coalition's goals, and her actions would play a role in furthering the antidictatorial cause. As she would have never been in a position to make the choices she did without her family ties, her story is an important illustration of the role of families in the struggle against the military dictatorship. Her experience also illustrates the dependence of the FMLN (and all guerrillas) on a vast, often unrecognized, base of support: without tens of thousands like Florencia, the FMLN almost surely would have been quickly defeated.

The oldest of four girls, Florencia was born in the town of Santa Tecla in 1952; her mother was a seamstress, and her father a chauffeur for a wealthy family. Even though her father drove for a living, on Sundays he would take his daughters for long drives into the countryside. "I remember that on various occasions we would go and pick up sisters, that is, Catholic nuns, we would pick them up in the mountains, right? And we would return to the city. . . . What I really noticed at that time was that they did not sit in the passenger seat but instead they lay down in the backseat, where feet are supposed to go. They would be hidden, and I said to myself, why would the sister do that?" (interview, June 24, 1996). Having been raised to be respectful, Florencia never directly asked why the sisters chose to ride in such an uncomfortable space. But eventually, the reason occurred to her. "Then with time I realized that my dad collaborated . . . between '62 and '65 . . . my dad was collaborating with the movement, with the insurgents."

In the 1970s, opposition politics again touched on her family life, as Florencia would discover one day when she found her mother crying. "I said to her, Mom, why are you crying? And she said to me, oh, daughter, I can't tell you. . . . My grandmother arrived, my mother's mother, and they began to cry together. And then I discovered that all my uncles, on my mother's side, belonged to the guerrilla movement that was beginning at that time. . . . They had seized one of them and they were torturing him" (interview, June 24, 1998). They knew that he was being tortured and denied food in a cell in the basement of the police station, because one of the police officers made her mother's acquaintance and told her. But he also offered a way out of this terrible situation.

The officer was already old, very old, and he said that if my mom came by that night to sleep with him, the next day he would give my uncle food . . . and that he would get a new jail cell and that he would help to get my uncle out. So to stop seeing my grandmother's suffering, my mother did it. They did give food to my uncle the next day, and they changed his cell and in a month they let him go. But my mom didn't just go that night instead she had to spend a number of nights with that man. (Interview, June 24, 1996)

Through these experiences Florencia stayed at the margins of revolutionary politics, well aware of the terrible consequences for those who dared to oppose the dictatorship. It wasn't until 1978, when she was already married with children, that she became directly involved in the revolutionary struggle. Again, she became involved through her family and, again, she did not initially even realize that she was involved.

One day she happened to run into one of her aunts, whom she had not seen in a long time. As she would later learn, the meeting was not coincidental but rather planned; her aunt, who lived and worked with Cayetano Carpio, had a job for Florencia.[25] "She said that she wanted to

---

25. Salvador Cayetano Carpio (1919/20–1983) was a Communist Party activist who broke with the party to initiate the armed struggle by founding the Popular Forces of Liberation (Fuerzas Populares de Liberación) in 1970. Eventually, the FPL would be the largest of the five parties that made up the FMLN, while the Communist Party, a party that had rejected armed

help me economically. . . . I can get you a position with the National Police." Some time later, an old family friend who had become a police officer came to her house to offer her a position preparing meals in the police station. Out of work and having trouble making ends meet, Florencia was more than willing to accept the job.

She began her new job in 1980 or 1981, at the height of the brutality in the police stations of El Salvador. "Blindfolded people would be brought into the police station and they did not register them, right?[26] At that time I was learning so many things. . . . Once there was a young girl that they had tied up and blindfolded and they had abused her in the room where they tortured people. . . . It hurt me so much to see her at that moment: raped, beaten up, tied up, blindfolded, and hungry" (interview, June 24, 1996). Florencia offered the girl some coffee and held it up to her lips so she could drink even though she was tied up. The girl asked if Florencia could contact her family, to let them know where she was, promising that even under torture she would never give away her secret. So Florencia agreed to make the phone call. "And that was when I began my work of helping all the prisoners."

In 1989, Florencia would fall under suspicion. When her bosses realized that she had relatives who were involved in the guerrilla struggle, she was taken into custody and tortured psychologically for eleven days: woken each time she managed to fall to sleep and asked the same questions over and over. But they never got any information; she did not belong to any revolutionary organization and so had no information to give. Frustrated, the police eventually released her; shortly afterward she would be fired from her government job.

Had it not been for her family network, it is unlikely that Florencia would have found herself doing the highly dangerous humanitarian work that she did for years. While she could have chosen not to take such risks, and nobody ever directly asked her to take them, Florencia's story shows the importance of family networks in shaping the context in which women eventually made those life-and-death choices.

---

struggle since its founding in 1930, would join with the FPL in the FMLN guerrilla coalition in 1980 (McClintock 1998, 254–55; Montgomery 1995, 102–4, 169; Wickham-Crowley 1992, 337).

26. If the police registered someone, they were unlikely to kill that person, since there would be a record that the last time the individual was alive was in police custody. To obscure the fact that they frequently murdered people, the police often did not register prisoners, but simply "disappeared" them.

Family networks were the single most important network that channeled the women I interviewed into revolutionary activism, but they were not the only one. The next most common experience before joining the guerrillas was participation in student organizations. Fourteen of the thirty-five women (or 40 percent) told me about participating in student protest activities before they became revolutionary activists. Since to be in student organizations one needs to be a student, it is not surprising that they were more highly educated than the average Salvadoran. Nearly half, or 46.6 percent, had gone to college for at least some a period of time, 33.3 percent had attended at least some high school, and 20 percent had attended at least some grade school.[27] Nationwide, in 1980 (the last year for which complete data are available), only 2 percent of all women had attended or completed college, 6.6 percent had attended high school, 58.3 percent had attended grade school, and a full 33.1 percent had not gone to school at all (Valdés and Gomáriz 1995, 101). These findings from El Salvador further confirm a widespread finding discussed in the Introduction to this book, that students are the sector that most consistently leads revolutionary movements.

There are many reasons for the prominence of students in revolutionary politics. First, students are likely to be young, and thus relatively free of family responsibilities. Their youth means that they are often more willing than older people to take on extremely serious risks and maybe to be somewhat oblivious to the severity of those risks.

Second, students tend to live far less structured lives than people who work for wages in the formal sector. Given the unstructured nature of student life, a student activist can often fit revolutionary activities into her regular schedule without attracting too much attention. In contrast, those who work regular hours in the formal sector, such as factory workers, would be immediately noticed if they failed to report to work for even a few hours.

University students in countries characterized by great economic inequality and political authoritarianism face a series of contradictions. Most of them are in training for professional careers that would, in theory, allow them a certain degree of material comfort and security. One might expect their relatively promising opportunities to make them strong supporters of the status quo. However, under conditions of political

27. Of the 30 who told me about their educational histories, 6 had college degrees (including one who had a medical degree), 8 had attended some college, 4 had high school degrees, 6 had attended some high school, 4 had grade school (sixth-grade) degrees, and 2 had attended some grade school.

authoritarianism, many of them can only look forward to being denied the fruits of their labors if they do not support the dictatorship and play by its clientelistic rules. While members of other sectors, such as peasants or the urban poor, are far more exploited, university students are more likely to understand their exploitation in political terms, and to hope that, by eliminating the dictatorship, they could create the opportunities that they see as rightfully theirs.

Finally, students work with ideas. They often spend long hours reading about and debating the meaning of such abstract values as democracy, freedom, justice, and equality. The contradiction between those values and the reality of Salvadoran life in the 1970s and 1980s drove many of them to become revolutionary activists.

Ana Guadalupe Martínez was one of the many student activists who became guerrillas.[28] Although her parents did not encourage her to oppose the dictatorship, she would eventually become a combatant and second in command of the ERP, one of the five groups that made up the FMLN. Born in 1952 on her grandparents' farm, she was the second child and first daughter of a family of four children. Her father, a retired military officer, made his living in agriculture; however, her parents would move to the provincial city of Santa Ana so their children could go to high school, an opportunity that was not available to rural children.

It was in Santa Ana, in 1967, that Ana Guadalupe Martínez first became aware of the political world, when her teachers went on strike. "For me, the strike was a discovery. First of all I did not know that strikes existed and that a strike was when people did not go to work. And secondly, the motivations that brought on the strike . . . demands for better salaries and for a social security plan for teachers. That was when I really discovered the other part of the world that I had not known" (interview, July 29, 1996). Her parents were not pleased that their daughter was so interested in supporting the strike. Although her mother believed that it was right that teachers should have better working conditions, she did not want her young daughter to participate, because she worried for her safety. "The first thing she brought up is that the National Guard could grab you and then anything could happen." Yet Martínez did not give up her interest in supporting the teachers, especially not when she discov-

---

28. In the 1980s, Ana Guadalupe Martínez was the second in command of the second largest of the organizations that made up the FMLN, the ERP. In the 1990s, she would be elected to the Legislative Assembly. At the time of my interview in 1996, she was serving as vice president of the Assembly, representing the Democratic Party (Partido Demócrata, or PD), a party that formed when the FMLN divided in 1995.

ered that her father's sister, who was a schoolteacher, was also one of the founding members of the Asociación Nacional de Educadores Salvadoreños (ANDES), the union that led the strike. "For me that was like a confirmation that what I was doing was the right thing, and that it was even just."

Still, she was hardly a political activist when she entered the university to study medicine. In fact she described student politics as "a strange world" that was interesting but hard to understand. But in 1969, six months into her first year in college, the students went on strike to pressure for changes both at the level of the university curriculum and in the larger world.

That was the time when the antiwar movement was most active in the United States and a proposal was sent from the University of [California,] Berkeley, to the University [of El Salvador] to hold a week of protest against the war in Vietnam. . . . And a proposal was made to hold a peaceful march, we were going to walk, to all participate in an activity that would be both physical and very adventurous because to go from Santa Ana to San Salvador in two days of marching, all of the young people with music, with guitars . . . it was the first political action in which I participated, within the student movement. And of course there were leaders there who explained to us . . . what the war in Vietnam was about, what the North Americans were doing in Vietnam. (Interview, July 29, 1996)

That experience left her wanting to learn more about the war in Vietnam. She would find some of the answers in the pages of *Life* magazine.

For me it was quite a discovery to see the magazine photographs of mutilated children, of children who had been burned with napalm, of women who had been torn apart by the bombs that the North American soldiers dropped. . . . And from that point on I participated in the student political activities to help make sure that things like that would not happen. And that was just the same time when the revolutionary armed groups were emerging. And without knowing anything else, along with some others, I began to participate in the ERP, in an armed organization. (Interview, July 29, 1996)

Ana Guadalupe Martínez had initially entered medical school so that she could carry out the values "that my mother had taught me, in other words, humanitarianism, an attitude of service to others." But after four years of study there, she decided that the best way to live out her mother's values would be to break out from the sheltered life that her mother had planned for her, by becoming one of the first to join the underground struggle.

After student organizing, the next most common organizing experience, prior to joining the revolutionary coalition, was participation in Catholic Church organizations.[29] Ten of the thirty-five respondents (or 28.5 percent) mentioned their previous church activism, teaching catechism, studying the Bible in base community groups, bringing material relief and literacy training to the residents of San Salvador's enormous shantytowns. In the years following the 1968 bishops' conference in Medellín, the message of liberation theology, that Christians had an obligation to work for the kingdom of God in this world rather than passively awaiting the next world, was a message that resonated throughout Latin America. While that message and the movement it engendered was an important factor in the rise of the revolutionary politics in Nicaragua, it was in El Salvador that liberation theology really ignited, in large part because of the figure of Archbishop Oscar Romero.

When Oscar Romero was chosen to be archbishop of San Salvador in 1977, many assumed that his career as archbishop would be as quiet and uncontroversial as it had been when he had been a priest. That might have happened except for the political atmosphere at the time. In the first months of 1977, the government's violence against the Catholic Church was intense: two priests were murdered, ten were exiled, five were tortured and then expelled, and three others were detained and beaten.

Far from his being the quiet supporter of the status quo, for which some had hoped, Oscar Romero would end up being the single most important voice of opposition to the political and economic violence of the time. Sunday mass, said by Romero and broadcast nationwide over the archdiocese's radio station, was the most listened to show in the country. It was also an important source of information: near the end of the mass, Romero always announced all documented cases of those who had been killed or tortured or had otherwise suffered political violence in the past week, whether at the hands of the government and its affiliates or at the hands of the guerrillas. Since there were always many more victims of right-wing than of left-wing violence, the military government was particularly threatened by Romero, eventually murdering him as he said mass in March 1980 (Montgomery 1995, 92–97; Peterson 1997, 60–66).[30]

29. The impact of the liberation theology movement is a theme that runs throughout Vázquez, Ibáñez, and Murguialday's excellent study of the role of women within the guerrilla organizations in El Salvador during the war and postwar periods. See especially their discussion of the impact of radical Catholicism on the sexuality of guerrillas (Vázquez, Ibáñez, and Murguialday 1996, 69–70).

30. The United Nations' truth commission later determined that Romero's murder had been ordered by Roberto D'Aubuisson, deputy director of the government intelligence agency known

But this instance of right-wing brutality, would backfire as had so many others; many of the women I interviewed noted that the murder of Archbishop Romero was a turning point in their political thinking. For instance, Gloria, who was only eleven years old at the time of the murder, told me that it affected her whole family. "Just like in all of El Salvador, it had quite an impact" (interview, July 23, 1996). Later on, as a college student, Gloria would be active in a student group that was affiliated with the ERP, one of the five groups that made up the FMLN.

The final organizing experience that was mentioned by a significant number of women was participation in some sort of labor union.[31] Seven out of thirty-five (or 20 percent) had belonged to a labor union (four of these unions were urban; three were rural) before joining the FMLN or another revolutionary organization. Of course, membership in one preexisting network did not preclude membership in another. Those women who belonged to multiple networks over the course of their lives, such as Ninoska, were especially likely to eventually confront the military regime.

Ninoska was born in 1942 in a small town in the department of La Paz to a mother who was only fourteen years old and single. Her mother lived with her in the house of her grandparents until Ninoska was three, when she got married, leaving Ninoska with her parents. So Ninoska was raised with her grandparents, aunts, and uncles, helping them with their agricultural work—raising yuca, corn, beans, pineapples, and sugarcane—for sale in the village and for the family's own consumption. At the same time she was learning about the world around her, both in school and through talking with her grandfather. Ninoska identified those conversations as her first political experience. "At night, when we were all peeling the yuca, my grandfather . . . would talk to us. My grandfather is a survivor of the massacre of 1932.[32] . . . Of course everybody was forbidden to

---

as ANSESAL, founder of several death squads, and founder of the Nationalist Republican Alliance (Alianza Republicana Nacionalista, or ARENA), the right-wing political party that would control the Salvadoran presidency from 1989 into the early twenty-first century (Montgomery 1995, 213–15, 242).

31. Three women participated in organizations that were not mentioned by the others. One participated in a rural cooperative, one participated in an urban neighborhood improvement association (Comité Promejoramiento del Desarrollo Comunal) and one woman, a Mexican citizen who eventually joined the FMLN, had previously participated in an FMLN solidarity group in Mexico City.

32. The massacre of 1932, often simply called "la Matanza," (the Massacre) in El Salvador, was the military's response to a series of protests against Depression-era economic policies, a military coup against the moderate reformer Arturo Araujo, and a fraudulent local election in January 1932. The leader of the uprising, Farabundo Martí, was executed during the Matanza, along with 25,000 to 30,000 others, fewer than 10 percent of whom had even participated in the protests. People who wore indigenous clothing were particularly targeted and as a result of

talk about it and he spoke to us in a very low voice. He told us that there had been this war, that there was a lot of injustice, that there was a lot of hunger, that there was a lot of misery and that was what led to that uprising" (interview, July 24, 1996). When Ninoska completed sixth grade, one of her aunts invited her to move with her to the city of San Salvador, where she could study nursing. So she did so and, as a fourteen-year-old nursing student, was sent into some of the poorest parts of the countryside, including the department of Chalatenango, on a government vaccination campaign. There she first saw the poverty that she had only known about through her grandfather's stories, for though her own family was poor, they always had some food in the house. "Nobody ever said anything and I didn't ask but we would arrive at many houses where we were going to vaccinate children, where the child was eating maybe a tortilla with salt and a tomato, a tortilla with a little water with lime and salt, and the children would not even have clothing . . . there was no need to ask questions, you could see hunger in their faces."

After the vaccination campaign, Ninoska returned to San Salvador, where she received her nursing degree, and at the age of seventeen, she began to work in the government maternity hospital. The hours were long, from 8:00 A.M. to 6:00 P.M. or sometimes from 6:00 A.M. to 8:00 P.M. "The work days were awfully long, we didn't have vacations. . . . And if a woman got pregnant she was out of a job. And they paid very little: twenty days after we got our [monthly] salary we had no money, the money did not stretch far enough to feed our families." So when one of her co-workers suggested that they form a labor union, Ninoska agreed.

While their initial pleas to the president for better working conditions were ignored, by 1965, the union had enough support to organize a public protest. "We held our first march to the president's house, all of us were dressed in white. Only the uniformed nurses went. The men did not join us, they didn't think it was important."

Little by little, working conditions did begin to improve as a result of their protests; in 1965 their salaries were raised by ten colones per month, though their requests for medical benefits and one free day per month

---

the Matanza, open indigenous culture largely ceased to exist in El Salvador, as the survivors changed their clothing style and language, trying to blend in with the mixed-race population. The Matanza ushered in the longest uninterrupted military dictatorship in Latin American history, and the memory of it would forever mark Salvadoran politics: the guerrilla coalition founded in 1980, the Farabundo Martí National Liberation Front, or FMLN, would be named after the martyred leader of 1932, while one of the death squads of the 1980s would be named after the president who oversaw the murders of 1932, General Maximiliano Hernández Martínez (Byrne 1996, 23; Montgomery 1995, 35–37; see also Anderson 1971).

were denied. In 1966 they were granted five free days per year then two free days per month and in 1967, after continued organizing, the nurses were granted three free days per month. Over the course of years of organizing, the government eventually conceded an eight-hour workday and even retirement benefits. But Ninoska's days as a union organizer reached their end in 1979.

There was an organization called ORDEN that did not approve of our work within the labor union. Within the hospital there already was pressure, threats, accusations. And things were already impossible, at that time Carlos Humberto Romero was president.[33] And in the cafeteria where we ate, in the hospital, there was a photo of that Carlos Humberto Romero. And when a nurse was eating—we were all sitting around, doctors, midwives, everybody—that nurse grabbed some refried beans that had been fried hard and she threw the beans at the wall. And bull's-eye! the beans hit the middle of the photo. That was why we were imprisoned. (Interview, July 24, 1996)

Even though Ninoska had nothing to do with throwing the beans, she was one of those who was punished most severely, since she was a union organizer. She was suspended for fifteen days without salary, "and then all sorts of real intense pressure started, they even threatened to disappear us." Ninoska knew she should take those threats seriously, so she quit her nursing job. Besides, by the late 1970s, she was already busy with her work in the church and the emerging human rights movement.

In 1972, Catholic Church workers arrived in the neighborhood where she lived, with her husband and children, to talk about the Bible. After participating in a series of ten talks, one could sign up for a two-day retreat, which Ninoska did. "In that retreat one got a deeper view of what our religion was about: Jesus' commitment to human beings. . . . That also motivated us to discover the needs of the community. . . . The community where I lived was poor, since when we arrived in the neighborhood, there were no streets, there was no electricity, there was no water. It was very rustic. So then we began to work in the community." Under the leadership of the church, newly inspired by the liberation theology

33. Carlos Humberto Romero, a military officer, became president in 1977 as a result of a fradulent election that ended when at least four dozen peaceful demonstrators were killed and the opposition candidate, Ernesto Claramount, was forced to flee into exile. As those who enter politics by the sword often exit by the sword, Romero himself was forced into exile when his government was overthrown in a coup in 1979 (Montgomery 1995, 71–75).

movement, Ninoska and her neighbors set out to put the Bible into practice, to build their community in a literal way.

After several years of slow fund-raising and negotiations with local landowners, the neighborhood had a chapel, a grade school, and a community center. Energized by that success, they moved out to a nearby neighborhood where people were even poorer, living in shacks they had put up themselves. Volunteering to help their neighbors, Ninosky and her fellow helpers would build a total of 243 houses. "We all worked, men and women, and there was mutual respect, it was quite lovely. We did that through the orientation of the church, with one helping another."

The next plan was to build a clinic. But it was never built, since by the late 1970s, community organizing, like other forms of organizing, was increasingly risky. And if organizing under threat of persecution was difficult for everybody, it was especially difficult for Ninoska, since she was facing a personal crisis: her brother, a law student, had been disappeared during a march, on July 30, 1975.

In the months that followed her brother's disappearance, Ninoska searched for him, like many others who had lost relatives in the repression of that demonstration. While she had not directly confronted the government before, Ninoska's experiences in organizing with the church served her well, for it was Archbishop Oscar Romero who helped put her in contact with others who were also searching for their relatives.

He told us, look, if you are to organize you will have to have greater strength. Get together, form a mother's committee and embark on your struggle, which is a very noble struggle. You will have to build a road where there is no road, you will have to open a space amid rows of sharp rocks. . . . We were twelve women . . . only women, that is how COMADRES was born, it was called the Committee of Mothers and Relatives of El Salvador [Comité de Madres y Familiares de El Salvador]. (Interview, July 24, 1996)

So Ninoska became a founding member of COMADRES. Through a variety of means, including letters, demonstrations, hunger strikes, sit-ins, international speaking tours, and a meeting with the pope, the women of COMADRES called the world's attention to the brutality of the Salvadoran regime. While they gained the release of a number of political prisoners, most of the disappeared, like Ninoska's brother, were never found.

Ninoska's story illustrates the importance of preexisting networks even in the case of the human rights groups that employed an apolitical discourse. While the women of COMADRES felt compelled to take great personal risks because of their apolitical love for their family members, they knew how to organize because most of them, like Ninoska, had previous experience in the liberation theology movement (Schirmer 1993, 36–37; Stephen 1994d, 2).[34]

None of the women I interviewed had belonged to a further sort of preexisting network—women's organizations—before joining the revolutionary coalition. But given that there was a tradition of women's organizing against the dictatorship throughout twentieth-century El Salvador,[35] it seems probable that for some women, a women's organization would have served as a preexisting network. Among the women I interviewed, a few mentioned that their mothers or grandmothers had belonged to a women's group, though I would categorize those memories under family traditions of resistance rather than preexisting networks.

In addition to family traditions of resistance and membership in preexisting networks, the last personal factor that explains why certain women chose to join the revolutionary coalition is year of birth or age. Nearly all were young when they joined, as was Lucita, who had only completed fifth grade when, at the age of twelve, she joined the FMLN along with other members of her family in the rural province of Chalatenango. Fourteen years later, once the war had ended, she moved to the city of San Salvador, where she worked as a secretary for the FMLN and attended college courses, thanks to educational benefits she received through the demobilization process (interview, July 1, 1996).

At twelve, Lucita was unusually young when she joined the guerrilla army, although she was certainly not the only rural dweller to join so young. It was much more common for rural girls than those from urban areas to join the guerrillas at a very early age, largely because rural combatants often joined the FMLN as part of a family, as they fled the violence that was much more generalized in the countryside than in the city in the late 1970s, when Lucita joined the guerrillas. But while most waited a

---

34. In a presentation at the 1998 meeting of the American Political Science Association, Cathy Lisa Schneider made a similar point regarding the Mothers of the Plaza de Mayo, the Argentine human rights group that publicly confronted the military regime that had kidnapped their children. The mothers of Argentina, like the mothers of El Salvador, employed an apolitical maternal discourse. Yet according to Schneider, the founding members of that group had not been apolitical women. Instead, they were Peronist party activists who first sought help from their party. After they were rejected by the leaders of the Peronist party, they organized themselves independently by drawing on the skills they had learned in their earlier days as party activists.

35. On early to mid-twentieth-century women's organizing, see AMPES 1981, 8–11; DIGNAS 1993, 86–106; García and Gómáriz 1989, 203–29; Gargallo 1987, 58–59; Hipsher 2001; Moreno 1997, 11–38; Navas 1987; Soro 1992, 1–19; Stephen 1997, 67–84.

few more years to join the guerrillas than did Lucita, in El Salvador, as in Nicaragua, guerrillas and other revolutionary activists were consistently young.

The women in my sample who had been involved in the revolutionary opposition in the 1970s and 1980s were born between the years 1941 and 1971. Thirty-one of them were born between 1950 and 1971, while only four were born in the 1940s. On average, they were born in 1958. With a few exceptions, they were young, relatively free of family responsibilities, and willing to take significant personal risks at just the time that the political crisis that had been building for several generations was reaching the breaking point.

A woman who was born in 1958 would have been an impressionable fourteen-year-old in 1972 when the Christian Democratic Party led an opposition alliance, the National Opposition Union (Unión Nacional Opositor, or UNO), that took the military party (Partido de Conciliación Nacional, or PNC) at its word when the PNC promised to respect the results of the presidential election. That election, which the UNO won only to see the electoral results annulled by the military, was a formative moment for many. "[My mother] spoke against the PNC to us. And she went to vote for the UNO and we were with her morally since we could not vote. But I applauded" (interview, August 1, 1996). The year 1972 saw "the famous electoral fraud. I could not vote but I actively participated in all the activities. For me that was a turning point" (interview, July 15, 1996).

Another formative incident occurred in 1975, when a student demonstration that had begun in protest of the government's spending thirty million dollars to host the Miss Universe pageant, ended in bloodshed. When more than two thousand students, mostly from the University of El Salvador, marched toward a central plaza downtown, they "found themselves surrounded by units of the National Guard with all avenues of escape cut off. The troops—without provocation according to eyewitnesses—opened fire on the demonstrators, leaving at least thirty-seven dead and several dozen more 'disappeared'" (Montgomery 1995, 67). More than one of the women I interviewed mentioned that they themselves had participated in such demonstrations and would have been there to face the army's gunfire that day if others had not stopped them. "The massacre of 1975 was a very hard thing because I had wanted to go to the demonstration but the teachers locked us in the school. [Then an] hour later we heard the ambulances, the machine gun fire" (interview, August 1, 1996).

When a last attempt was made by a coalition of military and civilian reformers to break the escalating cycle of political violence through a progressive coup in 1979, the activist born in 1958 would have been twenty-one. If she was enrolled at the highly organized University of El Salvador at the time, as were many of the women I interviewed, she and her classmates would have already been preparing to respond to the collapse of the last attempt to avert civil war. In January 1980, reformers resigned from the coup coalition as they protested the failure of the military to stop the death squads. In March 1980, the death squads finally did away with their most prominent opponent, Archbishop Oscar Romero. So when in October 1980, the five guerrilla organizations came together in the FMLN coalition, formally marking the beginning of the civil war, she was ready to go underground with the FMLN.

GENDER RELATIONS IN THE MONTAÑA

In the lore of guerrilla politics, the *montaña* is apart from the rules of daily life, a wild place where student radicals become toughened as they work side by side with peasants, where ethnic differences cease to have social meaning, where men treat women as equals (see, for example, Cabezas 1985; Luciak 2001; Pearce 1986, 124–27; Rodríguez 1996a, 1996b).[36] Lucita's words reflected this tradition when she answered my question about relations between men and women within the FMLN. "[They were] like normal relations between brothers and sisters. There was equality, there was no discrimination, not like in normal life. The physical differences were the only ones" (interview, July 1, 1996). At the time of the interview, Lucita was continuing her work within the FMLN and had never worked with the emerging feminist movement. No doubt her recollection of the 1980s was shaped by her experiences in the 1990s—our memories of the past are always shaped by the present. And perhaps Lucita experienced her years in combat as liberating, especially when compared with what she called "normal life." But others remembered their guerrilla years somewhat differently.

36. One famous reference to the Salvadoran montaña has sometimes been misinterpreted by native speakers of English. The guerrillas would say that, since in El Salvador, there is no montaña, the Salvadoran people themselves had to act as the montaña. That phrase is sometimes explained with the claim that El Salvador has no mountains, despite the fact that it is one of the most mountainous countries in Latin America. In fact, montaña is a far more mythic concept, the word meaning roughly uninhabited place, liberated territory, a space outside the control of the national authorities. So the claim is not that El Salvador is flat, but rather that the guerrillas could not have survived for years in the densely populated mountains of El Salvador without at least tacit support from the vast majority, who helped hide them from the authorities.

Like Lucita, Olga, who headed the FMLN Women's Secretariat (Secretaría de la Mujer) after the war, remembered significant gender equality when she was a guerrilla, but unlike Lucita, she remembered that there were some limits to that equality.

There was respect between men and women. It was not like they would say, since you are a woman you can't do that. . . . But perhaps women did not rise up to the same leadership positions. . . . If a man was punished they would not send him to the kitchen and in a woman's case they would. . . . There was disrespect at times, but I don't think that was true in all the zones. . . . [For example, in] Guazapa women were given leadership positions just like men. . . . They did discriminate against us for being women, but we did not see it at the time, we didn't pay much attention. It hasn't been until now that we have realized that they discriminated against us. Now we do care about the discrimination that occurred. (Interview, June 25, 1996)

Military organizations are contradictory things from the perspective of gender relations. On the one hand, it was in the FMLN army that Lucita, Olga, and thousands of other women learned skills, gained independence, were treated with new respect by men, and were empowered by the very thought that they were taking action and fighting back against the military dictatorship. Yet military organizations, even guerrilla organizations, are hierarchical, nondemocratic, and often defensive of the status quo. Marianela discovered that the organization she initially experienced as liberating became less so as it became more militarized.

Marianela, born in 1960, was raised in the town of Suchitoto, the 3rd of 5 children. At the age of twelve, she moved with her family to San Salvador, where as a teenager, she would join church groups that taught shantytown dwellers to read, eventually working in a health clinic run by the General Association of University Students (Asociación General de Estudiantes Universitarios, or AGEUS), an affiliate of the FPL. In 1980, she dropped out of college to join the FPL, going off to the war front, the province of Chalatenango, where she worked in health care and as a community organizer. In 1982, she gave birth to a girl, leaving her with an FMLN collaborator in San Salvador so that she could return to the *montaña*. For in some ways, life there was good, despite the war. "I always felt a lot of camaraderie, 'equality,' in quotation marks. In fact my first bosses were women. Later on I felt things had changed, especially when they militarized all the structures. [In] '83 the way we interrelated changed" (interview, June 24, 1996). In 1984 or 1985, she found herself at the head of a unit of fifteen in which ten were men who did not want to be there; having been wounded in combat, they were sent to work in a health unit headed by a woman. "I had to show them that I could be the boss, that I knew how to yell out an order. That was the measure that showed if I deserved their respect. After a while I earned the respect of some of the *compañeros*." Yet some remained so disrespectful that she was forced to request their transfer. Marianela speculated that part of the problem was her role as a leader of the health workers, a nonmilitary unit. "The female combatants were quite respected. They had to show that they really could do the same as everybody else."

Like Lucita and Olga, Marianela felt that throughout the war "relations between men and women were generally quite egalitarian" even in the case of women like her who worked on the war front as noncombatants. But that equality was compromised "to the extent to which we fell under the influence of militarization, verticalism, the notion of authority figures. . . . I feel like the first years were the best."

As the 1980s wore on and no end of the war was in sight, Marianela became increasingly tired of living far from her daughter, who was growing up in San Salvador without her. In 1987, without asking permission, she left for San Salvador. "At first I felt horribly guilty. I faced two difficult choices, as I would say, between my two loves" (interview, June 24, 1996). She requested permission to stay in San Salvador; permission was denied, but she stayed anyway, working as a messenger for the guerrillas, until the 1989 offensive, when she left her daughter again to work as a nurse.

Shortly after the offensive, she began "to be in contact with the women's movement." It was not that she sought them out but she was sent to work with the Coordinadora Nacional de Mujeres Salvadoreñas (CONA-MUS) in 1990, since "people from the FPL were there. That was when I began to learn about gender theory. . . . For me it has been quite an experience." By sending her to CONAMUS, Marianela's superiors certainly did not intend to turn her into a feminist activist. The reason for forming women's organizations had simply been for the women to provide support work for the guerrillas, as they always had. But the feminist theory she learned in CONAMUS, and a series of organizations after that, offered Marianela a framework within which she could explain her earlier experiences in the *montaña*. In the final years of the civil war, many other women found themselves in similar situations.

Yamilet, whom I introduced earlier in this chapter, shared many of Marianela's experiences. Although they belonged to different parties within the FMLN, she too would be sent by her party to work within a women's organization; like Marianela she would find herself reevaluating her past through the framework of feminist theory.[37]

Initially, like many of the women who had originally joined the move-ment as students, she felt that she was treated differently from the major-ity of her fellow guerrillas, that they saw her as less capable than they were, not so much because of her sex but because of her social back-ground, because she was urban and college educated. "Almost all of the others were peasants and I was not a peasant and I think that people treated me differently." Thinking back on her experiences intercepting government radio transmissions, from the vantage point of the postwar period, she noted that "there was sexual discrimination but I didn't see it that way at that time. The sexual rudeness was terrible. In the armed group where I was [the Communist Party, or PC] there was never a woman commander. . . . [But] in other parties there were" (interview, June 27, 1996).

In the middle of the war, about 1984 or 1985, plans were made for women's organizations. Initially, those plans were not shaped by the women within the guerrilla ranks, but by the male leadership, to avoid what Yamilet called "the couple problem." She explained, "Couples were very unstable, the woman was always to blame for that. So they began to promote women's organizations, always keeping this problem in mind, and also to help maintain supply channels" (interview, June 27, 1996). Each of the five organizations had its own women's association, that of Yamilet's Communist Party was called the Association of Progressive Women of El Salvador (Asociación de Mujeres Progresistas de El Salvador, or AMPES). But since all five organizations were united in a common front—the FMLN—women from all the organizations occasionally met to coordinate their work, with sometimes surprising results.

We would talk about things. There was one leader in the FMLN who would use his military status to seduce young women. And we discovered that he did this to all the women of the FMLN . . . he even put his troops at risk so that he could see one of his

37. Marianela belonged to the FPL, while Yamilet belonged to the Communist Party. While women frequently mentioned differences in their perceptions of the role of women between the different parties, I could find no clear pattern of differences based on party affiliation. All five groups within the FMLN formed women's organizations in the mid to late 1980s to provide rearguard support, organizations that went on to seek autonomy from their founding parties in the 1990s. In all five parties women could be found in positions of great authority; yet at the same time, I heard stories of sexual discrimination from women in each of the parties.

girlfriends who lived in the village. We decided to go to the leaders of the FMLN and to denounce him publicly and it was quite something. . . . That was like setting off a bomb in the FMLN because they had had other things in mind when they set up the women's movements. (Interview, June 27, 1996)

For a brief time, the new women's groups were able to successfully pressure for a few changes. For instance, cigarettes were given out at FMLN meetings although almost none of the women smoked. So the leadership agreed to also distribute items that the women could use: candy, underwear, sanitary napkins. And on March 8, International Women's Day, the men agreed to cook for the women. "Just on that day, but it was something."

But the organizations that had first emerged in 1984 and 1985 were to quickly disappear when the FMLN changed its military strategy. The new strategy "required a new structure. Before, we were in large groupings which really allowed us to meet." Afterward the groups were tiny. If there were five in the group, often only one was a woman. "That was a shame, but we understood that it was necessary. And that from that point we could not maintain the organizations we had created and the war effort practically used up everything we had."

In addition to there being a strategic necessity for this shift, it is possible that, from the perspective of some of the leaders of the FMLN, the fading away of the women's groups that they themselves had promoted was a good thing. "All of the leaders were afraid of us, since, well, they all had their histories" (interview, June 27, 1996).

In 1986, Yamilet requested a transfer to the city, and in December of that year, she was captured by the Treasury Police (Policía de Hacienda), the agency that had "the reputation for being the most brutal" of all the state agencies (Montgomery 1995, 134). But she was relatively lucky; her mother had known when she was taken away, since they ransacked the house. "My mom filed a complaint with the International Red Cross. I was presented to them on my tenth day in captivity." Yamilet was held prisoner for a year at the Ilopango prison, but she was not murdered, since the military had admitted to holding her.

In prison, she was active in COPES, the political prisoners' organization, and through the organization she learned of conditions in the prisons. "There I learned about cases of raped women, women who were pregnant because of the rapes, thousands of cases of torture, especially in the case of those who were captured on the war front or in rural areas." She came to recognize how men and women were treated differently. Although both men and women were tortured, "in addition the women were tortured in a different way, rape, degrading your body, that sort of thing did not happen to men. I was one of the women who wrote down the testimonies" (interview, June 27, 1996).[38]

In 1987, President Napoleon Duarte decreed amnesty for political prisoners, and Yamilet went free. "From that point on I did human rights work. . . . I became more interested in working specifically with women." In 1988, while she worked in human rights groups under the coordination of the Communist Party, two life-transforming events occurred: she gave birth to a daughter and the Communist Party gave birth to ADEMUSA, yet another attempt by the party to form a women's organization that would work on human rights and provide rearguard support for the war effort. So she went to work for ADEMUSA, but with a different attitude from what she had had the first time the party had sent her to work with women. Now she felt that "we needed to stop putting off our interests as women."

In 1989, Yamilet was sent to participate in the Standing Assembly of Central American Women (Asamblea Permanente de Mujeres Centoamericanas) as a representative of ADEMUSA. In that meeting they discussed the ongoing Escuipulas talks and what life would be like after the war. "Of course, we began to question a lot of things within the party. The priority was always the triumph. And we were always given the same

---

38. Others have found that the Latin American military dictators tortured in a gender-specific way. While men were systematically tortured in custody, women were both tortured and raped. Also, they were tortured psychologically in ways related to their roles as mothers and wives, sometimes being raped in front of their children and husbands. Ximena Bunster-Burotto argues that psychologically, women tended to endure worse torture than men. "[T]he torture of men, while horrible, has as its object something less than the extinction of their sexual, gender identity. The primary form of sexual torture of men is . . . placing them in powerless situations where they cannot defend a female prisoner . . . from brutal sexual torture performed in their presence. Women's torment is . . . systematically directed at her female sexual identity and female anatomy" (1986, 306–7; also see Schirmer 1993, 43).

While Bunster-Burotto's claims about the difference in patterns of torture are probably true in general, they may not be true in cases when women were the activists and nonactivist male relatives were captured as substitutes. That happened to the husband of Julieta, an activist in the Salvadoran Women's Movement (Movimiento Salvadoreño de Mujeres, or MSM). After the 1989 offensive in San Salvador, the death squads came looking for Julieta. She was not home, so they took her husband, even though he had never been involved in politics. They tortured him for fifteen days, finally letting him go. "Because of the way I am, they said to him, who gives the orders in your house? It is your wife. Aside from the beatings the hardest thing was the psychological part" (interview, August 2, 1994). Perhaps, in a twisted way, the torturers respected male guerrillas or social activists who acted in an appropriately manly fashion and so did not directly attack their masculinity. But in the case of Julieta's husband, who was a failed man in their eyes because he refrained from controlling his woman, his torture included attacks on his masculinity.

tasks. And additionally they didn't even know anything about the work that we did."

In December 1989, the FMLN attempted another final offensive, seizing control of sections of the capital, including middle-class neighborhoods that had never been directly touched by the war. But the mass insurrection that had occurred a decade earlier in Nicaragua, bringing down the dictatorship, was not to take place in El Salvador. Instead, the guerrillas lost control of the capital.

In the days and months that followed, the army would exact its revenge. Since guerrillas were difficult to capture, popular organizations, some of which had some ties to the guerrillas, some of which did not, bore the brunt of that revenge. "After the offensive ADEMUSA was one of the organizations that was repressed the most . . . they ransacked our office four times. I was taken prisoner again: four and a half months." Released from prison in the final months of the war, Yamilet joined those ADEMUSA activists who wished to pull away from the Communist Party, to devote themselves more fully to the women's work that the party had started. Yet while she herself favored breaking away, she did not do so without recognizing the intricate links between the guerrilla movement and the independent feminist movement that it had inadvertently engendered. "I came to feminism through the revolutionary struggle. That's why it happened" (interview, June 27, 1996).

3 Also a Women's Rebellion
THE RISE OF THE ZAPATISTA ARMY

In the early hours of January 1, 1994, a new year and a new political era were born in southern Mexico. In the first hours of the new year, the Zapatista Army for National Liberation (Ejército Zapatista de Liberación Nacional, or EZLN) took control of seven cities in one of the poorest and most repressed corners of Mexico: the state of Chiapas. The most significant of the cities taken by the rebels was the capital of indigenous Chiapas, San Cristóbal de las Casas, a colonial-era town still characterized by colonial-era politics. It was a woman, Major Ana María, who led the takeover of San Cristóbal. With the hope that politics would not be exclusively for and by men this time, other men and women participated at the major's side. Subcommander Marcos, the chief spokesperson for the rebels, described the takeover:

Only the indigenous men and women under her command are witness to the moment in which the major, a rebel indigenous Tzotzil woman, takes the national flag and gives it to the commanders of the rebellion. . . . Over the radio, the major says: "We have recovered the flag. 10–23 over.". . . It is 0100 hours of the new year for the rest of the world, but she has waited ten years to say those words. She came to the mountains of the Lacandón jungle in December 1984, not yet twenty years of age and yet carrying the marks of a whole history of indigenous humiliation on her body. In December 1984, this brown woman says "Enough is Enough!" but she says it so softly that only she hears herself. In January 1994, this woman and several thousand indigenous people not only say but shout "Enough is Enough!" so loudly that all the world hears them. (Marcos 1996a)

The Zapatista rebellion was many things. Focusing on its political and cultural content, some have called the Zapatista movement an "indigenous rebellion" (Soriano Hernández 1994, 17; Morquecho 1994, 148; Lloyd and Pérez Rosales 1995, 7), an "American intifada" (Jaimes Guer-

rero 1995, 189), and a movement for "constitutional democracy and social reform" (Castañeda 1995, 85; Fox 1994a, 17). Alternatively, a focus
on its economic characteristics has led others to call the movement a
"peasant rebellion" (Collier 1994, 7) and a "rebellion against a new global
strategy of accumulation" (Harvey 1994, 35).[1]

These labels all highlight aspects of the Zapatista rebellion. During the
course of about ten years of organizing in the Lacandón jungle, the Zapatistas mobilized a broad coalition behind their rich body of political
thought. All of the above labels describe some element of the movement.
So my goal here is not to dispute these characterizations[2] but to add one
of my own: the Zapatista rebellion is also a women's rebellion. Women
are well integrated into the Zapatista forces, constituting about one-third
of the combatants and half of the base of support of the EZLN (Marcos
1995c; Olivera 1996, 49; Ross 1995, 289; Stephen 1994a, 2).

At this point, readers who are familiar with the cases of Nicaragua and
El Salvador will find this statistic unsurprising; in fact, the percentage of

---

1. One thing the EZLN is not is a revolutionary movement in the same sense as the FSLN
of Nicaragua and the FMLN of El Salvador. Both Central American guerrilla movements sought
to seize control of the state through armed overthrow while the EZLN had goals that theoretically could have been met without overthrowing the state: democratization, redistribution, land
reform, national sovereignty, ethnic and gender equality. But since meeting those goals would
have been nearly impossible under the system of one-party domination that characterized Mexico (and especially the state of Chiapas) at the time when the EZLN emerged, the Zapatista
agenda can reasonably be called revolutionary.

Six and a half years after the Zapatistas' public emergence, the seventy-one-year hold on
national power that the Party of the Institutional Revolution (Partido de la Revolución Institucional, or PRI) had enjoyed came to its end with the election of Vicente Fox of the right-wing
National Action Party (Partido de Acción Nacional, or PAN) as president in July 2000. Yet even
when the PRI's grip on national power was at its weakest, it remained fairly strong in the state
of Chiapas. In the July election, the ruling party took eleven of the twelve congressional seats
from the state (Cuéllar and Urrutia 2000), though, a month later, in August, the PRI lost its hold
on the governorship to Pablo Salazar, representative of the opposition coalition, Alianza por
Chiapas. Salazar, who like many opposition politicians in Mexico, had been a member of the
PRI for most of his career (until 1999), was the first gubernatorial candidate from the opposition
to ever be elected in the state of Chiapas (Becerril 2000; SIPAZ 2000).

The differences between the EZLN and earlier Latin American guerrillas, and the reasons for
those differences, will be addressed in the conclusion to this chapter.

2. I would dispute one fashionable characterization of the EZLN, namely, the claim that
the EZLN is a postmodern movement. Despite its use of new technology, especially the Internet,
to build international support, and despite its greater attention to identity politics (both ethnic
and gender issues) than previous guerrilla movements, most of the demands of the EZLN are
highly modern: democracy; dignity; and access to basic resources, most fundamentally, land.
Melissa Forbis eloquently addresses the question of the Zapatistas and postmodernity: "There
has been a tendency to analyze the EZLN as postmodern rebels and internet warriors—although
the majority live without electricity, much less telephones or computers. This focus says more
about our own postmodern condition and how we processed the event, and less about the reality of being indigenous in Chiapas. Viewed in this manner, the Zapatistas are denied an agency
that they have fought hard to create" (2000, 2).

female armed combatants was nearly the same in all three cases. But we *should* be surprised by the numbers of female Zapatistas, for if there is any one thing that characterizes all the Maya Indian groups from which the vast majority of Zapatistas come, it is that women within those groups normally lead extremely restricted lives (see Eber 1995; Falquet 1995; Garza Caligaris 1991; Olivera 1996, 1995, 1994; Rovira 1997, 1995; Ruiz Ortiz 1991; Toledo Tello 1986).

There are many indicators of women's second-class status within their communities. For instance, they are often expected to wait until the men finish eating before they can begin to eat; under the conditions of scarcity that are prevalent within those communities, the end result is that women eat much less than men. When they are invited to meetings, which they often are not, women sit separately from men. In 1994, I attended a meeting in the indigenous town of Morelia, in the center of Zapatista territory; the male leaders of the community made the mistake of thinking that since we foreign visitors wanted to meet with "the community," we were only interested in talking to men. When the confusion was cleared up, the women were invited (over the town megaphone), and they arrived by the hundreds, with their young children.

Probably the most important mechanism by which indigenous girls are controlled is their being raised monolingual (in an indigenous language) in contrast with their brothers, who often have access to school, where they learn to read and write Spanish.[3] Indigenous women's limited formal education, compared with that of men, means that they have few opportunities to support themselves in a society in which Spanish is the language of money. Some indigenous women do end up getting to go to school for at least a few years, but those are usually the ones who, for whatever reasons, are particularly rebellious from an early age. The story of Juana, a Tzotzil Indian who was the second born of six but the first daughter, was terribly common. She told me that her childhood was "very difficult, I had almost no childhood, we had almost no money. They didn't want me to study because I had to help my mother in the house

---

3. Seven different indigenous languages and Spanish are spoken within the state of Chiapas, making organizing between communities difficult for men as well as women. But organizing is even more difficult for women, as they are less likely to be able to speak Spanish than men. Illiteracy is also a serious problem in Chiapas, a state in which 33.12 percent of the population is illiterate, compared with the national average of 12.44 percent. Not surprisingly, more women than men are illiterate: 37.5 percent of women cannot read, compared with 22.4 percent of men. In the predominantly indigenous municipalities of Altamirano, Margaritas, and Ocosingo, adult female illiteracy is much higher than the state average: 64.11 percent, 59.5 percent, and 60.5 percent, respectively (Hidalgo and Monroy 1994, 22).

because I was the oldest of all the girls. And my dad told me no, because you are a girl. When I was little I accepted it, but later on my dream was to become a star because I had seen television in the house of my aunt. I asked, to be a star, what should one do? She told me, study." So Juana begged her father to reconsider his rule that girls should not study and he relented, but he imposed strict conditions, telling her:

"You can go to school but you will have to carry firewood and water first and if not, you will go to school without eating as a punishment." I would go for firewood at 5:00 in the morning. . . . Often I barely arrived and had breakfast and I was late to school. [Because I was late] they punished me, making me get down on my knees or they hit my fingers on the chalkboard, very hard. I finished grade school at the age of 15 after a lot of sacrifices. Despite everything I got very good grades. (Interview, July 19, 1997)

These sorts of stories, of early intrafamilial struggles for the most minimal opportunities, were told over and over again by the indigenous activists whom I interviewed in Chiapas.[4] While girls and boys were not treated perfectly equally in Nicaragua and El Salvador, the women I interviewed in those countries did not tell such stories of educational opportunities denied, at least not to the same extent. Yet even for the Central American women, who were all fluent in their national language, and who were not systematically denied access to school, joining the guerrilla coalitions meant confronting gender barriers. If the women of Nicaragua and El Salvador had to take uncommonly big steps to cross gender barriers and join the guerrillas, then the women of Chiapas had to make giant leaps to overcome their barriers.

The significant presence of women within the Zapatista coalition tells us at least two things. First, gender relations were in transition in the years leading up to the rebellion. Had that not been the case, those

4. As I noted in the Introduction to this book, the women I interviewed in Chiapas differed from those I interviewed in Nicaragua and El Salvador, a result of the fact that I did my research during the war in Chiapas and during the postwar period in Central America. Many of the Central Americans I interviewed had been active in the guerrilla movements (and in the Sandinista revolution); by contrast, none of the women I interviewed in Chiapas had participated in the EZLN, to my knowledge. So when I refer to the indigenous activists I interviewed, I am referring to women who were active in various social movements or organizations, most of which would be considered part of what has been called the "new Zapatista movement" (Leyva Solano 1998, 35–55) or what I have referred to as the revolutionary coalition (see note 2 in the Introduction for an explanation of this concept).

The nature of my data means that I am not able to fully evaluate some of the personal factors that may have led women to join the EZLN. A more thorough study of the personal histories of the women of the EZLN will have to wait until the war has reached its end.

women who became combatants would not have been available for mobilization into such nontraditional roles. Second, the presence of women in the rebellion, both in their numbers and in their demands, indicates that the rebellion itself will continue to transform gender relations in Chiapas. I will argue that the Zapatista rebellion can be called a women's rebellion because of its origin, which is the focus of this chapter, and in its demands, which will be addressed in the chapter's conclusion.

BEFORE THE REBELLION

The site of the Zapatista rebellion, the southern Mexican state of Chiapas, is both very poor and very rich. One indicator of the extreme poverty of the majority of the residents of Chiapas is malnutrition. Almost 67 percent of the population of the state has been identified as malnourished; about half of those people (33 percent of the state's population) are "severely malnourished." The average resident of Chiapas is much poorer than the average Mexican: in Chiapas, 22.3 people per 100,000 die each year as a result of nutritional deficiencies, whereas in Mexico as a whole, an annual average of 10.5 per 100,000 die as a result of such deficiencies (Hidalgo and Monroy 1994, 23). Access to public services is another indicator of the well-being of a population. In Chiapas, 44.6 percent of all houses lack access to indoor plumbing (in other words, sewage systems), while at a national level, "only" 21.47 percent of Mexicans lack access to indoor plumbing (Hidalgo and Monroy 1994, 22).

These numbers actually underrepresent the poverty of the indigenous population of Chiapas, since they are an average of the terrible conditions under which most indigenous people live and the better conditions that characterize the lives of most ladinos (people of mixed race who speak Spanish). Not surprisingly, in official records, indigenous people and ladinos are not distinguished. But regional distinctions provide some indication of this disparity. In the municipality of San Cristóbal, where most of the relatively affluent ladinos of the eastern third of the state live, 17.3 percent of houses lack electricity and 31.1 percent lack running water. In contrast, in the three mainly indigenous municipalities to the east of San Cristóbal (which are now at the center of the rebellion), access to basic services is much less common. In Altamirano, 74.2 percent have no electricity; 64.3 percent have no running water. In Las Margaritas 67.1 percent have no electricity and 76.9 percent have no running water. In Ocosingo the numbers are similar: 67.9 percent lack electricity; 57.4 percent lack water (Hidalgo and Monroy 1994, 22).

But as suggested by the title of Thomas Benjamin's history of Chiapas, *A Rich Land, a Poor People* (1996), the poverty of the indigenous residents of Chiapas is not due to a shortage of natural resources. In some ways, Chiapas is one of the richest states of Mexico. Although Chiapas is relatively small, with only 3 percent of the country's population, it is an important source of raw materials. Chiapas supplies 54 percent of Mexico's hydroelectric power, 13 percent of its gas, and 4 percent of its oil. In a country in which corn is the main staple food, Chiapas plays an important role by supplying Mexico with 13 percent of its corn (Collier 1994, 16).[5] And just as these macroeconomic indicators tend to gloss over ethnic differences, they also minimize sex differences. The conditions under which most indigenous women live are grim. Malnutrition and shoddy health services are terribly common, leading to one of the highest rates of maternal mortality in Mexico: more than 8.5 of every 10,000 women in Chiapas are victims of maternal mortality each year (Garza Caligaris and Cadenas Gordillo 1994, 96).

Reproductive issues provide other measures of the traditional subordination of indigenous women. Within indigenous communities, contraception is frequently unknown. In one study, 28 percent of Tzeltal women and 52 percent of Tzotzil women did not know of any contraceptive method (Bellato cited in Barrios Ruiz and Pons Bonals 1995, 26). Contraception is even less frequently used (the same study found that 75.7 of Tzeltal women and 88 percent of Tzotzil women had never used contraception). Low levels of contraceptive use and early marriage for both women and men (Barrios Ruiz and Pons Bonals 1995, 27) mean that birthrates are high. However, this may be changing: one doctor told me that about 60 percent of young indigenous women now use contraception, although its use remains low among older women (interview with author, February 1995).

Pressures for early marriage have an important effect on women's lives in ways that go beyond birthrates. Because young men are not granted the privileges of adulthood until they marry, they have an incentive to seize unwilling women and force them into marriage. Also, parents sometimes resolve disciplinary or economic problems by selling their daughters into marriage or servitude (Garza Calgaris et al. 1993, 7, 32, 38). But marriage, even with all these limitations, is often a woman's best option. Should a young woman have a child out of wedlock, she is considered the

---

5. For more on the political-economic factors that set the stage for the Zapatista rebellion, see Rus 1995; Tejera Gaona 1996; Villafuerte Solís and García Aguilar 1994.

same as a widow and may only marry a widower, a man who usually is far older than she is and who is interested in marriage only to have someone to cook and clean and care for his children (Olivera 1994, 63).

For a long time, probably hundreds of years, most indigenous women in Chiapas lived under these conditions: heavily controlled by their fathers and husbands, often malnourished, always in danger of dying from minor complications in childbirth. But even before the Zapatistas officially emerged in January 1994, there were challenges to these circumstances. Just as Mexico has changed in the past generation, so has the state of Chiapas; these changes have had a significant effect upon gender relations in indigenous communities.

GENDER RELATIONS IN TRANSITION: STRUCTURAL CHANGES

As I have already suggested, one of the roots of the Zapatista rebellion was frustration over the conditions of economic inequality and political repression under which the indigenous majority of Chiapas lives. Perhaps inevitably, social tensions were engendered by the highly unequal distribution of land and of other basic goods in the state. Big landowners kept those tensions under control through the use of what were called white guards *(guardias blancas)*, or private police forces, forces that periodically threatened or killed Indians whom they saw as troublemakers.[6]

Beginning in the 1970s (especially in the north of the state), many indigenous people began to directly challenge the power of the big landowners, challenges that included seizing tracts of land. At that point the state government stepped in violently on the side of the landowners and their white guards: life in the countryside of Chiapas became characterized by what Amnesty International called "a pattern of deliberate political killings" (quoted in Benjamin 1996, 234). Other human rights organizations consistently identified Chiapas (along with the state of Oaxaca) as "the Mexican state with the most official violence" (Rus 1995, 71).[7] But as in Nicaragua and El Salvador, inequality and political violence were not enough, on their own, to fuel a rebellion.

6. For many years, the white guards enjoyed the formal approval of those who ruled over the state of Chiapas. In 1961, Governor Samuel León Brindis decreed that ranchers would be allowed to legally carry arms and hire private police forces. Official support for the white guards was rescinded in the early 1990s, as part of the process of agricultural modernization that led to the NAFTA accords. Nonetheless, those private police forces continued to exist, on occasion joining with public police forces to battle peasants in disputes over land (CIACH 1997b, 1–2).

7. It is important to note that the Mexican government has generally ruled through incorporation far more than through repression, in sharp contrast with the Somoza dictatorship of

A number of changes occurred in Chiapas beginning in the 1970s that pushed people into seeking new solutions for old problems. These changes included growth in independent peasant unions, colonization of the jungle, the rise of new industries (such as trucking and tourism) and, more recently, changes in the international political economy, including those brought about by NAFTA (North American Free Trade Agreement), that led to the end of the possibility of legal land reform (Collier 1994).[8]

Material changes are critical to understanding the roots of the rebellion. But to fully understand these conditions, we have to consider the different ways in which economic change was experienced by men and women. To understand why a full 30 percent of the Zapatista combatants are women, it is important to understand the gendered impact of structural changes in the years leading up to the rebellion.

In response to demands for land reform from the 1950s onward, the federal government of Mexico encouraged colonization of the jungle that covers the eastern third of the state of Chiapas. By the 1980s, an estimated 150,000 migrants had settled in the Lacandón jungle (Benjamin 1996, 205). It was in the jungle that men and women from different towns, different linguistic groups, different religions, all came together. There they came to realize that they were united by common grievances. The jungle would become the birthplace of the Zapatista rebellion.

The move to the jungle was experienced differently by women and men. Although many women had to be forced to join their husbands in migrating there, the long-term effect of the move was to cut some of the traditional ties that had constrained women's autonomy (Garza et al. 1993; Rovira 1995, 16–20; Townsend et al. 1994, 21). Because women

---

Nicaragua and the military dictatorship of El Salvador. Nonetheless, the governments of the state of Chiapas sometimes used violence against social movements in ways reminiscent of their Central American counterparts (official violence is discussed in Benjamin 1996, 234–35; Collier 1994, 40–41, 46–49, 78–79; Harvey 1998, 60, 92–117; Tejera Gaona 1996, 312–13; Womack 1999, 162–71).

    8. The modern Mexican state emerged out of the Mexican Revolution of 1910–17. The constitution, written in 1917, reflects that revolutionary heritage in multiple ways, including a guarantee, through Article 27, of a continual process of land reform. That does not mean that land disputes were always decided in favor of the tillers, nor that they were resolved rapidly or without violence. But it does mean that, until 1992, the Mexican state regularly resolved land disputes in favor of peasants, making it quite unusual within Latin America. That possibility of receiving land through legal petition was cut off in 1992 when President Carlos Salinas de Gortari reformed Article 27 to eliminate the promise of land reform. This move, which made investment in Mexico more appealing to foreigners and nationals who had money to invest, also made life more desperate for the huge majority of Mexicans who had no money to invest. In short, the amendment of Article 27 eliminated the hope that landless peasants might someday receive land through land reform.

had been more linguistically isolated than men before the move to the jungle, the move had a greater effect on their ability to communicate with others. Growing up in the highlands, many women had been kept out of school by their parents and so they were both illiterate and monolingual.

But in the jungle, linguistic isolation from the Spanish-speaking world, and from speakers of other indigenous languages, was broken out of necessity. Members of ethnic groups that had lived in separate communities back in the highlands formed mixed communities in the jungle. Sometimes people from different indigenous ethnic groups married. In those cases "the couples communicated in the husband's language, and so many women became bilingual since they were 'socially' obliged to do so" (Rovira 1995, 17). It is true that the subordination of women was reflected in the husband's ability to impose his language, as opposed to his speaking in the wife's language or in some combination of the two languages. But subordination sometimes has unintended consequences. In this case, it meant that women were more likely to develop linguistic skills that made them crucial to the survival of the new communities—and to the survival of the guerrilla army that was to form in the jungle.

Just as indigenous migrants to the jungle were transformed by their experience, so too were many who came from every other state in the Mexican union, including those of the far north (Leyva Solano and Ascencio Franco 1996, 50–52). In the jungle those migrants from outside Chiapas, and especially their children, would be the creators of a "sense of community" that contrasted in important ways with what had existed in the villages that they had left (Ascencio and Leyva 1996, 154).[9] For one thing, an indigenous language—Tzeltal—was the common language, not Spanish; though Spanish was also spoken. The community sentiment would be an indigenous one, but in an inclusive, rather than exclusive, way.

This inclusive indigenous identity would be reflected with time in the Zapatista's own inclusive indigenous sentiment and it was reflected, thousands of times over, in the experiences of people like Carolina, who was born in the jungle to a mother from the state of Tabasco, and a father from Tila (in Chiapas). Although they spoke Spanish in their home, their daughter would become an activist in an autonomous indigenous women's group, perhaps because of her having spent her formative years in the jungle community. "From the time I was small I couldn't study

---

9. On the political and social implications of migration to the Lacandón jungle, see also Acevedo García 1995 and Mendoza Ramírez 1995.

well, I finished grade school. There was no high school in the community. We would have to go all the way to Ocosingo to go to high school [and it was too expensive]. . . . I speak Tzeltal, Spanish, and Tzotzil. I learned languages in the community, Tzeltal when I was fourteen years old, from neighbors. Here [in San Cristóbal] I learned Tzotzil" (interview, July 8, 1997). Both in the jungle and later in San Cristóbal, Carolina was active in indigenous women's organizations, though she herself was not raised as indigenous. That is what I mean by the sense of community that is at once indigenous and inclusive: it included all who identified with the indigenous struggle, which would become the Zapatista struggle, against a government with a long history of engaging in unequal and sometimes violent clientelistic exchanges with the indigenous communities of Mexico; counting on those communities to provide votes for the ruling party, while neglecting to provide them with the most minimal services.

At the same time as many migrated to the jungle in search of land, many other residents of the highlands remained in their highland communities. Those communities were not economically static. While some peasants continued to attempt to make a living off the densely populated and mountainous land, others entered new occupations. These new jobs (especially in the petroleum, trucking, and tourism industries) brought them into contact with people outside their native villages.

The transformation of employment in the highlands had mixed implications for gender relations. The increased importance of money in the highland economy (as opposed to subsistence production) and men's relative advantages over women in earning money (since some lucrative professions, such as trucking, were culturally closed to women) meant that the traditional economic interdependence of men and women evolved into a situation in which women are "both more dependent on men than men are on women, and more dependent on men now than they were in the past" (Flood 1994, 156; also see Eber 1995, 69–70, 241–42; Rosenbaum 1993, 126).

But while women were more dependent on men than the other way around, in the sense that women were not as able to earn cash, they were not necessarily more dependent in other senses. The two most lucrative new opportunities for men, in trucking and the oil industry, meant that men left their women behind in their communities for long periods of time, requiring the women to take on new responsibilities and allowing the women to gain new skills and confidence. While the custom of leaving women behind to run the household and cornfield goes back centuries in indigenous Chiapas, for as long as plantation owners have hired seasonal labor, that practice became more widespread with the growth of trucking and oil.

Increased monetarization also pushed many indigenous women into the labor market. Monetary activity took various forms. Most indigenous women who entered the market did so as producers or vendors in the ladino-dominated cities, selling items that ranged from woven goods to food to the pine needles used in religious ceremonies. Another option, for young women who had received some formal education, was to seek work as bilingual teachers. A third option was to work as a maid in a ladino home in the city.

But there were costs to these strategies. Women who ventured out of the confines of their villages, even in order to raise the cash necessary to survive in those villages, were often ostracized. A strategy that was undertaken to hang onto the old way of life often had the opposite effect. In a few extreme cases, women were murdered by their own relatives for stepping out of the bounds of their proper roles through the cooperative movement (Nash 1993, 127–29, 141). In many cases, the solution to the ostracism generated by limited economic independence was to seek greater independence by moving for good to one of the cities of Chiapas (Flood 1994, 165).[10]

Women, equipped with new independence and new skills—but also new grievances—became open to mobilization directly in the EZLN, or indirectly into a social movement that sympathized with the EZLN. Commander Susana, a Tzotzil Indian, discussed how her experience as a maid in San Cristóbal would eventually lead her to join the Zapatista Army. "The work was hard. I came to think that living like that, why am I suffering far away? And why don't I go home? I returned to my community and I commented to all my *compañeras* that they abused us, that this shouldn't be. My boss beat me. I thought about it some more and I learned about the Zapatista Army. I thought some more, deeply, and I thought it is not good that they treat us so badly" (quoted in Rojas 1995a, 60). Susana first mobilized women in her community and then traveled with the EZLN. Thus, the injustice that she experienced as a maid in San Cristóbal, and the courage to leave her community that she also gained through that experience, was communicated throughout the state, even to women who had not yet ventured out of their native villages.

In the decades leading up to the Zapatista rebellion, many men and

---

10. In the period from 1980 to 1988 alone, the urban population of Chiapas increased "from 700,000 to more than 950,000" (Rus 1995, 84)

women, like Susana, moved away from the highlands, organizing new sorts of communities in the jungle, the cities, and other rural areas. That migration was to transform indigenous Chiapas. Because of migration, according to the anthropologist Jan Rus, "there is probably not a family in the Highlands that does not have brothers and sisters, sons and daughters, who participate in each of the new kinds of organizations. All of these people are in contact, visiting each other, talking, weighing strategies and alternatives" (1995, 85; on the political implications of migration, also see Tejera Gaona 1996, 304–10).

Those family networks would facilitate the organization of a statewide movement like the EZLN, for as I noted in the cases of Nicaragua and El Salvador, family ties are always some of the safest bases for recruiting into a guerrilla army. Family networks may be an especially important way in which women are recruited into guerrilla armies, given that women are excluded from some of the preexisting networks through which men may be recruited.

All these above changes in material conditions had the effect of transforming the lives of many indigenous women because they opened up the possibilities for comparison. As long as the vast majority of indigenous women remained isolated by geography and language, there was little chance that they would be mobilized by a movement like the EZLN. For such mobilization to occur, some women had to gain the opportunity to compare.

Many different occurrences over the past forty-some years created opportunities for comparison; these occurrences included the move from the highlands to the jungle, the acquisition of new linguistic skills, and the experience of being a vendor, bilingual teacher, or maid. Comparison allowed some women to recognize the patterned nature of social inequality in Chiapas, a radicalizing realization.

GENDER RELATIONS IN TRANSITION: ORGANIZING

The Zapatista rebellion grew out of the conditions of material inequality that I had outlined so far, in combination with particular organizational opportunities and constraints. Opportunities existed because the Mexican state has traditionally ruled through controlled mobilization, a system of social control that is known as corporatism. Playing by the rules of the corporatist game (including voting for the ruling party, the PRI, and only organizing through its social movements) has sometimes brought rewards to the players, rewards such as access to land or to other government largesse.[11]

This system of controlled inclusion distinguishes Mexican politics from the politics of violent exclusion in the Central American countries that also gave rise to guerrilla movements. But in some ways, Chiapas has as much in common with Central America as it does with Mexico City. It was the combination of potential organizing opportunity combined with significant constraints on legal reform that created the EZLN.

By this point, it should not be surprising that extreme social inequality and governmental violence would have combined with new organizational opportunities to create a guerrilla organization like the EZLN. After all, that is basically the story of the guerrilla wars in Nicaragua and El Salvador. And seen from the perspective of the north and center of Mexico, Chiapas looks an awful lot like Central America. But from close up, nobody would think that Chiapas is a twin of to either Nicaragua or El Salvador.

In Nicaragua and El Salvador, attempts to peacefully organize were regularly and violently put down for generations up to the time of the armed rebellions. Not so in Chiapas: though the long arm of the PRI was not always generous in the resources it handed out in the peripheral state of Chiapas, there can be no doubt that Chiapas is part of Mexico. It was the closing off of prior opportunities for organizing (Harvey 1994, 28)—as opposed to the complete absence of organizing opportunities—combined with the opening of new opportunities that were not easily controlled by the PRI, that led to support for armed rebellion. This was especially true in the periphery of the periphery: the Lacandón jungle in the eastern third of Chiapas.

The first groups that tried to organize the new arrivals to the jungle were religious. As far back as the 1940s, Protestant missionaries with links

11. The Party of the Institutional Revolution (Partido de la Revolución Institucional, or PRI) has consistently dominated elections in state of Chiapas, especially in those voting districts with the highest percentage of indigenous voters. George Collier observes that in the 1988 election, "which opposition parties vigorously and effectively contested in northern and metropolitan Mexico, 89.9 percent of Chiapas voters, including impoverished Indian peasants, allegedly turned out for the PRI" (1994, 17, also 79–81). Héctor Tejera Gaona documents electoral results from the 1980s, finding that districts with large percentages of indigenous people overwhelmingly favored the PRI with up to 98 percent of votes going to the official party, according to official figures. Just as remarkably, he found that rural districts (where it is more difficult for voters to get to the polls, and where one would expect low turnouts) were the districts with the highest turnouts in Chiapas. In those districts up to 87 percent of voters supposedly turned out to vote (1996, 320–25; for electoral figures from 1976, 1982 and 1988, see Francisca Alicia Pérez Grovas cited in Guillén 1995, 43–44; for electoral figures from 2000, see Cuéllar and Urrutia 2000).

to the Summer Institute of Linguistics attempted to organize the colonists, with the support of the government, to encourage individualism and to reduce the role of traditional religious and cultural practices. At least numerically, they enjoyed considerable success: in 1960 fewer than 5 percent of the jungle's residents identified themselves as Protestant, while by 1990, 25 percent identified themselves that way (Harvey 1994, 29).

But for the purposes of tracing the roots of Zapatismo, the most important religious organizing was that of the liberation theology–influenced church under the bishop of the Archdiocese of San Cristóbal, Samuel Ruiz. This is not to say that the church had any intention of creating a guerrilla movement, but simply that the church's advocacy of basic human rights had the effect (in a state where basic human rights were often ignored), of preparing some indigenous people for later mobilization in the Zapatista army. Starting in the 1960s, Catholic missionaries began to work in the jungle and highlands; three decades later, more than seven thousand indigenous lay workers organized their communities into small groups (Eber 1995, 223). Unlike their Protestant counterparts, they actively encouraged cooperatives and the restoration of traditional practices.

A key turning point was the 1974 Indigenous Congress held in San Cristóbal under the sponsorship of Bishop Samuel Ruiz. Ironically, representatives of the state government had asked Bishop Ruiz to organize the conference. He had agreed to do so on the condition that it be a serious event, by and for indigenous people. Agreeing to that condition meant that the government gave up its traditional control over indigenous organizing. The conference was remarkable, for "it was the first official meeting of Indians not convened for the government to tell Indians what to do" (Collier 1994, 62). Many of the leaders and organizations that would eventually come to support the armed uprising by the mid-1990s traced their roots back to the church-sponsored conference of the mid-1970s.

Although the church-sponsored Indigenous Congress of 1974 was held in the central highlands of Chiapas (in the city of San Cristóbal) and though the church's organizing was carried out throughout the state of Chiapas, it was in the Lacandón jungle where the new liberation theology–influenced church had the most influence.[12] The church ended up filling an organizational vacuum in the jungle, a vacuum that did not ex-

12. On the Archdiocese of San Cristóbal and its role in the jungle, see also Harvey 1998, 1994; Guillén 1997, 1995; Legorreta Díaz 1998; Womack 1999, 119–61, 198–208.

ist in the highlands, where the national government had a strong presence through a wide array of agencies.[13]

Women were actively targeted for mobilization by the liberation theologians going back at least to the mid-1960s.[14] This holistic mobilization effort included discussing the Bible; teaching literacy (in both Spanish and native languages); advocating for human rights; providing health services; and aiding women in forming economic projects such as cooperatives, communal cornfields and corn mills, chicken production, vegetable gardens, and craft cooperatives. All these projects were part of a process of claiming the "dignity" of each woman—*dignity* being a frequently used word. Sister Caridad explained the process:

Each pastoral team includes a group of women. In each community we promote groups of women through the word of God because these are extremely religious people. At its base, the word of God is about equality. Paul says that there are no women, there are no men, there are no Greeks, etc. Women have to understand that because of their own dignity, they are the equals of men. If it happens that men don't let them go out of the house by themselves, the word of God has something to say about it. People's thinking is changing. . . . The contribution that the church's work can make is to help women grow in consciousness and political commitment. . . . All the women who participate in the church also participate in other organizations. I think all of them do. What helps the church is that because of our equality we have the right to participate and also because the word of God urges us to change the world.

When I asked her how they were going to do this, she replied: "It's the people who have to do it for themselves. Today the people have taken control of their lives. They are looking for autonomy, that may be a step forward. I don't know what will come next. I think that my work is to accompany and to help and to enlighten. This work is very slow but there is no hurry" (interview, December 17, 1995). Sister Caridad's words reflect a common process in Catholic base communities. This process starts with

13. Diana Guillén listed forty-six state and parastatal agencies that had a presence in Chiapas on the eve of the Zapatista rebellion in 1993 (1997, 23).

14. The Archdiocese of San Cristóbal has been working with indigenous women for a long time, probably longer than any other group in the state. In 1995, I interviewed thirteen women who did pastoral work with indigenous women and found that they had been working in indigenous communities for an average of nine and a half years, with individual experiences ranging from thirty-two years to six months. None of the women I talked to were originally from Chiapas, though they assured me that there were indigenous women from Chiapas who did the same sort of work they did.

reevaluating everyday experience through the light of the Bible ("If it happens that men don't let them go out of the house by themselves, the word of God has something to say about it"). It then moves on to applying those new insights in the public world ("All the women who participate in the church also participate in other organizations").

I don't think Sister Caridad overstated the impact of this work. Many other women who work with indigenous women, who are not affiliated with the church, also mentioned the prior work of the church as critical for preparing women for mobilization in other social movements. For instance, a social worker named Claudia told me she had more success organizing indigenous women in health projects if those women had previously been popular church catechists. "There were years in which the archdiocese accompanied; it said that women and men were equal. The truth is that the archdiocese was a very important factor in getting men to realize that women are equal" (interview, December 15, 1995).

Perhaps in recognition of the critical role the church played in setting the stage for future mobilization, relations between secular feminists and church workers are quite close. But there are some significant differences. As one observer suggested, "The church's work with women is very progressive at the level of social participation, but anything that has to do with the body, such as abortion and contraception, that is simply not acceptable" (interview, January 1995). Nonetheless, by questioning entrenched social structures, and encouraging women to organize to transform those structures, the Catholic Church did play an unintended role in preparing women for mobilization as Zapatistas.

But despite the great importance of the church, it could not serve the needs of all the new arrivals in the jungle. Ultimately, the residents of the jungle were too pluralistic in their religious affiliations to be mobilized by any single religious organization, even one as ecumenical as the liberation theology movement often was. A group that hoped to attract all the residents of the jungle would have to appeal to secular values such as pluralism and democracy. In 1978, a group called Popular Politics (Política Popular) started to make such appeals.

Popular Politics was a Maoist-inspired movement led by refugees from the student movement that ended with the government's massacre of students in Mexico City's Tlatelolco Square in 1968. Popular Politics self-identified as Maoist, and indeed it was, in a number of ways: in the social sector it sought to organize, that is, the peasantry; in its hope to win over those peasants through the construction of liberated zones; and in its expectation that this would be slow work, carried out over many years. But it did not act in the Maoist tradition of seeking power through the barrel of a gun. In fact, other organizers in the jungle sometimes criticized Popular Politics for its willingness to negotiate and compromise with the government (Collier 1994, 64–65, 70–73; Legorreta Díaz 1998, 94–109).

The secular outsiders from Popular Politics entered a society that was organized both by the radical Catholic activists already mentioned and by a number of peasant union federations. Over the course of about a decade, these organizational currents flowed side by side. But eventually, many came up against the limitations of pacifistic organizing, as the debt crisis, the elimination of government support for peasant farmers, the end of land reform, and continued governmental violence and corruption all contributed to a growing belief that reform, within the framework of legal politics, was simply not possible (Benjamin 1996, 235–45; Collier 1994, 78; Escalante Gonzalbo 1995; Harvey 1998, 1994, 30–35; Leyva and Ascencio 1996, 148–73). The process that had begun with a peaceful Congress in 1974 turned into an armed rebellion by the mid-1990s.

Where do indigenous women fit into this strategic shift? As is the case in discussions of the influence of the radical church on indigenous communities, accounts of the secular organizing that laid the groundwork for the EZLN (in other words, Popular Politics and the peasant unions) fail to mention the differential effect of these strategies upon men and women. My guess is that when observers write of how indigenous "peasants" were organized between the mid-1970s and the mid-1990s, this really means "peasant men," since indigenous life in Chiapas tends to be strictly segregated by sex. But that does not mean that women were unorganized during the second, secular wave of organizing that culminated in the Zapatista uprising. It just means that they had separate organizations.

Starting in 1986, the first women's groups, which were devoted to feminist studies and discussions of violence against women, began to be organized in San Cristóbal. These groups were mainly composed of people who were affiliated with the university, or who did intellectual work, such as schoolteachers; the majority of participants were mestizas (non-indigenous women) who were not originally from the state of Chiapas. The groups were always small and often short-lived.

The first group, the Women's Promotion Committee (Comité Impulsor de Mujeres)[15] was to promptly divide in two over a disagreement about whether the group should be composed of only women, or of both

---

15. Another woman I spoke to gave me a somewhat different name, but it had the same basic meaning. She told me that the group was called the Promotion Group for the Support of Women's Organizations (Grupo Promotor de Apoyo de Organismos de Mujeres).

women and men. The new co-ed group that resulted from the split was known as Antzetik (*women* in Tzeltal); as late as 2000 it was still devoted to studying gender issues. By themselves these groups did not have a major impact on life in Chiapas, and their names were never widely known, but they did have a far-reaching influence, in that many of the leaders of the broad-based women's movement of the 1990s were first politicized through those small groups.

Those little groups set the stage for the occurrences of 1989. That year was critical for women's organizing, for that was when a coalition first came together in response to a wave of rapes in San Cristóbal. The reasons for the high rate of rape were unclear, but they may have been related to the fact that San Cristóbal is a city that attracts significant numbers of outsiders (tourists from the rest of Mexico and foreign countries, along with migrants from the mainly indigenous highlands of Chiapas).

The high incidence of rape certainly had something to do with the tradition of impunity for those with ties to the ruling party. For instance, one man, who was widely believed to have raped fifty foreign women, was released because of his ties to the PRI. Other accused rapists, who were members of a progovernment union (the Confederación de Trabajadores Mexicana, or CTM), were also released. In a third case, the rape victim captured the rapist's identification card, but even that rapist went free. Not only were the accused men not brought to trial, but visibly injured rape victims were doubly victimized by the police: taunted, asked if they liked it, dismissed as not having been virgins to begin with. The last straw was a series of eight rapes that were reported in a single week in one neighborhood of San Cristóbal. María Patricia, who was active in responding to the rapes, discussed the violent political context of the times:

Around the end of 1988 [Governor] Abselón Castellanos leveled a community; people were disappeared near Palenque. . . . In 1988 we became aware of very selective violence against indigenous people. More repression began with [Governor] Patrocinio [González]. He started to strike leaders: it was very serious and very selective. Fray Bartolomé was born.[16] *In 1989 there were a series of rapes in broad daylight. The scandalous part is that all the rapists went free.*

16. The Fray Bartolomé de las Casas Center for Human Rights (Centro de Derechos Humanos "Fray Bartolomé de las Casas") was founded by the Archdiocese of San Cristóbal in 1989 in response to the wave of political violence that María Patricia discussed. The center's work was very much informed by the liberation theology movement within the church, as illustrated by the following quote from the center's informational pamphlet: "As a Christian organization the Center aims to be faithful to the Gospel's message to help, accompany, and promote all human beings who make just demands, recognizing in them the presence of our Savior."

In response, a demonstration was called on Mother's Day (May 10) in the central square of that colonial city.

The demonstration united between one hundred and three hundred women who had never worked together, including church women, housewives, university students, and indigenous women. Out of that demonstration emerged the Women's Group of San Cristóbal (Grupo de Mujeres de San Cristóbal), originally formed to address the issue of sexual violence and eventually extending that agenda to include domestic violence. After the May 10 protest, a group of women requested a meeting with the governor, Patrocinio González. They were somewhat surprised by the outcome of that meeting, during which, according to María Patricia, they confronted the governor with

a series of problems in the city, lack of security, etc. We also proposed solutions: to create a special agency for sexual crimes like there was in Mexico City. He said yes but not because he was such a feminist. . . . Afterward all the responsibility was dumped on us but it was an accomplishment. They thought that we weren't going to accept. . . . But they didn't even give us a single sheet of paper. I had to go to the Public Ministry and force open a space. They were really rude, they would say "sit down" and there was no place to sit. My boss was one of the officials that I had denounced. [They gave us nothing more than] a single salary and it was very small. They wouldn't even lend me the key to go to the bathroom. The women from the group brought chairs, a bookcase. We had to go all the way to Tuxtla Gutiérrez [the capital] to protest so they would give us a typewriter. (Interview, July 12, 1997)

The Women's Group of San Cristóbal made considerable concrete gains in a short time but like the study groups of a few years earlier, it was to fragment shortly after its creation.[17] Lina discussed the disagreements that led her and other women to leave the Women's Group to form the Collective of Autonomous Women in Struggle (Colectivo de Mujeres Autonomas en Lucha "La Ciclamina," or COMAL).

For some reason the group divided again. Some women wanted it to open up, they wanted to talk about free and voluntary maternity, legalization of abortion, the

---

17. In 1990 the Women's Group of San Cristóbal formed a Support Center that addressed issues of domestic and sexual violence for children and women. That same year they had a radio show, and they were heavily involved in supporting the governmental center for victims of sexual crimes that María Patricia spoke about. Throughout the 1990s, they continued their work in favor of reproductive health and against violence through popular education, research, and medical, legal, and psychological attention for victims of domestic or sexual violence (interview with Paloma, December 4, 1995; also see Freyermuth Enciso and Fernández Guerrero 1995).

topic of lesbians, that among other things. There was a consensus that no, they were only going to work on violence: domestic violence and rape. . . . So we began to meet, the same old rebels, since by that point we were already notorious. We formed a group that was called . . . the Collective of Autonomous Women in Struggle [Colectivo de Mujeres Autonomas en Lucha, or COMAL]. We included the part about autonomous because other groups were always affiliated with either the government or the church. (Interview, June 27, 1997)

As in Nicaragua and El Salvador, autonomy was becoming an important issue within the women's movement of Chiapas. But it played out differently there. First of all, the ruling party in Mexico, the PRI, was far more willing to attempt to co-opt opposition groups than either the Somoza regime or the Salvadoran military government had been. In those countries, women's groups did not have to address the issue of how much autonomy to seek from the old regimes, since they were in clear opposition to those regimes. Where autonomy was an issue in Central America was in relation to the guerrilla movements (and the political parties they would become). Of course, that had not yet become an issue, at least not publicly, in Chiapas in the late 1980s.

Another critical difference with Nicaragua, and to a lesser extent with El Salvador, was the weight of the Catholic Church within civil society in Chiapas. The difficulties of attaining autonomy in two directions—from the PRI and from the church—would become clear when, to the surprise of many, abortion was legalized in Chiapas.

In 1990 the governor of Chiapas, Patrocinio González, unilaterally depenalized abortion while claiming that this action was a response to a request from the Women's Group of San Cristóbal.[18] María Patricia explained how they responded:

We said, that's not true, right in front of the journalists. And it's a cardinal sin to call the governor a liar in front of journalists. [We said it couldn't have been us] because we use gender-neutral language [and] . . . the civil code said "he who

18. González's proposal would have permitted abortion with the agreement of both members of a couple or just the consent of the woman (if she was single) as long as the abortion was performed within the first ninety days of pregnancy. Abortion was depenalized on December 9, 1990, and, under pressure from the Catholic Church, that legal change was "suspended" twenty-two days later. Three years and four months later, González's change to the penal code was overturned by acting governor Javier López Moreno. The new penalties for abortion were increased, both for the woman who had the abortion and for the doctor who performed it, with a new exception for pregnant women who were suffering with AIDS (C. Rodríguez 1994, 135–37; also Guillén 1995, 57–58).

aborts," and with that we were quiet. Obviously we paid a price for that. . . . There were horrible demonstrations. Seventeen thousand signatures against abortion in those days. The whole discourse swept us away. The group was broken, it divided. The majority of the people who had been involved on May 10 [in the demonstration] were from the CEBs [Christian base communities]. For 2 months no one would sell me anything in the market. (Interview, July 12, 1997)

But if González was not really responding to the demands of women's organizations by depenalizing abortion, to what was he responding? The intended audience was probably the Catholic Church, which was busily promoting human rights in indigenous communities, a real threat to the power of the ruling party. Many activists in the growing movement saw the governor's move as an attempt to separate the secular feminists from their new religious allies; to pressure the church to stop its organizational work with indigenous people in exchange for a repenalization of abortion; and to break up the women's movement itself, in which the majority of activists were Catholic.

Natalia, who was active with indigenous peasant groups at the time that González depenalized abortion, suggested another theory, that the real target of the law was not the church as much as indigenous women. "The penal code [would have allowed] abortion for economic reasons, family planning, [and] genetic malformation. It was obvious that family planning was for the indigenous zones" (interview, June 13, 1997). To be eligible for an abortion for reasons of family planning, the pregnant woman had to prove that she already had "too many" children, say five or six. Natalia's theory, that the depenalization of abortion was part and parcel of the González administration's attempts to control indigenous communities, does not exclude the first theory: that the purpose of the legal change was to divide those who would promote human rights within those communities. Natalia herself observed that "even within the movement itself we were divided by the pressure of the church because many worked in the communities" (interview, June 13, 1997).

At about the same time as urban women were organizing into nongovernmental organizations, rural women were organizing into economic cooperatives in response to the monetarization of the rural economy, discussed earlier. Easily the most prominent economic cooperatives were the artisan collectives that appeared in starting in the 1950s. Building on a traditional indigenous women's skill—the weaving and embroidery of intricate clothing—the cooperatives allowed thousands of women to earn small amounts of cash, often without leaving their villages.

The artisan cooperatives were heavily promoted by the government, especially through the National Indigenous Institute (Instituto Nacional Indígena, or INI), which started organizing women's artisan cooperatives in the 1950s (Eber and Rosenbaum 1993, 166). The Indigenous Institute would go on to found cooperatives all over the state, including the Independent Organization of Indigenous Women (Organización Independiente de Mujeres Indigenas, or OIMI) in 1990 and J'Pas Joloviletik (Tzotzil for "Women Who Weave") in 1984, both weaving cooperatives with their headquarters in the city of San Cristóbal. The other major weaving cooperative based in San Cristóbal was Sna Jolobil (Tzotzil for "House of the Weaver"), which was founded in 1970 with the support of foreigners and ladinos that were not affiliated with the INI or other government agencies. By the mid 1990s, 2,320 women belonged to these three cooperatives along with numerous other women who belonged to others based elsewhere in the state.[19]

In some ways, the rise of autonomous peasant women's organizations runs parallel to that of autonomous peasant men's associations. Just as many of the peasant union federations were originally formed on the initiative of the official party, so too many of the peasant women's organizations were initially created by government institutions, later gaining autonomy (Olivera 1994, 66). Many indigenous activists first became mobilized through various government programs in the 1980s, but became disillusioned because of what they saw as the government's indifference toward indigenous people and, in some cases, because of outright governmental fraud (on these organizations, see Eber 1995, 237–39; Freyermuth Enciso and Fernández Guerrero 1995; Hernández 1995; Olivera 1994, 65–70).

In a weird and unintended way, it was the PRI itself that was directly responsible for creating most of the organizations that would form part of the loose Zapatista coalition after 1994. Of course, the original aim was not to sponsor opposition groups, but to create organizations that would be loyal to the PRI, the same clientelistic strategy that had effectively guaranteed nearly seven decades of uninterrupted party rule. While one could argue that the Somoza regime and the Salvadoran military regime also "created" opposition groups through their exclusionary policies, the promotion of civil society was much more direct in the case of the PRI. Although almost none of the political activists I interviewed in Nicaragua and El Salvador had ever had anything to do with the old regimes in their

19. Eight hundred and seventy women belonged to JPas Joloviletik, 1,000 belonged to San Jolobil, and 450 belonged to OIMI in the mid-1990s.

countries, most of the women's movement activists in Chiapas had, at some point or another, been part of a PRI-sponsored organization.

In addition to the women who became politicized through government-sponsored economic collectives, thousands more were involved in smaller groups that were affiliated with autonomous peasant organizations. For instance, Carolina's first political experience occurred in the Lacandón jungle at the age of sixteen. "I spent a year in Independent ARIC, Union of Unions [ARIC (Asociación Rural de Interés Colectivo) Independiente, Union de Uniones], I taught them to make bread. Two hundred and fifty women were organized, what we wanted was five pesos per person to buy the materials. It was good work that God gave us. We sold a lot of bread right in the jungle" (interview, July 8, 1997). The resources generated through such women's groups within the peasant movement were important for the women who were involved and allowed them to gain more independence than they might have otherwise enjoyed; in Carolina's case, it allowed her to move to the city of San Cristóbal and to continue her education. Moreover, such groups helped many women learn how to organize.

A final change in the organizational map of Chiapas that indirectly helped lay the groundwork for the rebellion was the arrival of the Guatemalan refugee camps. Although I have never found any evidence to support the Mexican government's initial accusation that the EZLN was run by Guatemalans (or, for that matter, that there is a single Guatemalan within Zapatista ranks), the mere presence of more than one hundred thousand refugees from a thirty-some year guerrilla war had an impact on many residents of Chiapas. Clearly the Guatemalan experience, in which around 110,000 (mainly indigenous) people were killed, is not something that any opposition group would wish to replicate. But lessons may be drawn from defeats as well as from victories.

Moreover, the story of the Guatemalan refugees is not all one of defeat. More than one observer commented to me that Guatemalan refugee women were among the best-organized women in the state of Chiapas.[20] Several of the women I interviewed who worked with indigenous women from Chiapas in the 1990s had worked with Guatemalan refugees during the 1980s. Those activists sometimes told the stories of those highly organized indigenous women in the refugee camps, to motivate indigenous women from Chiapas to organize and improve their lives. As one noted, "I was always talking to the indigenous women about the refugees." That

20. For a study of one of the most prominent groups of Guatemalan refugee women, see Organización de Mujeres Guatemaltecas Refugiadas en México "Mamá Maquín" 1999.

indirect contact may have helped many of the women who would become Zapatistas to develop an international vision of their situation and
how to change it, even if they never personally met any of the refugees.

Over the past generation or so, a number of changes had the cumula-
tive effect of breaking the physical and intellectual isolation that had characterized the lives of most indigenous women. Those changes meant that
many women were available for mobilization, either as Zapatista combatants or, more often, as members of the Zapatista's base of support. The
presence of so many women within the Zapatista coalition helped place
gender issues on the agenda from the first day. That does not mean that
the Zapatista army is a feminist army. But it does mean that the public
emergence of Zapatismo would have irreversible effects on indigenous
women and on the organizations that seek to mobilize those women.

CONCLUSION: A NEW SORT OF GUERRILLA MOVEMENT

By itself, a shift in gender relations did not create the EZLN. But, as I have
shown in this chapter, it was one of the causes. Leaving this factor out of
an explanation of the rebellion would result in an incomplete view of political change in southern Mexico. It is possible that the Zapatista rebellion
would have occurred even without a prior shift in gender relations. At the
same time, it is possible that the rebellion would have occurred without
the prior mobilization efforts of the church, or without the closing of the
land reform option by the Salinas administration, or without any one of
the other factors discussed in this chapter.

But perhaps not. Perhaps the particular combination of factors that
came together (including changes in women's roles) was the only combination that could have engendered rebellion. After all, significant upris-
ings like that of the EZLN are fairly rare; at the very least it is clear that no
single one of the factors, in isolation, would have been sufficient to cause
a rebellion, much less such an unusual sort of rebellion.

The EZLN has been called a movement of "armed reformists" (Castañeda 1995), for its aim is to democratize the state, not to overthrow it. It
is a movement that put women's equality on the revolutionary agenda
from the very first day of the public rebellion, a movement that, at least at
the level of discourse, is highly inclusive.[21] Marking the 505th anniversary of the Spanish Conquest, Marcos noted:

21. Not all Zapatistas share the highly inclusive sentiments of Subcommander Marcos. In
sharp contrast with Marcos's frequent inclusion of gays and lesbians in the Zapatista coalition,

This 12th of October, we indigenous people are no longer the only indigenous. Men and women of different races and colors, but of the same nationality, share our misery and pain; workers of the countryside and city stuck in the ditch of unemployment, women who are raped and abused by powerful influences, young people assassinated by lawless soldiers, little children obliged to swallow the neoliberal nightmare, old people thrown out like garbage, students who are beaten and persecuted by police with academic standing, gays and lesbians attacked for being "different.". . . If today we are all Indians according to the racist mind of Power, today we all should be Indians. (Marcos 1997; also see CCRI 1996; EZLN 1995, 67–69; Marcos 1996b)

In many ways, the first public years of the EZLN differed greatly from the first years of the Nicaraguan FSLN or the Salvadoran FMLN. Lisa, an activist in the Zapatista Front (or FZLN, one of the unarmed offshoots of the EZLN) compared the EZLN with earlier guerrilla movements in Latin America:

This struggle has a different transcendence than the others because it is very complete from the beginning. I think that it has learned from the earlier processes and it has gone beyond them. Obviously as a woman I am very interested in taking on women's struggles. [In FZLN meetings] we have begun to talk about the fact that one cannot be a Zapatista and an oppressor. And it is incongruent to be a revolutionary and to block women's liberation. (Interview, June 26, 1997)

But the Zapatista movement was not necessarily so different from other movements, so "complete," from the very beginning, if one traces the beginning back before 1994. Considering the predecessor of the EZLN, a group called the Forces of National Liberation (Fuerzas de Liberación Nacional, or FLN), one finds a group that Lisa might not recognize, but one that would be familiar to students of earlier guerrilla movements. When the FLN was first founded in the northern city of Monterrey in 1969, it was typical of the movements of that era, according to John Womack. "They were all male, in their 20s, passionately anti-Soviet

---

was the following exchange at an international meeting in La Realidad, deep in the Lacandón jungle: "[A] feminist foreign journalist asked a group of 10 Zapatista women fighters, dressed in woolen ski masks and pastel cotton house dresses, what they thought of the lesbian movement. The fighters whispered among themselves. One offered an answer that made it clear they did not understand the word lesbian. When journalists helped them with a brief explanation, they whispered some more. 'That doesn't exist here' one Zapatista women answered curtly" (Preston 1996, A5). Such accounts suggest the need for caution when interpreting official Zapatista communiqués, and for a realization that there are many versions of the Zapatista agenda.

(therefore as well hostile to the Mexican Communist Party), passionately pro-Cuban and Che-Guevarist, most of them from locally respected families, and graduates of the State University of Nuevo León" (1999, 190).

In 1980, after having formed active cells in six states (including Chiapas) plus Mexico City, the leadership of the FLN wrote and published forty-two pages of statutes "to regulate its new clandestine forces and organize them into the already then named Zapatista Army of National Liberation" (Womack 1999, 191). Those statutes suggest that the FLN saw itself as a typical guerrilla movement of its day. It opposed "U.S. imperialism . . . the Mexican bourgeoisie and its puppets who form the bourgeois Mexican state." Like their fellow Latin American guerrillas, its members promised to utilize a "political-military" strategy, including "the creation of mass organizations" under the guidance of a guerrilla force that would act as "the vanguard of the revolution." That revolution, in turn, would be framed by "the science of history and society: Marxist-Leninism, which has demonstrated its validity in all the victorious revolutions of this century" (Womack 1999, 192–94).

In the 1980 statutes, the rural branch of the FLN was already called the Zapatista Army of National Liberation, the EZLN. By the time the guerrillas went public in 1994, the name "FLN" had been dropped altogether. But more had changed than the name. Gone were the references to Marxist-Leninism, to the bourgeoisie as enemy, to the vanguard party that would guide the revolution.

Why did the classically Marxist FLN evolve into the unorthodox EZLN? One possibility has already been detailed in this chapter: being a multiethnic, dual-gender movement that arose out of a climate of significant political and religious pluralism, the EZLN could not be doctrinaire if it was to hold that coalition together. Neil Harvey (1998) has suggested that when the outsiders from the FLN arrived in the Lacandón jungle in 1983, they had little choice but to adapt to the needs and customs of the area. The locals wanted literacy training, lessons in Mexican history, and help in setting up armed self-defense patrols. So that is what the FLN organizers initially provided, though none of those items were on their own agenda.

At the same time, locals very clearly did not want the outsiders to do anything that would threaten their customs. At first the Zapatistas seemed to be just such a threat. When the Zapatistas behaved in a way that would have been typical of clandestine guerrilla armies—preparing food and weapons under cover of darkness—many thought they were engaging in witchcraft. To try to avoid frightening the people they hoped to recruit, the FLN leaders had to act more openly within the community (Harvey 1998, 164–66).

Given the statutes of the FLN, written just three years earlier, it seems clear that the first Zapatistas to organize in the jungle would not have independently chosen such an unorthodox agenda and such unorthodox organizing strategies. But they did not have to accept the new agenda and strategies. They could have refused to take the lead of the locals, either trying to impose their agenda on the jungle residents or leaving in search of a new place to organize. Instead, they stayed, becoming less Marxist and more indigenous in the process.

So the very local needs of everyday life in the jungle could explain the evolution from the FLN to the EZLN. Other clues may be found in Mexican politics, at both the state and national level. While the Central American rebellions were nationwide (though there the guerrillas obviously enjoyed more support in some parts of their respective countries than in others), the EZLN was a movement with a strong base in only one of the thirty-one states in Mexico. Even if all residents of Chiapas were to support the rebels (which was far from the case), the Zapatistas could never hope to overthrow the Mexican government on their own. Moreover, the chance that they could mobilize support outside of Chiapas behind a movement to overthrow the state was extremely minimal. In most of the rest of Mexico, the ruling party had employed a much more inclusionary strategy than in Chiapas, and so it enjoyed more popular support than did the government of the state of Chiapas or the governments in those Central American countries where guerrilla movements took hold.[22]

---

22. One could reasonably object that the PRI's Mexico has always differed from the Central American dictatorships that engendered guerrilla movements, and so the FLN should have differed from other Latin American guerrillas at its founding in 1969. But while Mexico has always differed from Central America, it is also true that 1969, Mexico under the PRI was far more like the Central American dictatorships than it was by 1994. Nineteen sixty-eight was the year of the massacre of hundreds of peaceful student protestors at Tlatelolco Square in Mexico City, a massacre that ended the student movement and sent movement survivors into a sort of exile in the poorest regions of the country, where many of them formed such groups as the FLN. In the following decades, the PRI returned to its clientelistic or inclusive strategies in an effort to regain lost legitimacy. By the late 1980s, in many parts of the country, politics opened up considerably: elections were more likely to be openly contested and opposition candidates who won the vote count were more likely to be permitted to take office, especially outside the predominantly indigenous south. In July 2000, the PRI lost the presidential election for the first time since its founding seventy-one years earlier, though it retained control over the majority of the congressional seats in the state of Chiapas. A month later, that control over Chiapas was challenged when, for the first time since the founding of the PRI, the PRI lost control of the governor's office to Pablo Salazar Mendiguchía, the candidate of the opposition alliance and a former PRIista (Becerril 2000).

It is at the level of national politics where one finds what may be the most obvious force that shaped Zapatismo, since the Zapatistas (like all guerrillas) made a series of demands of the state, even if they did not aim at overthrowing it overtly. The party that they confronted, the PRI, was well entrenched and could claim a revolutionary heritage of its own. Having evolved out of the Mexican Revolution of 1910–17, by the time the Zapatistas emerged on the public scene, the PRI had ruled over national politics, without interruption, for nearly seventy years.

Like the Somoza regime of Nicaragua, and the military rulers of El Salvador, the PRI used violence against political opponents, but generally in a much more selective way than in Central America. Like the Somozas and the Salvadoran military, the PRI used elections to create an illusion of democratic rule, but generally in a much more sophisticated way, and sometimes, especially in the north of the country, those elections were actually meaningful. Unlike its counterparts in either Nicaragua or El Salvador, the PRI used a wide array of clientelistic strategies to tie people to the regime. If the PRI's rule was dictatorial, and many would say that it was, it was an inclusive dictatorship, in sharp contrast with the exclusive dictatorships of Central America.

Some political regimes are much more vulnerable to revolution than others; regimes such as that of the PRI are extremely unlikely to be overthrown by an armed group. The regime type most likely to be overthrown is what Timothy Wickham-Crowley has called patrimonial praetorian regimes, or mafiocracies. The Sandinistas were able to overthrow the Somoza mafiocracy because of Somoza's remarkable lack of support in civil society and the broad class base of opposition to the family dictatorship (1992, 299). In contrast, the FMLN faced an impersonal military regime with strong links to the economic elites of El Salvador, the sort of regime that has proved to be "consistently able to suppress revolutionaries, even those with deep and widespread peasant support" (1992, 299). A further type of regime, electoral democracies, are the least vulnerable to revolutionary overthrow.

It is easy to categorize the regimes that confronted the FSLN and the FMLN, but what sort of regime confronted the EZLN? An inclusive dictatorship is not one of Wickham-Crowley's categories, yet that term describes the nature of the PRI's system better than any of his three terms. Chiapas, and Mexico as a whole, was far enough from being a true electoral democracy during the first decade of the Zapatista's existence (roughly 1984 to 1994) to allow for the growth of such a guerrilla movement, and to explain the nationwide outpouring of support when they made their public appearance.[23]

But the very real democratic elements within the Mexican regime (especially since the highly contested election of 1988) and the PRI's preference for controlled inclusion over exclusion helped to explain why the Zapatistas chose to forge a reformist movement. It is an armed guerrilla force, to be sure, but one that is less doctrinaire, and more inclusive, than any seen so far in Latin America. This is logical enough given that the EZLN emerged against a regime that used a combination of authoritarian and democratic tactics with which to maintain its power; a traditional military organization would have had little chance of engendering the popular support needed for the Zapatistas to succeed.

Finally, one might look internationally to explain the nature of Zapatismo. The Zapatista Army, one of the first major guerrilla movements to emerge in the post–cold war world, seemed to have been shaped by that new world. The end of the cold war meant that the discourse of Marxism-Leninism was no longer as compelling as it had been for earlier guerrillas, who had something to gain through appropriating a Marxist discourse and analysis, namely, the material and ideological support of Cuba (Castañeda 1994, 51–89) and possibly that of the Soviet Union. During the cold war, seeking support from fellow revolutionaries by using their language was a smart and even necessary move (whatever the actual beliefs of the guerrillas), for they could count on the rapid and often violent opposition of the U.S. government, sometimes even to attempts at moderate and legal reform.[24]

Such outside factors probably will not shape the calculations of the Latin American revolutionaries who follow the Zapatistas if they noted

23. Although Mexicans generally opposed the Zapatista's use of violence, they did not oppose their goals. Surveys showed that 61 percent of the residents of Mexico City supported the Zapatista's goals on January 7, 1994. That percentage had risen to 75 percent by February 18 just as the first peace talks between the EZLN and the government were beginning (Golden 1994c, 5). Support for the Zapatistas was to remain fairly steady over time: a nationwide poll conducted in August 1996 found that while almost 76 percent thought that the EZLN was doing the best it could to achieve peace through dialogue, only 22 percent thought that the government was doing the best it could (*La Jornada* 1996a, 1996b). In August 1998, a poll of 4,854 Mexicans from twenty-three states found that 57 percent thought the government was not working toward peace, whereas 49 percent thought the EZLN was not doing everything that it could (Gil Olmos 1998).

24. The most infamous examples of the U.S. government opposing the reformist Left in Latin America (and thus driving many leftists into the arms of the guerrillas) were the fall of the Arbenz government in Guatemala in 1954, and the fall of the Allende government in Chile in 1973, both overthrown in military coups with strong material and moral support from the US Central Intelligence Agency or CIA.

the Clinton administration's apparent disinterest in the Zapatista rebellion. The passing of the cold war means that revolutionaries will have a harder time finding outside governmental allies, but it also means that they will confront fewer outside enemies.

Even though Mexican guerrilla movements were not eligible for Cuban support,[25] the guerrilla movements that formed and fought during the era of the cold war were influenced by one another. While there were important differences between the Latin American guerrillas of the cold war era, depending on factors like the strategy they employed and the areas of their country in which they operated (especially if they were largely urban or rural), Forrest Colburn's (1994) claim that there were remarkable intellectual similarities among the guerrilla leaders of that era— including commitments to socialism, to popular mobilization under the guidance of a vanguard party, to Marxism-Leninism—was illustrated by the FSLN and the FMLN, among many others.

International alliances help explain the nature of Zapatismo from 1994 onward in a negative way, that is, in the absence of strong opposition from the U.S. government and in the absence of the socialist paradigm that framed opposition politics during the cold war era. They also help explain Zapatismo in a positive way. The international Left was far more feminist in the 1990s than it was when the FSLN was created in 1961, or even when the FMLN first was formed in 1980.

On January 1, 1994, the very first day of the rebellion, the Zapatistas made a series of feminist demands, demands unlike any made by previous Latin American guerrillas. On that day the rebels distributed copies of a twenty-page booklet called *El despertador Mexicano* (The Mexican alarm clock).[26] Pages 17 and 18 of the booklet were devoted to a list of women's demands, known as the Revolutionary Women's Law,[27] in sharp contrast

25. Since, in the Western Hemisphere, the Mexican government was one of the few allies (or at least not antagonists) of the Castro government, the Cubans had a policy of not lending support to guerrilla movements in Mexico (Castañeda 1994, 85).

26. Translated excerpts from this text are available under the title "Declaration of the Lacandón Jungle," in Marcos 1995b, 51–54 and Womack 1999, 247–49. The original text is available on the EZLN and FZLN websites.

27. Revolutionary Women's Law:

In its just struggle for the liberation of our people, the EZLN incorporates women into the revolutionary struggle without concern for their race, creed, color or political affiliation, the only requirement is to take up the demands of exploited people and to commit to obey and enforce the laws and regulations of the revolution. Additionally, in light of the situation of working women in Mexico, the following just demands for equality and justice are incorporated into the Revolutionary Women's Law.

First—All women, without regard to their race, creed, color or political affiliation have the right to participate in the revolutionary struggle in any place or degree in accordance with their will and ability.

to the original agendas of earlier guerrilla groups in Latin America, which barely mentioned gender issues, if at all.[28] That the women's demands were listed near the end of the booklet is also telling, of course. Women's demands would rarely be at the top of the Zapatista agenda during the first years of the public rebellion. Yet those demands never disappeared completely either, and they were to fuel a dramatic increase in the numbers of organized women, and the coherence of the women's movement, in Chiapas and in Mexico as a whole.

The first sentence of the Revolutionary Women's Law reads much like so many earlier declarations of independence, inviting women to join a universal struggle against oppression without specific reference to gender inequality. "[T]he EZLN incorporates women into the revolutionary struggle without concern for their race, creed, color or political affiliation, the only requirement is to take up the demands of exploited people and to commit to obey and enforce the laws and regulations of the revolution." But at that point the similarity ends, for the Zapatista document goes on to list ten specific women's demands.

The list includes demands that were directed at the government, as is typical of guerrilla demands, insisting on women's right to have access to primary health care and education. But some of the demands were made to a different audience, addressing fellow guerrillas and fellow indigenous people: insisting on women's right to participate in the decisions made in their communities, to choose how many children to have and when to have them, to avoid forced matrimony, to live free from violence both in

---

Second—Women have the right to work and to receive a fair salary.

Third—Women have the right to choose the number of children that they can have and care for.

Fourth—Women have the right to participate in the concerns of their communities and to be elected freely and democratically to political offices.

Fifth—Women and children have the right to primary health care and basic nutrition.

Sixth—Women have a right to an education.

Seventh—Women have the right to choose their partners and should not be forced to contract matrimony.

Eighth—No woman should ever be hit or physically abused by her relatives or by outsiders. The crimes of attempted rape and rape will be severely punished.

Ninth—Women can occupy positions of leadership in the organization and can hold military ranks in the revolutionary armed forces.

Tenth—Women will have all the rights and obligations that are spelled out in the revolutionary laws and regulations.

28. While the earliest platform of the FMLN of El Salvador did not address gender issues, the Nicaraguan FSLN's formal platform (first presented in 1969) contained a few feminist elements, explicitly condemning discrimination against women, and calling for equality between women and men (FDR/FMLN 1986, 205–9; FSLN 1986, 81–189; Lobao 1990, 222–23). But the Sandinista's Historic Platform, though unusual in mentioning the problem of gender inequality, did not go nearly as far as the Zapatista's Revolutionary Women's Law in addressing that problem.

and outside their homes. In the long history of guerrilla politics in Latin America, the personal had never been analyzed in such explicitly political terms.

According to Zapatista spokesperson Subcommander Marcos, the Revolutionary Women's Law came out of a series of meetings with indigenous women in dozens of communities in the months leading up to March 1993. In that month, according to Marcos, the "first uprising of the EZLN" occurred when Commander Susana read the Revolutionary Women's Law to an audience of "nervous" men and "singing" women (Marcos 1994, 69; Rovira 1997, 110–17). The women's movement activists I interviewed agreed with this account, although several suggested that the impact of the Revolutionary Women's Law was greatly limited by the fact that some women who entered the Zapatista forces after the law was presented did not even know of its existence. Paloma, an activist in the Women's Group of San Cristóbal, had a rather ambivalent answer when questioned about the meaning of the Revolutionary Women's Law:

What I think is that the EZLN is not a feminist movement but rather a movement that is military, hierarchical, and authoritarian. Not all of them have gender consciousness but some of them do. The EZLN is not against working with women, but I think that it has been a little careless about work with women. The topic of women always is treated as less important than the other topics. But it does try to break with a patriarchal system. We had an interview with some of the commanders about unjust punishment in the case of women who had been raped [and] who did not get to participate in the decisions. And they told us that they recognized their faults, they promised to work so that women's situation would change. The fact that an indigenous woman, with a military rank, can wear pants and take up arms is an incredible accomplishment. One female commander told us that it was not hard, that life in the communities was harder. (Interview, December 4, 1995)

While it would be wrong to exaggerate the feminist elements within the EZLN agenda—it was, after all, a military organization dominated by men—it would be equally wrong to dismiss those elements out of hand. The organization's apparent openness to criticism by external feminists was just one measure of the difference between this guerrilla uprising and the many that preceded it.

The difference in the initial gender demands made by the EZLN, when compared with the less extensive ones made by the FSLN and FMLN during their guerrilla years, may very well have been due to the changed nature of international civil society, to the increased prominence of femi-

114

nism within international leftist thought, and to the Zapatistas' need to seek support from international civil society in the post–cold war world. Speaking to the international Left, through the Zapatista websites or through the multiple international assemblies that would be held in Zapatista territory, required speaking an international language, and one of those languages was feminism. That is not to suggest that the women of Chiapas themselves were uninterested in greater equality, simply that there was some sort of combination of local and international interests at play, a combination that was often hard to disentangle.

4 Rethinking Women and Guerrilla Movements
BACK TO CUBA

T he guerrilla wars did not play out the same in each country discussed in this book. In Nicaragua, the guerrillas successfully overthrew the old dictatorship in 1979 and governed for more than ten years; in El Salvador, the decade-long guerrilla war ended in 1992 in a negotiated settlement; in Chiapas, the guerrillas never even tried to overthrow the state, though their project was not necessarily less transformative.[1] But despite those differences from the perspective of the state, the stories were very similar, if seen from the perspective of gender relations. In all three places, a significant percentage—perhaps as many as a third—of the guerrillas were women. In all three countries, many of the women who had been mobilized in the guerrilla movements and the revolutionary coalitions would go on to become feminist activists, an unintended outcome of the revolutionary movements that I analyze elsewhere.[2]

---

1. These cases are so different that most theorists of revolution would categorize the Sandinista revolution as "successful" and the other two cases as "unsuccessful," since the FMLN of El Salvador did not manage to overthrow the old regime and the EZLN of Mexico did not try to do so. But I think the concept of success is in need of qualifications.

Analyzing guerrilla groups from the perspective of whether they succeed in overthrowing the state is only one way to understand them. An approach that centers on the experiences of individual revolutionaries, as I have used in this book, lends itself to entirely new understandings of guerrilla movements. For instance, Nicaragua and El Salvador may be understood as examples of a successful and an unsuccessful revolution, if they are considered from the perspective of the state. But they are similar sorts of cases from the perspective of those who fought in the guerrilla movements and the revolutionary organizations. In both Nicaragua and El Salvador, the experience of armed struggle for social transformation had a similarly transformative effect on those who participated. In both cases, the guerrilla struggles engendered the same sort of autonomous feminist movements, even though the guerrillas "succeeded" in one case, and "failed" in the other.

2. In Nicaragua and El Salvador, vibrant autonomous feminist movements emerged after the wars. In Chiapas, before the war had even ended, women's rights activities grew and consolidated both in women's organizations and within the nationwide indigenous rights movement. For an analysis of the legacy of revolutionary movements and the kind of feminist organizing they have engendered, see Kampwirth (in progress; 1998b; 1996a).

In this concluding chapter, I will compare the roles played by women in the revolutionary movements in Nicaragua, El Salvador, and Chiapas with their roles in the Cuban guerrilla struggle, a comparison that allows me to refine my arguments by introducing variation into the analysis. In other words, comparing will allow me to evaluate an outcome that did not occur in any of the three cases analyzed so far. Cuba, where guerrillas would successfully overthrow the Batista dictatorship in 1959, is a good test case, since relatively few women participated as combatants in the guerrilla phase of the Cuban Revolution. To find some explanations for why few women participated, I will revisit Cuba in the 1950s, analyzing it through the framework of the theory developed over the course of this book to explain the role of women guerrillas in the cases of Nicaragua, El Salvador, and Chiapas.

During the Cuban guerrilla struggle that began in 1953 with the assault on the Moncada army barracks, few women were directly engaged in combat roles. It has been estimated that women constituted about 5 percent of the guerrillas, most of whom seem to have been mobilized as students (a common conduit for male and, especially, female guerrillas as is shown in Chapters 1 and 2 and the Appendix). Many women played critical support roles during the guerrilla days but rarely found themselves in leadership or combat positions (Foran, Klouzal, and Rivera 1997; García Oliveras 1979; Maloof 1999, 26–27; Jaquette 1973; Lupiáñez Reinlein 1985; Reif 1986, 155; Smith and Padula 1996, 22–32; Wickham-Crowley 1992, 21).

The Cuban Revolution marked the close of an era in which the public face of Latin American guerrilla armies was mostly male. Why was that? What happened in Latin America, between 1959, when the guerrillas of Cuba's 26th of July Movement overthrew the Batista dictatorship, and 1979, when Nicaragua's dual-gender FSLN overthrew the Somoza dictatorship?

As I outline in the Introduction, and illustrate in the three chapters that follow, certain changes in Latin America in the years following the Cuban Revolution help explain the large numbers of women who participated in late twentieth-century guerrilla movements in the region. I argue that a combination of structural, political, ideological, and personal factors came together to make it possible for many women to join guerrilla movements in Nicaragua, El Salvador, and Chiapas, summarizing that argument in a chart in the Introduction.

While Cuba is an imperfect test case, since I must rely on secondary sources, I think it is worth trying to shine the light of my findings backward in time—to the years leading up to the 1959 overthrow of Batista—to see how they may help explain the role of women in the Cuban guerrilla struggle. Looking back at the beginning of the Cuban revolution should also help sharpen my theory of women and guerrilla struggle by distinguishing between factors that were present in Cuba as well as in Nicaragua, El Salvador, and Chiapas, and factors that were absent in Cuba but present in the other three cases.

Structurally, the situation in Cuba in the 1950s could have allowed for women's mass entry into the guerrilla army. A process of land concentration and mass migration was under way, similar to the process that the residents of Nicaragua, El Salvador, and Chiapas experienced in the decades preceding their guerrilla wars. As in the other cases, many rural elites consolidated their landholdings in response to growing global demand for tropical products: in the Cuban case, that product was mainly sugar. Sugar had dominated the Cuban economy since the colonial era, and its dominance only grew in the decades leading up to the Cuban guerrilla struggle. After 1925, sugar accounted for some 80 percent of exports, taking up more than 50 percent of the cultivated land (Pérez-Stable 1993, 16).

The ever growing role of sugar plantations had measurable effects. Comparing the late 1940s with the mid-1920s, Marifeli Pérez-Stable found that "per capita consumption of a variety of products declined. . . . While population grew 41 percent, consumption of rice expanded 22 percent, wheat flour 38 percent, potatoes 5 percent, coffee 29 percent, legumes 40 percent, cotton textiles 8 percent" (Pérez-Stable 1993, 20). As big landowners sought to consolidate ever larger holdings, they found that the government often sided with them as they evicted small farmers. "From 1940 to 1959, landowners were winning 75 percent of their eviction lawsuits" (Wickham-Crowley 1992, 119), among them cases against squatters who had worked the same plot of land for more than three decades. Eviction rates were especially high in the region of the country—the Sierra Maestra—where the guerrillas would enjoy the most support.

During the 1940s and early 1950s, the balance of the rural economy shifted; as increasing numbers lost access to land, they entered the ranks of rural wageworkers. According to census data, in 1946 about 57 percent of Cubans were rural wageworkers; by 1953, at least 60 percent of the Cuban population made a living through rural wage labor (Rojas Requena, Ravenet Ramírez, and Hernández Martínez 1985, 53). But as it turned out, it was quite difficult to get by working for wages in an economy dependent on sugar. The nature of sugar production meant that a tremendous demand for labor during the harvest was followed by many months with little demand. "In the mid-1950s, one-third of the labor force did not hold full-time jobs. During the dead season, overt unemployment rose to 20.7 percent; underemployment averaged 13.8 percent throughout the year. . . . Urban-rural disparities highlighted the magnitude of the problem: 71 percent of the urban labor force and 64.3 percent of the rural had full-time jobs year-round" (Pérez-Stable 1993, 27).

As in Nicaragua, El Salvador, and Chiapas, many experienced the changes in the countryside as a crisis, and many of those desperate rural dwellers responded to the crisis by migrating. By the 1950s, Cuba was ranked in the top five Latin American countries by a variety of development indicators, including urbanization. More than half of all Cubans lived in urban areas as early as the 1930s and the majority of those urban dwellers lived in the capital city, Havana. By the year when the 26th of July Movement first emerged—1953—57 percent of the population was urban, according to census figures (Foran, Klouzal, and Rivera 1997, 19; Luzón 1987, 212; Pérez-Stable 1993, 5, 14, 28; Rojas Requena, Ravenet Ramírez, and Hernández Martínez 1985, 20). These figures need to be read as rough estimates, for the definition of *urban* varied considerably from study to study.[3] Nonetheless, they illustrate a process of societal movement that might have set the stage for the mass mobilization of women into the revolutionary coalition.

In Cuba, as in Nicaragua and El Salvador (the cases for which I have similar data), women were somewhat more likely than men to live in cities in the years leading up to the guerrilla war.[4] In the cities, females were more likely to be available for mobilization into the revolutionary coalition than in the countryside: they were more likely to attend school, to have the opportunity to join groups that might act as preexisting networks, and to be able to join a revolutionary group against the wishes of

3. One review of population studies explains how the criteria for the definition of *urban* varied from study to study: "1899–1907 and 1919: localities with 1000 or more inhabitants; 1931, 1943: existence of a postal address; 1953: existence of particular public or social services in localities of 150 or more inhabitants; 1970: existence of 4 or more urban characteristics in localities of 500 or more inhabitants" (Rojas Requena, Ravenet Ramírez, and Hernández Martínez 1985, 20).

4. "Considering 1953, the rate of masculinity of the whole population was of 1.053 men per 1.000 women. But for the urban population it was 1.004 and for the rural population it was 1.177. . . . The rural areas were the place where men were concentrated, given the need for male workers in the sugarcane fields" (Luzón 1987, 107). A very detailed chart of occupations broken down by men and women is available in Foran, Klouzal, and Rivera 1997, 20. It is consistent with Luzón's observation that men were more likely to live in rural areas because they were more likely to be employed in agriculture. Data on the sex ratio in Nicaraguan cities is reported in 26 n. 5; data on the sex ratio in Salvadoran cities is reported in 54 n. 15.

their parents, or, thanks to the anonymity of city life, often even without their parents' knowledge.

This is not to suggest that young women who lived in small towns could not be mobilized into a guerrilla movement under any circumstances; clearly some of them were, at least after the 1960s. But the chances that a young woman would be mobilized were diminished to the extent that her daily life was constrained. The reality of small-town or rural life—lived under the gaze of watchful neighbors and relatives, often without access to secondary school and the opportunities to join student organizations—made it less likely that a young woman could join the revolutionary coalition, except in those cases when whole families joined.

The constraint of rural life seemed to be determinative in the case of early and mid-twentieth-century revolutionary movements. In his analysis of the Latin American guerrillas who were active between 1956 and 1970, including those in Cuba, Timothy Wickham-Crowley observes that he could not find any case in which there was "female predominance in either numbers or power within a movement, nor . . . a single case of a female peasant joining as an arms-bearing guerrilla regular" (1992, 21). In Cuba, the majority of male guerrillas were from rural areas, and many rural women (like rural men) participated in the revolutionary coalition in various support roles. But the women who played the most prominent roles (midprestige or high-prestige guerrillas) were largely, if not entirely, from the cities. "Women guerrillas [in Cuba] were from middle-class backgrounds, educated, and probably white" (Foran, Klouzal, and Rivera 1997, 32).

Another structural factor that affected whether a young woman was available for mobilization was family structure. Girls often found that they were freer to act without strict parental supervision if the head of their household was a single woman than if they lived in a nuclear household, for a single mother was likely to be as occupied with raising money to support her children as with supervising those children. Presumably, this argument about single-female-headed households would apply to boys as well as girls. But given that in many countries, boys are freer to act without adult supervision than girls (see, for example, Lancaster 1992), it may be the case that boys are available for mobilization under a much wider variety of circumstances than are girls.

It seems that a smaller percentage of Cuban households were headed by single females in the decade when the guerrillas formed than would be the case in Nicaragua or El Salvador in the years when the FSLN and the FMLN sought to mobilize people. In 1953, according to the census, men headed 86 percent of the households nationwide; women headed 14 percent. The most urban province was the one with the greatest number of female-headed households: 19.67 percent of households in the province of Havana were headed by women, as against 80.3 percent by men. In the more rural Oriente province, where the bulk of the revolutionary war was fought, 13.32 percent were headed by women and 86.67 percent by men (Pérez Rojas 1979, 30–31). Another study reported a lower percentage of female-headed households in 1953: 9.6 percent headed by women, 32.4 percent by both sexes, 54.2 percent by men (Reca Moreira et al. 1990, 30–31).[5]

Studies suggest that between a quarter to a third of the Central American households were headed by women in the years leading up to the guerrilla movements, while, at a national level, no more than 14 percent of households were female headed in Cuba.[6] If these figures are accurate, then more cohesive and controlling families could help explain the limited role that young women played in the Cuban guerrilla war. The structural change that could have allowed for the mobilization of large numbers of women into the 26th of July Movement—migration—might have

5. Differences in the findings may be due to the fact that the two studies used somewhat different categories (Pérez Rojas divided households into two categories, while Reca Moreira et al. divided them into three) or it could be due to differences in the samples in the two studies. Moreover, marital status is not as objective a question as one might think: men and women varied on whether they thought they were married. Since the number of men and women in the population was roughly equal, if 50 percent of men reported they were married, about 50 percent of women should have reported the same. In fact, the percentages differed: in 1953, while 35 percent of men reported they were married and 17.7 percent reported that they were in consensual unions or common-law marriages, 37.7 percent of women reported that they were married and 20.6 percent reported that they were in consensual unions (Reca Moreira et al. 1990, 61). So only 52.7 percent of men claimed to be married or in a marriagelike relationship, while 58.3 percent of women considered that they were in such a relationship, possibly because of differences in perceptions about when a temporary separation during the harvest season had become a permanent separation, with women hopeful that their husbands would return even after the men had decided to abandon their families.

6. In Nicaragua, as I reported in Chapter 1, a series of studies conducted between 1950 and 1979 varied widely in their findings regarding single-female-headed households: ranging from 10.4 percent of households to 48 percent of households, with most studies reporting that between a quarter to a third of all households were headed by single women. In El Salvador, as I reported in Chapter 2, a series of studies conducted between 1950 and 1978 also varied in their findings: from a low of 9.2 percent of rural households headed by women in 1970, to a high of 39.5 percent of poor urban households headed by women in 1978. On average about a third of households were found to be headed by women.

While I have never seen a quantitative study of family structures in Chiapas, many studies of the impact of globalization on life in Chiapas make reference to its impact on families. Households that were formally headed by single females were uncommon in indigenous Chiapas, but the numbers of households that were effectively headed by single females for much of the year (as their husbands worked far from their village) seemed to be on the rise in the decades preceding the rebellion.

been mitigated by the tighter controls kept over young Cuban women, who were more likely to live with both parents than in either Nicaragua or El Salvador at the equivalent time.

That the relative cohesiveness or looseness of family ties played a role in making young people available for, and interested in, mobilization in the revolutionary coalition was suggested in a study of the Federation of University Students (Federación Estudiantil Universitaria, or FEU) and the Revolutionary Directory (Directorio Revolucionario), both Havana-based predominantly student groups that participated in the movement against Batista (Suchlicki 1969, 71). "It is significant to note that several of the FEU and Directorio members were from areas other than Havana and many came from poorer or working-class homes. Living away from their families and exposed to the loneliness of a new urban environment, these students stayed close to the campus and were apparently more prone to political involvement than the average city student" (72–73). Suchlicki's comments support the hypothesis that young people were more likely to be mobilized when they were free from family control, and when they were in search of the camaraderie of a student group, a home away from home.

The sort of structural upheaval that transformed Cuban society in the decades leading up to the guerrilla war shared many similarities with the structural upheaval that would later transform Nicaragua, El Salvador, and Chiapas. In all four cases, economic globalization drove a string of common events, including land concentration, migration to cities, and increases in the numbers of single-female-headed households (though such households seemed to have been less prevalent in Cuba). Yet Cuban women were less likely to have participated as combatants in the Cuban guerrilla struggle than in the guerrilla struggles elsewhere that would follow it.

One way to interpret this finding would be to eliminate structural conditions as a factor that shaped the gender composition of the guerrilla forces. For similar structural conditions should produce similar outcomes. If similar structural conditions are associated with different outcomes, it means that the structural factors were not causal, at least not in a direct way. Some have suggested that if we cannot find a clear correlation between structural factors and the rise of guerrilla movements, then we should discount structural factors in favor of other factors, such as those of a political nature (Grenier 1999, 12–17; Seligson 1999, xi).

With regard to the question that has dominated revolutionary studies—under what circumstances have revolutionaries succeeded in overthrowing states?—an important distinction is lost in finding that structural conditions are not directly causal, and then leaping to the conclusion that they are therefore not causal in any sense. If structural conditions were truly irrelevant in setting the stage for guerrilla struggle, then one would expect no pattern in the structural makeup of the countries that have experienced significant guerrilla movements. Rich countries would be just as likely to experience significant guerrilla movements as poor countries. But in fact, revolutions have not occurred in the rich countries of the world, at least not during the twentieth century.[7]

But even if structures should not be dismissed as a factor that set the stage for revolutions, perhaps they should be discounted as factors that allowed for women's mass mobilization into the guerrilla movements. Perhaps the ideological and political factors were the only ones that mattered in mobilizing women. While my findings from Nicaragua, El Salvador, and Chiapas suggest that ideological and political factors were more important, I would not dismiss the role of structures.

If women joined guerrilla movements, that meant at least two things happened at the same time. First, women had to be available for mobilization, and second, they needed to be actively mobilized (through preexisting networks, and by guerrillas who were interested in mobilizing them). It was in the first step—availability—that structures made a difference. Structural changes, especially mass migration, were critical in making women available for mobilization. As long as most women were constrained by traditional structures, they could not be mobilized. It was once the material conditions of many women's lives changed—once they were free of the social controls of small-town and patriarchal-family life—that they were available to be mobilized. Of course, many who were available would never be mobilized, but without availability, mobilization was impossible.

So I would not erase structural factors from the chart in the Introduction that outlines the causes of women's mobilization. Instead, I would

---

7. See Colburn 1994, 8 for a chart of the twenty-two countries that had a revolution during the post–World War II period. All of them were in the third world, a region characterized by high levels of poverty and inequality (though as his chart shows, there were considerable variations between the countries). If structural factors played no part in the rise of mass guerrilla movements, one would expect to find some examples of revolutions in the first and second worlds as well. Many argue that in 1989 there were revolutions across the second world (in the countries of Eastern and Central Europe); however, Colburn does not include them in his list of revolutions, presumably because they did not fit his definition of revolution: "a violent change of government followed by an assault on established political and economic orders by new and determined political elites" (1994, 7).

qualify that section of the chart identifying structural factors as necessary but not sufficient conditions. Structures set the stage for the political drama to come, but they did not make the guerrilla movements form, any more than stages cause theatrical events to spontaneously generate. Structural factors did not make women join guerrilla movements once those movements had formed, either. But if the structural conditions are wrong, then even determined guerrillas will have little success in their attempts to mobilize a mass movement of men or women.[8]

Revolutions always occur in a structural context, but they are not made by structure alone. As Marifeli Pérez-Stable argued in analyzing the factors that led to the overthrow of Batista by Castro's 26th of July Movement: "Sugar monoculture constituted the structural context that allowed social revolution to happen. Sociopolitical dynamics explain how it was actually made" (1993, 7). In a parallel fashion, I would argue that structural factors were the context for women's mobilization, while sociopolitical factors explain how women were (or were not) mobilized.

What sociopolitical factors shaped the gendered outcome of the Cuban guerrilla war? Remember that in Nicaragua, El Salvador, and Chiapas, one of the ways that many women were first politicized was through the Catholic Church. Timing is one reason that the Cuban Catholic Church could not have played this sort of role. While the Catholic Church certainly existed in Cuba in the decades before the 1959 triumph of the 26th of July Movement, the liberation theology movement did not. Liberation theology would not be born until the 1968 bishops' conference in Medellín, Colombia. Instead, the Catholic Church that shaped Cuban culture in the prerevolutionary years was a church of the old school, a church that most certainly did not try to mobilize women to question social inequality and to organize against it.

There were Catholic organizations that sought to mobilize women in the days before Vatican II (1962–65) and the Medellín bishops' conference (1968), but those groups were limited in political impact because of the weakness of the church as an institution. "In the 1950s [the Cuban Catholic Church] had the lowest percentage of nominal (72.5%) and practicing Catholics (5–8%) in Latin America. Cuba also had the highest percentage of non-church members (19%)" (Crahan 1987, 4). The weak-

---

8. Wealthy countries have not been immune to guerrilla movements, as illustrated by the examples of the Symbionese Liberation Army, the Black Panthers, and the Weather Underground, all of the United States. But wealthy countries have been immune from guerrilla movements that generate enough of a mass following to come even close to threatening the state, precisely because the structural conditions for revolution are absent.

ness of the church was either caused, or illustrated, by a shortage of clergy.[9]

In response to that perceived weakness, church leaders formed two laypeople's Catholic groups in the 1950s: Catholic Action (Acción Católica) and the Young Catholic Workers (Juventud Obrera Católica, or JOC). Both these groups implemented programs that seemed designed to undermine the appeal of the Left, and to keep the faithful on the margins of opposition politics.

Catholic Action, intent on combating the appeal of socialism, initiated a series of projects aimed at identifying the needs of rural workers. The Young Catholic Workers attempted to compete with labor unions for the loyalty of workers and claimed 20,000 members. . . . Catholic Action and the Young Catholic Workers were aimed at maintaining traditional Catholic cadres drawn from the bourgeoisie within the church in the face of increasing societal pressures. In so doing they tended to insulate lay-people from secular organizations, thereby limiting their influence over movements such as Castro's. While some Catholics did participate in the insurrection against Batista, overall the Catholic Church did not play a major role. Although Catholics were generally anti-Batista, there was little feeling that their faith required them to participate in his overthrow. Rather there was a strong desire to appear neutral. (Crahan 1987, 4)

This is not to say that the hierarchy of the church was in favor of the Batista dictatorship. In fact, on occasion it directly opposed Batista.[10] Yet even during those moments when the hierarchy opposed the political dictatorship, it was silent on questions of economic or social inequality, in-

9. A 1957 survey of rural dwellers found that "[o]nly 53.51% of those surveyed had ever laid eyes on a priest and less than 8% had ever had any contact with one. More telling was the fact that only 3.4% of those surveyed believed that the Catholic Church would help them improve their lot. The vast majority (85%) of priests and religious were concentrated in Havana teaching in private schools rather than engaged in pastoral work. This meant that some urban neighborhoods were also without pastors" (Crahan 1987, 4).

10. The Cuban bishops called for Batista's resignation at least twice during his last year of rule, in February and again in early March 1958 (Wickham-Crowley 1992, 189–90), though it seems that opposition was ambivalent for in December of 1958, the bishops "rejected a request from the clergy to issue a pastoral letter concerning the insurrection" (Crahan 1987, 5).

Lower clergy and laypeople were involved in a much greater variety of anti-Batista activities, including combat. While most of the Catholic activists discussed by Manuel Fernández (1984, 23–34) were men, he does make reference to collaboration between a priest and Celia Sánchez, a major figure during the guerrilla period and later the common-law wife of Fidel Castro. "At that time Father Antonio Albizu, a Franciscan from Manzanillo parish, maintained contact with Celia Sánchez, who was very close to Fidel Castro, so as to lend his help to the combatants and resisters" (1984, 27; contacts between Albizu and Sánchez are also mentioned in Alfonso 1985, 36).

cluding gender inequality, the very issues that would be championed by the secular 26th of July guerrillas (Alfonso 1985, 23–31; Crahan 1987, 4–8; Fernández 1984, 23–34; Gómez Treto 1988, 9–10).

Perhaps no single factor distinguishes Nicaragua, El Salvador, and Chiapas from Cuba as clearly as liberation theology. In Cuba, where the local Catholic Church promoted traditional gender roles, either women were not mobilized in mass numbers or their mobilization was not acknowledged by the revolutionary leaders. The rise of liberation theology, with its call on all, male and female, to build the kingdom of God on earth, seems to have been central in preparing young women for unconventional lives and, perhaps more generally, for unsettling gender relations in the societies where the new theology took root. It did so both through the message of equality promoted by the liberation theologians, and through the base communities that were formed across those countries as a way of putting that new message into practice.

The other major ideological change that I identified as important in explaining the role of women in the FSLN, the FMLN, and the EZLN was the guerrillas' use of the mass mobilization strategy, a strategy of winning the hearts and minds of thousands through work that was political as well as military. In contrast, the Cubans did not use the mass mobilization strategy. Instead, Cuba was the place where the foco strategy was most successfully employed, where a small band of guerrillas overthrew a dictatorship, a feat that was not to be repeated.

One of the most prominent leaders of the guerrilla army, Che Guevara, explained what he called the "lessons of the Cuban revolution," a list of lessons that neatly captured the foco strategy. "1. Popular forces can win a war against the army. 2. It is not necessary to wait until all the conditions for making revolution exist; the insurrection can create them. 3. In underdeveloped America, the countryside is the basic area for armed fighting" (quoted in Loveman and Davies 1997a, 50; on foco strategy, see also Castañeda 1994, 73–74, 76–77). Guerrillas who used the foco strategy did not need to mobilize everyone who was potentially willing. In fact, they preferred to organize a small, dedicated, and competent band, an army of elite revolutionaries, rather than waste time tediously recruiting people who were ambivalent and perhaps incompetent. While there were a few women in prominent positions within the guerrilla movement, and many women who did support work, as a rule, women seemed to fit in the category of people who were not worth mobilizing.

Linda Reif has suggested that women were rarely recruited, citing "excerpts from Radio Rebelde broadcasts, the major revolutionary station,

[that] reveal no attempt to mobilize specifically women" (1986, 155). Various comments made by top leaders were consistent with Reif's observation. With regard to the failed attempt to seize the Moncada army barracks in 1953, Castro claimed: "If the Moncada had fallen into our hands; even the women of Santiago de Cuba would have taken up arms" (quoted in Lupiáñez Reinlein 1985, 157). Although that quote implies that women would not normally be willing to take up arms, in fact Fidel had not allowed women to participate in the attack on the Moncada, instead assigning them more appropriate duties like ironing uniforms or nursing injured combatants (Smith and Padula 1996, 24).[11] Similarly, Che Guevara discussed women's roles:

Naturally the combatant women are a minority. When the internal front is being consolidated and it is desirable to remove as many combatants as possible who do not possess indispensable physical characteristics, the women can be assigned a considerable number of specific occupations . . . in this stage a woman can perform her habitual tasks of peacetime; it is very pleasing to a soldier subjected to the extremely hard conditions of this life to be able to look forward to a seasoned meal which tastes like something. . . . The woman as cook can greatly improve the diet and, furthermore, it is easier to keep her in her domestic tasks; one of the problems in guerrilla bands is that all works of a civilian character are scorned by those who perform them; they are constantly trying to get out of these tasks in order to enter into forces that are actively in combat. (Quoted in Loveman and Davies 1997, 111–12)

From Che's perspective, the positive reason to encourage women to work as cooks rather than combatants was that women were more tolerant of such duties.

There was also a negative factor that could have shaped the decision not to recruit women, an arms shortage, which shaped "the selective character of access to the Sierra" (Marel García 1996, 42). Given the sexist assumptions inherent in the comments made by guerrilla commanders Che and Fidel, selectivity would have meant excluding most women. Again, some women did end up in combat positions, at least periodically, but they were not actively recruited in the way that thousands of women would be by later Latin American guerrilla movements.

---

11. Fidel Castro seemed to have changed his position with time, for in 1958, a small brigade of about fourteen women, the Mariana Grajales Brigade, would be formed, reportedly with Castro's strong support (Smith and Padula 1996, 30).

The analysis of Cuba up to this point shows that while structural factors seemed to have made many women available for mobilization, ideological factors—the nature of the church and the strategy employed by guerrilla leaders—kept all but a few from being actively mobilized. What about the personal factors that could have set some on the revolutionary path? While there are some personal questions that I cannot address, since I did not do extensive interviews in Cuba (issues like how family traditions of resistance shaped women's early political thoughts, or the average age when women chose to join the revolutionary movement), the existing secondary literature does provide clues regarding preexisting networks.

As already noted, the church groups that existed in Cuba in the years leading up to the guerrilla war were not very suitable as preexisting networks, since the goals of their founders were to demobilize and depoliticize members. In contrast, labor unions often did serve to channel male union activists into revolutionary activities in Cuba. But few, if any, women would become revolutionaries through the labor union movement, for a number of reasons. First, most women were not employed in the formal sector in 1953, the year of the guerrilla movement's emergence. Only 13 percent of them were recognized as part of the economically active population in Cuba, a smaller percentage than in other parts of Latin America at the same time (Luzón 1987, 190; Pérez-Stable 1993, 32). Second, women tended to be greatly underrepresented in unionized industries.

Before the revolution, an estimated 11.8 percent of the employed miners, craftsmen, and industrial workers in Cuba were women. But they were concentrated in a few industries, especially the textile industry, where some 46 percent of them were employed, and which—apart from the major textile center at Ariguanabo—was predominantly made up of unmechanized small shops. Another 37 percent of them were in the food and tobacco industries, and the rest of them were thinly distributed in other industrial occupations. (Zeitlin 1967, 124)

And even in those industries in which women were concentrated, like tobacco and textiles, they were represented by male union leaders. One study of the role of labor unions in the overthrow of Batista mentioned a few women, among them Haydée Santamaría and Melba Hernández, who sought to build links between the guerrillas and workers, but they themselves were not workers.[12] That female workers rarely were political

---

12. "Haydée Santamaría was born and raised at the Constancia sugar mill in the Las Villas province, where her father ran the carpentry shop. She and her brother Abel felt compassion for

activists is further illustrated in a 119-page-long analysis of the role of unions in the guerrilla war that provides multiple lists of union activists, all of whom were male (Instituto de Historia del Movimiento Comunista y de la Revolución Socialista de Cuba 1985, 251–370).

The labor union movement, in which women were largely absent, contrasted sharply with the student movement. In Cuba (as would be the case in Nicaragua and El Salvador), the student movement served as a preexisting network that channeled many into revolutionary politics, both directly and indirectly, especially in the early days of the guerrilla struggle.[13] While men seemed to have held the vast majority of leadership positions within the student movement, some women were student leaders. Not only do studies of that movement record the names of a number of female leaders, but women also made up a fairly large minority of college students; at least a third of the people who completed university degrees in the 1950s were women.[14]

The influence of women within the student movement should not be overstated; many lists of student leaders of the 1940s and 1950s included few or no women. For instance, Julio García Oliveras listed the fourteen student leaders at the University of Havana who he thought "represented the most advanced ideas of the university student body" (1979, 28), a list that included many who would later become famous revolutionary leaders, such as Fidel Castro, Raul Castro, and Armando Hart. The list included no women.

At the same time, many of the lists of student leaders did include women. Moreover, in departments in which women often specialized,

---

the workers who suffered unemployment between sugar harvests. To escape their 'very reactionary' family, the two moved to Havana, sharing a tiny apartment, which in the early 1950s became the original headquarters of Fidel Castro's movement.

In 1952 Melba Hernández was a thirty-two-year-old lawyer whose legal skills would be crucial to Castro's rebellion. Her parents' home became an alternative meeting site for Castro's organization" (Smith and Padula 1996, 23).

13. "The majority of the men who were involved in combat on July 26th [the date of the 1953 attack on the Moncada] had been trained, in one form or another, in University practices" (García Oliveras 1979, 102).

14. Among the population six years of age and older, 1.4 percent of men and .7 percent of women had university degrees in the 1950s. But that figure included both recent college graduates as well as people who would have been of typical college age many decades earlier. If the numbers of families that sent their daughters as well as their sons to college had crept up over time, it is likely that the ratio of men to women was somewhat less than 2 to 1. Data on grade school and middle school enrollment in the 1950s supports that hypothesis, for the ratio of boys to girls was 1 to 1. Of boys age five to fourteen, 51.5 percent were enrolled in school, as were 51.6 percent of girls in that age range (Pérez-Stable 1993, 33). Seen another way, in 1953, women were somewhat more likely than men to have attended at least enough school to have learned how to read: 80.02 percent of females and 75.85 percent of males were literate (Schroeder 1982, 125; table V.2).

such as education or journalism, the lists of elected leaders sometimes included nearly as many women as men.[15] So women were hardly absent from university life, including organized university life. Many of the women who played significant roles in the guerrilla coalition—women such as Vilma Espín, Gloria Cuadras, and Isabel Girodana—could trace their political roots to the university organizations (see Smith and Padula 1996, 22–32). But it seems that, had they so chosen, the guerrilla leaders

15. A study of student activism at the University of Havana identified the following women as anti-Batista student activists: Susa Escalón, Berta Hernández, Eva Jiménez, Conchita Portela, and Zaida Trimiño (García Oliveras 1979, 49, 81, 171–72). Additionally, García Oliveras mentioned the bravery in combat, communications, or arms running of a series of other women—including Haydée Santamaría, Melba Hernández, Vilma and Nilsa Espín, Ansela de los Santos, Leyla Vazquez, María de los Angeles Pumpido, and Zaida Trimiño y Natalia Bolívar—without specifying if they were students or just based in Havana (1979, 192–93, 241, 244). At least some of them, such as Zaida Trimiño, had been student activists at the University of Havana, whereas others, such as Vilma Espín (who held a degree in chemical engineering from the University of the Oriente [Shnookal 1991, xi]) collaborated with the University of Havana students without being one of them (on student organizing at the University of Havana, see also Suchlicki 1969).

In his study of the anti-Batista student movement in Santiago de Cuba, José Lupiáñez Reinlein makes occasional reference to pro-Batista students. For instance, one group that he describes as "opportunists" and "homeland sellers" *(vendepatrias)* was composed of three men and one woman, Leyda Sarabia. In November of 1952, those pro-Batista students won a student election and the new vice president was Nieves Despaigne, "daughter of a sadly famous lieutenant of Batista's army"(Lupiáñez Reinlein 1985, 23, 109–10).

Lupiáñez Reinlein lists the following women as prominent in anti-Batista student activism at the Instituto del Oriente: Lutgarda Agüero, Carmen Cardona, Enma Rosa Chuy Arnau, Marta Correa, Gloria Cuadras, Asela de los Santos Tamayo, Nilsa and Vilma Espín, Electra Fernández, Cira Lujó, Nitza Madrigal, Nancy Ojeda, María and Ramona Ruíz Bravo, and Delfina Yero (Lupiáñez Reinlein 1985, 40–42, 50–52, 110, 116–17, 191, 229). One of those women, Martha Correa, a student activist at the Instituto de Segunda Enseñanza de Santiago beginning in 1952, listed a number of female students who were active as she was, before the 26th of July Movement first publicly emerged with the 1953 attack on the Moncada: Nancy Ojeda, Juanita y Carmen Yasells, Isabel Baltazar, Osmalizaán Belén, Marina Molleuve, Manuela Lavigne, and Rosa Pérez Cuitían. After the Moncada attack, according to Correa, dozens of new female students joined the movement, inspired by the examples of Haydée Santamaria and Melba Hernández (who were sentenced to seven years in prison for their supportive roles in the attack) (Lupiáñez Reinlein 1985, 162–63; Smith and Padula 1996, 24).

Not surprisingly, women were best represented at the normal school (teaching college) of the University of Oriente, constituting a third to almost a half of the people elected to positions in the Asociación de Alumnos de la Escuela Normal de Maestros; the association was part of the university-wide movement led by Frank País (often identified as someone who might have rivaled Castro had he lived to see the revolution). The following women from the normal school are identified by Lupiáñez Reinlein as having played prominent roles: Pilar Baquié, Ivonne Blanco, Gladys Brizuela, Ullo Isabel del Carmen, Eugenia Dominguez, Nancy Duharte, Xiomara Erice, Mirtha Fernandez, Noelia Ferrer, Adisdania Flores, Elia Freta, Elia Frómeta [same as previous name on list?], Cira Louhau [same as Cira Lujó?], Elvia Méndez, Raquel Mestre, Melba Olivares, Ena Rizo, Juana E. Sanchez, Ligia Trujillo, and Rafaela Tur (1985, 50, 91–92, 176–77). The other school at the Oriente where women were frequently elected to office was the school of journalism. The following journalism students held office in an anti-Batista student group in 1953: Evangelina Chió Vidal, Estela Flores Salas, Elizabeth Ginarte Tassé, Dolores Griñán Pérez, María Sossa Comas, and Rita Vázquez Pillot (Lupiáñez Reinlein 1985, 181–82).

could have recruited more vigorously from among the many willing anti-Batista activists who attended Cuban universities in the 1950s.

Recruiting women more energetically could have been beneficial for the guerrillas, from a military and strategic perspective. Women, like men, sometimes suffered government repression, ranging from being fired upon with water cannons during peaceful protest, to being tortured and murdered for carrying messages for the rebels (Lupiáñez Reinlein 1985, 114–15, 122; Smith and Padula 1996, 31). Yet despite the real risks that women faced, they were more likely to be overlooked by the security forces than were men. On more than one occasion, men and women participated together in some oppositional activity—a demonstration, an organizing meeting—at the end of which state security arrested or even killed the men, while the women went free (Lupiáñez Reinlein 1985, 196–99; Marel García 1996, 52). Che Guevara referred to the somewhat greater chance that a woman would escape the notice of security forces when he recommended that women should be the ones to carry messages or objects between groups of combatants: "[W]omen can transport them using a thousand tricks; it is a fact that however brutal the repression, however thorough the searching, the woman receives less harsh treatment than the man" (quoted in Loveman and Davies 1997, 111–12).[16] It seems that the Cuban guerrillas themselves thought they could benefit by recruiting more women, and yet they did not do so.

So why did the guerrillas choose not to vigorously recruit women into the movement? I already suggested many of the reasons: the need for small numbers of guerrillas due to the foco strategy, the shortage of firearms, and the sexism of guerrilla leaders. Moreover, it seems that mobilizing women would have been difficult. In all likelihood, considerably fewer women (as a percentage of the population) were available for mobilization in Cuba than would be in Central America (possibly because of differences in family structure and definitely because of the scarcity of potential preexisting networks, aside from the student network).

A final reason that could have played a role in the guerrillas' disinterest in recruiting women is historical. In 1959, when Fidel's 26th of July Movement overthrew the Batista dictatorship, feminism played little role within international left-wing thought. By 1979, when the FSLN overthrew the Somoza dictatorship, international feminism already held a sig-

---

16. My reading of the phenomenon of women receiving more lenient treatment (in Cuba and elsewhere) leads me to think that the leniency tends to diminish as the conflict wears on. At times, revolutionary women (and those wrongly accused of being guerrillas) sometimes were treated even more brutally than men, an issue I discuss in Chapter 2.

nificant place within the international Left. The influence of international feminists would only grow over the subsequent decades.

I make this argument about international feminism with some caution, for my findings regarding the role of feminism in motivating women to join the Nicaraguan and Salvadoran guerrilla coalition were clear: when interviewed, almost nobody said that a concern for gender equality factored into her decision. Where feminism seems to have mattered was not in influencing women at the time when they joined the guerrillas; instead, feminism seemed to have shaped the thinking of the mostly male leaders of the guerrilla forces. During the second half of the twentieth century, the possibility of generating international sympathy and sometimes material support became increasingly tied to the extent to which a revolutionary movement promoted women, both in the sense of whether women were present in the armed forces and in the sense of whether women's issues were on the agenda. As the twentieth century wore on, guerrilla leaders increasingly benefited from mobilizing women and publicly proclaiming their commitment to feminist values.

The EZLN of Chiapas, which emerged later than any of the other groups, is a particularly clear example of this. From the beginning of their public life, the Zapatistas' communiqués were highly inclusive (of gays and lesbians as well as women), promoting feminist values of equality and tolerance at the same time as many of the Zapatistas' indigenous supporters were unfamiliar with the concepts of gay rights or feminism, as I discussed in Chapter 3. That is not to say that the Zapatistas' promotion of gender equality was all for public show; many of the challenges to inequality that were made over the course of the 1990s were quite real, to the displeasure of some Zapatista men. Although the Cuban case suggests that guerrilla leaders would have been less inclined to mobilize women without international pressures to do so, once those women were mobilized, their revolutionary activism would sometimes lead them into the fight for gender equality, with or without the support of those who first mobilized them.

So comparing the 26th of July Movement with the FSLN, FMLN, and EZLN leads me to revise my original chart on the reasons for women's mobilization in two ways. The structural factors should be identified as necessary but not sufficient, as factors that set the stage but did not cause the drama. Further, an addition should be made to the chart, namely, the impact of international feminism. But international feminism does not belong in the category of personal factors (for it seemed to have had almost no effect on women's personal decision making). Instead, it was one of the ideological factors that shaped the guerrilla methods. The other factors that I originally hypothesized as important, especially the rise of liberation theology and the role of preexisting networks as a channel into guerrilla life, seem to have been confirmed (or at least not discounted) through comparison of the Central American and Mexican cases with that of Cuba. The revised version of the chart is on page 135.

CONCLUSION: NEW QUESTIONS FOR REVOLUTIONARY STUDIES

During the twentieth century, the field of revolutionary studies was dominated by two versions of a single question: Under what circumstances have revolutionaries succeeded in overthrowing states? or, Under what circumstances have states fallen to revolutionary movements? That question served the field well over the course of the last century, informing generations of interesting studies.

But perhaps a new century requires new questions. Perhaps it is now time to move on intellectually. There are a number of reasons to do so. First, the end of the cold war has changed both the resources available to revolutionary movements and the resources available to the dictatorships they opposed. Some have suggested that the age of revolution came to an end with the end of the cold war; others have suggested that revolutionary movements will continue to emerge as long as there is local injustice (see, for example, Goodwin 2001; Selbin 2001). A third position, one that I subscribe to, would be that the end of the cold war changed the international context in significant ways, but its termination did not always eliminate local grievances; in fact, it sometimes aggravated them. Under those circumstances, we will continue to see the periodic emergence of revolutionary movements, but ones that will differ from the Marxist-Leninist movements of the cold war era, ones that, like the EZLN of Chiapas, may not even demand the overthrow of the state. A statecentric approach may not serve us well if we hope to understand these post–cold war revolutionaries.

A second reason for expanding our questions, and increasing the pluralism of our methodologies, is that revolutionary movements in the post–cold war world are too complicated to be understood within the confines of a single question. Indeed, they have always been too complicated to fit well into those confines. Focusing our analysis on the moment of overthrow flattens the experience of revolutionaries, thus doing a real disservice to the revolutionaries themselves, and to those of us who study them.

Many interesting questions do not easily fit within the confines of the central question and so have not been asked. But by putting aside the

FACTORS THAT LED TO MOBILIZATION
OF WOMEN AS GUERRILLAS

STRUCTURAL CHANGES

Land concentration, increasing insecurity for rural poor
 (due to economic globalization and population growth)
 → male migration and often abandonment of families
 → rise in number of single-female-headed households
 → female migration (to cities or Lacandón jungle), which broke traditional ties,
  made organizing more possible

 Necessary but not sufficient

IDEOLOGICAL AND ORGANIZATIONAL CHANGES

Rise of liberation theology
 → growth of religious and secular self-help groups

Change in guerrilla methods
 → from foco organizing to mass mobilization
 → from military strategy to political-military strategy
 → from disinterest in, to interest in, mobilizing women in rresponse to international
  feminism

POLITICAL FACTORS

State response to those self-help groups was often repression
 → repression pushed many women into more-radical activities in self-defense

*Ineffectual state efforts to co-opt (especially in Chiapas) gave women new
 skills and new resentment*

PERSONAL FACTORS

Family traditions of resistance
*Membership in preexisting social networks (student groups, church groups,
 labor unions)*
Year of birth

COMBINATION OF ALL FACTORS

 → mobilization of women in guerrilla movements and other revolutionary organizations

central question, I was free to ask others. Those questions included, How does gender as a central category of analysis help to explain revolutionary movements? and How and why were large numbers of women mobilized into Latin American guerrilla movements beginning in the late 1960s? But these questions only scratch the surface of all the questions that could be addressed, if only the central question were set aside. In this book, I have touched on a few of the following questions, but there is still much exciting intellectual work to be done.

Under what circumstances (if any) can the coalition that overthrew the old regime be maintained during the revolution? Can the objections of those who are threatened by revolutionary transformation be mitigated so that they do not engender counterrevolutionary movements? Or would a nonthreatening program be so watered down as to be nonrevolutionary? Was foreign involvement in (or promotion of) revolutionary and counterrevolutionary movements inevitable during the cold war? Is it still inevitable? Does globalization make revolutionary success more or less likely? Under what circumstances have the guerrillas' goals (such as challenging social inequality and authoritarianism) been met without the price of massive revolutionary and counterrevolutionary violence being paid? Individuals who participate in guerrilla movements and revolutions also could be fruitfully studied. Many have debated their class identities (and to a lesser extent, those based on gender, ethnicity, religion, and geography), however, fewer have considered their motivations in joining these movements, their experiences within them, the influence of those experiences on their later lives, and how they remember the guerrilla struggles and revolutionary periods.

Under what circumstances are women available for mobilization? Do their motives differ from those of men? Do their experiences differ from those of men? How does the experience of participating in these groups change the lives of participants? How does it change their values? How does the impact of participating in the revolutionary coalition differ depending on their role within the coalition? How does that impact depend on their class background and ethnicity? Certainly one could fruitfully ask similar questions regarding people of various ethnicities, classes, educational backgrounds, and religious backgrounds. Looking at these factors will allow us to analyze the extent to which the revolutionaries succeeded in transforming their societies, in creating new men (and women), and in breaking down the old social and political barriers that contributed to the guerrilla wars in the first place.

Asking new questions will require looking beyond the moment of the overthrow of the old regime. By not privileging that moment, it will allow for more complicated understandings of revolutionary success or failure. Hopefully, this book is an early example of what will be a new, pluralistic, and intellectually fruitful trend in revolutionary studies.

Appendix
SOCIAL ORIGINS OF THE CENTRAL AMERICAN GUERRILLAS

By reviewing the literature on the social origins of the guerrillas in Nicaragua and El Salvador, and setting it in the context of my own study, I will address the question of who participated in the revolutionary movements in these countries, making three arguments. First, the literature has tended to be skewed in that it has underestimated the urban component of the guerrilla movements, perhaps especially in the case of the Salvadoran FMLN, a guerrilla army that was more rural than the Nicaraguan FSLN, but not as rural as has been claimed in much of the literature. Second, I wish to contest the idea, implicit in much of this literature, that guerrillas either were urban elites who were students at the time they were mobilized, or were unschooled rural peasants. In fact, many students had parents who were peasants or members of the urban poor, making them both students and of non-elite origin. That an individual could have been both of peasant origin and a student seems rather obvious, yet much of the literature implicitly discounts that possibility. Third, I will suggest that, on average, male and female guerrillas came from somewhat different social backgrounds, with female guerrillas more likely to have been students and of urban origin at the time they were mobilized than were male guerrillas.

My research samples in Nicaragua and El Salvador included more women of urban origin, and more women who were students, at the time of mobilization than might be expected from a review of the literature, if one focused on those works that depend heavily on data drawn from

---

1. This review addresses the guerrilla movements of Nicaragua and El Salvador, but not that of Chiapas, because my research sample in Chiapas included no guerrillas, to my knowledge, and so I do not have the sort of data that would allow me to address the question of the social origins of the women of the EZLN. Given the reality of conducting research during the war in Chiapas, the women I interviewed were somewhat different from those I interviewed during the postwar periods in Nicaragua and El Salvador. The women in my Mexican sample

journalists or interviews with guerrilla commanders.[1] But examining what I believe to be more-reliable sources—government records, demobilization data, and interviews with mid- and low-prestige revolutionaries—I will suggest that the guerrilla coalitions were more internally diverse than many have claimed. Of course, I am not the first to point to the diversity of those coalitions. My argument is quite consistent with that of such writers as Forrest Colburn, who has argued that the "key to successful insurrections has not been, as is so often romanticized, an alliance between guerrillas and peasants. Instead, what has been indispensable is the ability of the revolutionaries to weld together a broad coalition of groups" (1994, 46).

But what sorts of people made up these broad coalitions? Scholars generally agree that the top leadership of the FSLN of Nicaragua and the FMLN of El Salvador was composed of individuals who were mainly highly educated and of middle- or upper-class origin: the data supporting this is quite reliable, including such compelling sources as interviews with the guerrilla commanders themselves, the people I call high-prestige revolutionaries. Where there is far more debate, and far less concrete data, is with respect to the social origins of the vast majority of the members of the revolutionary coalition, the men and women I call mid- and low-prestige revolutionaries (see the Introduction for an explanation of these categories).

NICARAGUA

Carlos Vilas conducted what is probably the most carefully documented study of the origins of those who died in the war against Somoza, based on data collected in the early 1980s by the Nicaragua Social Security agency (known as INSSBI).[2] Vilas analyzed a random sample of 640 cases of people killed in the guerrilla struggle (of the 6,000 cases documented by INSSBI) and found that the single most common occupation was student (29 percent); followed by tradesperson (22 percent); worker or journeyman (16 percent); office employee (16 percent); technician, professional, teacher or professor (7 percent); small merchant or trader (5 percent); and finally peasant or farmer (4.5 percent) (1986, 112).

---

were those who worked with women (both in women's groups and in women's projects within mixed groups), many of whom were of indigenous origin. In effect, they were expert witnesses: many had worked with the Zapatistas, but none was publicly part of the EZLN.

2. The study was carried out to facilitate payment of pensions to the families of those who died.

He contrasted that study of what he called "the rank and file of the in-surrection" with a study of 113 cases of revolutionaries drawn from "the leadership cadre and notable militants" (1986, 113). In the study of top leaders, intellectuals and peasants made up a larger percentage, and workers a smaller percentage, of the sample than was true in the study of the rank and file (1986, 113–14).

Vilas also considered another way of judging class background, that is, by recording the occupations of the parents of those who died in the guer-rilla struggle, a measure that may be more meaningful given the young age of most of the guerrillas.[3] Vilas had data on the parents' occupations in 390 cases and found that the single largest category was self-employed (39 percent); followed by peasants or farmers (19 percent); small entre-preneurs, merchants, or traders (17 percent); office employees (9.5 per-cent); technicians, professionals, teachers, or professors (9.5 percent); and finally workers and journeymen (5 percent) (1986, 115).

So according to Vilas's study (the only one of its kind, to my knowl-edge), the FSLN was not simply made up of urban elites who gave orders to rural peasants. While people who fit into both those categories did par-ticipate in the Sandinista coalition, neither of those categories contained a large percentage of those who were killed in the fight against Somoza. A number of other scholars have painted a similarly complicated picture of the FSLN.

John Booth details the FSLN's successful recruiting efforts among a va-riety of sectors, including peasants, union members, students, and the ur-ban poor, arguing that the top leadership was mainly composed of people of middle- and upper-class origins (1985, 147–51; also 97–126, 271–72). Similarly, Mark Everingham notes that the "Nicaraguan revolution was not peasant, proletarian, or bourgeois. People of almost every social stra-tum actively participated in the overthrow of the Somoza dictatorship by contributing his or her might, mind, or money to collective action. On 19 July 1979, it was difficult to find a citizen of the country who did not talk like a revolutionary" (1996, 1). Farideh Farhi also argues that the Sandin-ista revolution was not fundamentally a peasant rebellion, instead de-scribing it as an "urban-based revolution," noting that "[t]he confronta-

---

3. "Seventy-one percent were between 15 and 24 years old when they died, a proportion almost three times higher than the weight of this age group in the demographic pyramid (20 percent)" (Vilas 1986, 108). On that same page, Vilas presented a very useful chart of the age and sex of the 640 people he studied, showing that only 6.6 percent of those who died were women. This finding was in notable contrast to the widely cited figure that about 30 percent of the Sandinista combatants were women.

tion with the regime was . . . carried out mostly in the urban areas" (1990, 81 n. 32).

Jeffrey Paige argues that the rank and file of the Sandinista coalition was made up of rural semiproletarians, along with members of the urban informal sector (1997, 30–31). While the last stages of the guerrilla struggle were fought out in most of the major Nicaraguan cities, it was "where the cotton fields met the city in the urban Indian *barrios* of Subtiava (in León) and Monimbó (in Masaya) [that] a critical point of social combustion was reached" (1997, 30; Paige draws these conclusions from a series of studies [see 379 n. 49]).

Timothy Wickham-Crowley argues that the leadership of what he calls the second wave of Latin American guerrilla movements (which included those of Nicaragua and El Salvador) "was drawn from privileged groups in society," a claim that is consistent with the findings of all the others. He also claims that "[v]irtually every report from the countryside, including a wealth of on-the-scenes reports by journalists,[4] confirms the largely, often overwhelmingly, peasant composition of the guerrilla armies." In the same section of his book, he mentions the significant role of the urban informal sector in the Sandinista guerrilla struggle (1992, 214–15).

Wickham-Crowley seems to use the word *peasant* as a synonym for *poor rural dweller* no matter how that person made his or her living. His category of peasant includes squatters, sharecroppers, semiproletarians, and proletarians (1992, 231–34). He goes so far as to suggest (citing Paige) that many of the urban dwellers who played such a significant role in the war against the Somoza dictatorship really were peasants as well: "The

---

4. Journalistic accounts may be poorly suited for analyzing the social background of rank and file guerrillas. One would expect that most of the residents of rural guerrilla camps would be from the countryside. But urban guerrillas were much harder to find, because they almost never grouped in camps, even when a guerrilla army had a sizable urban presence. Camps only existed where the guerrilla army controlled land, something that was rare in the cities except when the war was nearly won. Unlike rural guerrillas, who sought to control territory, urban guerrillas sought to blend into their surroundings: continuing to go to work or school and to live at home if possible. For obvious reasons, urban guerrillas who sought to go unnoticed would be harder for journalists to identify than rural guerrillas in camps.

Finally, there is reason to suspect the way that visitors to the camps decided who was a peasant. Journalists very rarely had the sort of time (or typically the inclination) needed to collect good data on occupation and class background. My guess is that they judged whether a group was composed of peasants by means of exterior markers (the way people dressed, how they cooked, or how they spoke), probably supplemented with a few conversations with camp members. But many people dress, cook, or speak like peasants (especially those who have lived in the countryside) despite having other occupations. Also, a number of women of urban origin told me that when they were sent to the camps in the countryside, they were looked down upon by rural dwellers for being urban and, therefore, soft. So they worked as hard as possible to prove themselves and to avoid appearing to be urban.

majority of peasants displaced by the growth of cotton estates had to find residence elsewhere, and a substantial portion of them ended up as residents in the peripheral *barrios* of the towns and cities of northwestern Nicaragua. From there many migrated to the cotton districts to pick cotton at harvest time, while retaining an 'urban' residence" (1992, 235).

It is certainly possible to argue that the Sandinista guerrilla struggle was a "peasant rebellion" if the word *peasant* is used so broadly as to include many urban dwellers. Such a broad definition has the advantage of highlighting cultural traditions and ties to family in the countryside, which played an important role in unifying the Sandinista coalition. Yet more is lost than is gained by such a definition, because, most important, most rank-and-file Sandinistas did not see themselves as fitting into the boxes of either peasant or educated urban elite. As Vilas found, only 4.5 percent of those who died in the war were identified as peasants or farmers by those who had known them, and only 19 percent of them had parents who were peasants or farmers (1985, 112–14).

Lynn Horton's excellent book, *Peasants in Arms*, sheds considerable light on the mechanisms by which the unsettling effects of export-oriented capitalism set the stage for the FSLN. Her findings, based on more than one hundred interviews with Sandinistas, contras, and their supporters in the mountain municipality of Quilalí, can help explain an apparent contradiction in the literature on the class background of those who joined the Sandinista guerrilla struggle. On the one hand, scholars such as Wickham-Crowley and Paige argue that the regions where the transition to export-oriented agriculture was most strongly felt (measured by the rise of "squatters" according to Wickham-Crowley and "rural semi-proletarians" according to Paige) were the places where the revolutionaries had the most success in recruiting people. On the other hand, Vilas found that very few of those who died in the guerrilla struggle were peasants or farmers.

Quilalí is a perfect place to try to sort out this puzzle, for it is located in the department (the rough equivalent of a state) of Nueva Segovia, one of the four departments in the northern mountains of Nicaragua that Wickham-Crowley identified as the "crucible of the revolution" (1992, 232). So who were the Sandinistas of Quilalí? One important sector that joined the guerrillas in Quilalí were *finqueros*, or ranchers, people who clearly had not lost the most in the economic transformation of the region. In fact, it was precisely because of their power in the region that they were the first to be recruited. "The FSLN, pragmatically recognizing that 'a finquero can recruit a colono, a poor peasant, but a poor peasant can never recruit a finquero,' would first win over a finquero and then give that producer the autonomy to build his own network of collaborators, which generally included his extended family and his workers and colonos" (Horton 1998, 69). Those ranchers who supported the Sandinista guerrillas did so for reasons that were largely political rather than economic, stemming from their traditional loyalties to the conservative party or their disgust with dictatorial nature of the Somoza regime (68–71; also Paige 1997, 356–57).

Many ranchers who did not support the Sandinistas had sons and daughters who joined the guerrillas anyway, without the knowledge of their parents, while they were high school students in the cities of Ocotal or Estelí (Horton 1998, 70). Although the inequalities they had observed in the countryside might have informed the decision of those sons and daughters to join the FSLN, it was only in the city where they could join independently of their parents, because it was much easier for them to act without their parents' permission or even knowledge in the city than back home.[5] Also, in the cities of the north of Nicaragua, the Sandinistas' clandestine networks (especially their student networks) were better developed than in rural Quilalí (70).

Horton found that the ranchers and the rural poor who supported the FSLN did so for somewhat different reasons. "[U]nlike the finqueros, who saw formal democracy as their principle goal, several poor peasants interviewed who collaborated and fought with the FSLN guerrillas report that they were attracted to FSLN class-related discourse. . . . 'They said that we were going to own things in common—the land, houses, animals; that we were going to have equality, which they always called communism'" (1998, 72–73). Despite the differences in their motivations, for Horton the critical point is that they mobilized together. In other words, in rural Quilalí there was no mass movement of poor people challenging their patrons by joining the FSLN; those who joined were mainly those who were encouraged to join by their patrons. "[O]n the eve of the revolution only a minority of Quilalí residents, perhaps one hundred or less, actively supported the FSLN guerrillas and the great majority of Quilalí peasants remained largely quiescent, as they had in earlier years" (1998, 74).

This is hardly surprising. The FSLN's promises of a new world of equality were of a utopian nature. Although such promises might have been

---

5. This would be true even in the cases of children whose parents lived with them in the city, for cities generally allow for more anonymity than rural areas, with less watchful neighbors. While rural young people sometimes found it difficult to join the FSLN if their parents disapproved, city youth could easily join with or without approval.

appealing, they were hardly reliable. In contrast, the minimal security offered by reinforcing the bonds of clientelism probably seemed to be a far more realistic survival strategy for most people. Moreover, the violence in the cities, especially the cities of the north, that pushed many into open rebellion against Somoza barely touched the lives of most who lived in the rural areas that surrounded those cities. "In the final days of the Somoza regime, the barricades rose again in Estelí and many of Nicaragua's major cities and finally Managua itself. Quilalí peasants heard distant bombing, saw the military planes and helicopters pass overhead, and listened to news of the combat on their radios" (Horton 1998, 75). Horton estimated that about twenty-five residents of Quilalí were killed during the insurrection, including both those on the side of the National Guard and those on the side of the FSLN. In contrast, in the nearby city of Estelí, thousands died during a series of direct confrontations with Somoza's National Guard. Citing a CEPAL study, Horton notes that "[f]or Nicaragua as a whole, it is estimated that at least 35,000 people were killed in the insurrection, largely in urban areas" (1998, 76).

Mountain dwellers in Nicaragua's rural north generally experienced the Somoza government as having left them alone, and so many of them resented the new Sandinista government's efforts to intervene in their daily lives. The difference between the Somoza and Sandinista eras, from their perspective, helps explain why a later guerrilla group—the contras—were very successful in mobilizing support in the rural areas of the north, though not in cities like Estelí.[6]

Horton's findings suggest that the structuralists may be right to look to the transformation of the rural class structure as a factor that set the stage for the successful guerrilla uprising. But since their data on the guerrillas was generally gathered at a distance—from journalistic accounts, information gleaned from the work of other scholars, or quantitative analysis of class structure—it was hard for them to know which individuals, within a rebellious region, were the ones who actually joined the guerrillas. In fact, Wickham-Crowley's theory that many of the FSLN supporters were displaced peasants who made a living as squatters, and who were motivated by fear of land insecurity, was apparently not true in Quilalí. "While Quilalí, like other agricultural frontier zones, had a large number of squatters, none of the peasants interviewed for this study identified as-

---

6. Most of Horton's book is devoted to explaining why a majority of the poor of Quilalí supported the contras.

saults on land security as a prerevolutionary source of conflict" (Horton 1998, 330 n. 5).

Vilas and Horton have shown through data gathered from those who lived through the guerrilla struggle that the majority of the guerrillas were not peasants who became semiproletarian as they were displaced by agroexports. Instead, many (perhaps most) of them were their children: 19 percent of those who died had parents who worked the land and 39 percent of those who died had parents who worked for themselves, probably a reference to work in the informal sector, which could have been rural or urban (Vilas 1986, 115). Scholars who have identified the displacement of peasants and migration to the cities as key mechanisms in the rise of the FSLN were right to do so, but that does not mean that it makes sense to call the Sandinista revolution a peasant rebellion. Instead, it was very much a rebellion of young people caught between worlds, many of these young people being students, of both rural and urban origin.

The findings of Horton and Vilas, along with my own interview data, show that to claim that people who joined Sandinistas were either students from elite social backgrounds or recently displaced peasants is to flatten reality. Viewed from close up, individual Sandinistas typically had far more complicated personal histories than that, as had their parents. It is worth contesting the notion that Sandinistas were either students or of peasant background (but never both) for a number of reasons, not least of which is that such notions fit neatly into stereotypes of peasants as stupid people.

Academic theories based on the assumption that students and people of peasant origin were categories that never overlapped may have evolved through the use of well-documented information about the top leadership of revolutionary organizations to fill out much thinner data on mid- and low-prestige guerrillas. The top leadership of the FSLN was quite clearly drawn from an unusually well-educated sector of the Nicaraguan population (people who had attended some college or at least some high school, including a number of university professors). Data on the personal histories of the top leaders indicate that most were privileged in class as well as in education, having middle- or upper-class parents. But it would be wrong to generalize from this information to conclude that the vast majority of high school and college students in Nicaragua were from affluent backgrounds.

In my study, most of the Nicaraguan women who had participated in the guerrilla movement or the revolutionary coalition were from poor families, while a large minority were from middle-class families.[7] Despite their modest backgrounds, many of them were high school or college students when they joined the FSLN, having managed to obtain scholarship money or having been lucky enough to have families that chose to devote their limited resources to their education (though often not those of their siblings) in light of their good grades or some other consideration. So the students who made up the explosively expanding university enrollments in the years that preceded the rise of the FSLN were hardly all from the middle or upper classes (see Wickham-Crowley 1992, 220 for an excellent chart documenting rising university enrollments).

EL SALVADOR

Many have argued that the Nicaraguan FSLN was a broad cross-class coalition, and that the very breadth of the coalition played a significant role in its eventual success in overthrowing the Somoza dictatorship. In contrast, these same scholars often argue, the class base of the FMLN was narrower, a fact that may have contributed to the FMLN's eventual inability to overthrow the military government of El Salvador (see the introduction to Chapter 2 for a list of comparative studies).

But how narrow was the class base of the FMLN? Was the main difference that the upper class split its allegiances in Nicaragua (some supporting Somoza to the end, while others cast their lots with the Sandinistas) while the upper class of El Salvador remained largely unified against the FMLN? Or was the FMLN more like the stereotypical peasant rebellion, in which only the top leaders—the guerrilla commanders—were college educated and from affluent, often urban, backgrounds?

A number of scholars who have considered the sorts of people who made up the FMLN have concluded that they were more like the stereotypical peasant rebels than were the Sandinistas. For instance, Hugh Byrne finds that the top leaders were largely of lower-middle-class or middle-class origin and that most of them became active while in high school or college, with a few leaders coming from peasant backgrounds. He argues that the base of the FMLN was overwhelmingly of peasant origin, noting that "[o]ne senior FMLN commander estimated that more

---

7. In the cases where I have data on their class backgrounds, fifteen were from poor backgrounds (with parents including peasants, bread bakers, construction workers, maids, and market vendors), and eleven were from middle- or upper-class backgrounds (with parents including teachers, landowners, housewives, owner of a public transportation company, and a senator).

than 95 percent of the guerrilla combatants were from the peasantry by the end of the war, as were four out of every five intermediate military commanders" (1996, 35). Byrne comes to his conclusions on the basis of "interviews and discussions with about half of the top leadership of the parties that made up the FMLN during the civil war and secondary information about many others" (1996, 50 n. 40). Like other scholars, Cynthia McClintock argues that the top leaders of the FMLN were mainly of middle-class background and that most of them studied for some period at the University of El Salvador (the UES). She provides nice biographical sketches of those top leaders, but as is the case with most of the other scholars who addressed this question, she has much better information on the top leaders than on either the midlevel leaders or the rank and file, citing her own interviews with top leaders and one midlevel leader, supplemented with journalistic and academic accounts of the FMLN, all of which tend to privilege top leaders over midlevel leaders or rank-and-file guerrillas (1998, 251–60).

In comparison with the top leaders, midlevel leaders seemed to be drawn from a wider variety of backgrounds; this group included teachers, students, peasants, workers, priests, and former members of the army and the National Guard. McClintock's data on what she calls the rank and file are far sketchier (based largely on journalistic accounts) and suggest that between 80 and 95 percent of the rank and file were peasants, many of whom had participated in church groups before joining (1998, 267–71).[8]

Both Paige (1997, 30–31, 379 n. 49) and Wickham-Crowley (1992, 236, 243–44) find that the mid- and low-prestige members of the FMLN were not peasants in the strict sense of the word (that is, very small landowners), but rather seemed to be mainly rural dwellers who made a good part of their living off land that was not their own: as wageworkers during harvest season. That is, they were largely rural semiproletarians. Additionally, Paige notes the important urban component to the Salvadoran revolutionary coalition, including members of the urban informal sector and activists in communist-affiliated labor unions.

Paige and Wickham-Crowley's findings on the rural component of the revolutionary coalition are not necessarily inconsistent with those of

8. McClintock's categories did not neatly coincide with mine. Her top guerrilla leaders and my high-prestige activists were basically the same people, and her midlevel activists would include my midprestige activists, but her rank and file would include some of my midprestige activists (since I consider all female combatants to be midprestige, given the position of women in nontraditional roles) along with my low-prestige activists. My categories are explained in more detail on pages 13–15.

Byrne and McClintock, for it is quite likely that the word *peasant* was used by journalists and top-level leaders to encompass all poor rural dwellers. Nonetheless, if that is the case, it points to the need for more careful studies, ideally based on interviews with rank-and-file revolutionaries themselves, to avoid such overly broad generalizations. As a general rule, we should be suspicious of data in which one group of people (high-prestige revolutionaries) present themselves, or are portrayed by others, as having complicated backgrounds—some were lower middle class, some were middle class, a few were of peasant origin, some went to high school, some went to college—while another group of people (mid- and low-prestige revolutionaries) are portrayed as having very simple backgrounds: they were peasants.

No doubt those same rural dwellers who supported the FMLN would have told more complicated stories of their own lives. For instance, they almost surely had political as well as class histories, probably having participated in other organizations—what I called preexisting networks—as did the former revolutionaries I interviewed in El Salvador. And some of them (perhaps most of them) must have been socialized into family traditions of resistance, as were many of the women I interviewed. Those political histories are touched upon by McClintock and Paige, when they mentioned church groups and labor unions, but with few details.

Political factors are the focus of Yvon Grenier's study. As have other scholars, he notes that nearly all the top leaders of the FMLN came out of the universities of El Salvador, especially from the UES. But unlike many other scholars, he observes that the FMLN could not be neatly divided into two groups: peasant followers and college-educated urban leaders. Rather than claiming that the rank and file were nearly entirely peasants, Grenier points to the urban university ties of many who were not top leaders. "The overwhelming majority of the FMLN leaders, probably most of its intermediary cadres and a good many of the rank-and-file had previously been rectors, professors or students at the UES (and to a lesser extent, at the UCA or the Jesuit college Externado San José)" (1999, 106). Unfortunately it is hard to evaluate that claim, since he does not explain what evidence he used to arrive at his estimate, nor does he specify what he means by "a good many of the rank-and-file."

Lynn Stephen portrays the rank and file of the Salvadoran guerrillas as a diverse group, a coalition that included urban as well as rural dwellers, along with teachers, students, church members, labor union activists, the urban poor, peasants, men, and women (1997, 62–65). Tommie Sue Montgomery also argues that the FMLN's supporters were not all peasants. Although the areas where the FMLN controlled territory were mainly rural and mountainous, their ability to control those areas was based in large part on a network of supporters in the cities.

The "people" also lived in the cities and kept the FMLN supplied with basic necessities. Charles Clements observed in Guzapa that "The vast majority of their supplies flowed to the rebels not across the border but out from San Vicente, San Miguel, San Salvador, and other cities. They relied on an impressive underground network of supporters who risked their very lives for the cause." Roberto Roca, a member of the FMLN General Command, said that "we could not establish hospitals in the war fronts if there were not an enormous popular network in the cities who buy one ampule of penicillin, sterilized water in tiny amounts—which in the course of two or three weeks allows us to stock a field hospital." (Montgomery 1995, 116, also 101–26)

Given that the FMLN was unsuccessful in its attempts to foster urban insurrections, while urban insurrections played an important role in the Nicaraguan guerrilla war, it is likely that the FMLN had a smaller urban network than did the FSLN. But it is also likely that the urban element of the FMLN coalition has been underestimated by scholars.

Not only did urban guerrillas have to lie much lower than guerrillas in rural camps (thus escaping the notice of journalists), but also women who were part of urban commando squads were less likely to formally demobilize under United Nations auspices (despite the material benefits that came with demobilization) than were women who played other roles within the FMLN. Since the FMLN never admitted to the existence of the urban commandos, women could not demobilize as such. Those urban commandos who did demobilize did so as though they had participated in the political structures, according to an excellent study by Norma Vázquez, Cristina Ibáñez, and Clara Murguialday, based on lengthy interviews with sixty women of the FMLN.[9] Of the women they interviewed, 47.5 percent never formally demobilized; of these, 45 percent had worked on the war front, and 55 percent had been part of the urban commandos (1996, 217).

The women who were interviewed by Vázquez and her colleagues lived in all the regions of the country in which the conflict was fought and

9. Vázquez and her colleagues analyzed a wide variety of topics, including motivations for joining the guerrilla coalition, sexuality within the FMLN, experiences of motherhood, religion, differences in the experiences of women of urban and rural origin, the nature of the demobilization process, and the experiences of those women in the postwar period.

included members of each of the five organizations that made up the FMLN. They were categorized depending on their ages and the roles they played during the war, categories that themselves tell much about the internal diversity within the FMLN:

Group 1: Women of urban origin who were based in guerrilla camps on the warfront and who were less than 20 years old when they were incorporated. . . . Group 2: Women of rural origin who were based in guerrilla camps and who were less than 20 years old when they were incorporated. . . . Group 3: Women of urban origin who were based in guerrilla camps and who were older than 20 years old when they were incorporated. . . . Group 4: Women of urban origin who participated in the urban commandos in San Salvador. . . . Group 5: Women who collaborated with the FMLN in the zones that the guerrillas controlled. (Vázquez, Ibáñez, and Murguialday 1996, 25)

Women of urban origin who joined the FMLN sometimes were assigned work in the rural guerrilla camps and sometimes given the job of urban commando. In contrast, all the women of rural origin were assigned to work in the rural areas. That rural women were not sent to the cities makes sense from a strategic perspective. First, there was plenty of work to do in the countryside (given that all the camps were all located there); second, effective commandos had to blend into their surroundings and a newcomer to the city would have a hard time blending in.

From the perspective of the literature on the social origins of the guerrillas, the finding that the FMLN leaders sent some urban women to the countryside, whereas they left all rural women there, is important, for it suggests that the role of urban women (and men) has been underestimated. Most observers have assumed that the vast majority of camp members were peasants (though some were of urban origin), while completely failing to count urban commandos, all of whom were of urban origin.

The women who served in the commando forces estimated that one in four urban commandos was a woman. Apparently, many of the urban women were originally mobilized through student networks. One out of every four of the women of urban origin specified that she was motivated to participate while studying at the UES, often almost immediately upon entering the university, at the average age of eighteen (Vázquez, Ibáñez, and Murguialday 1996, 105, 130), a finding that is consistent with Grenier's (1999) argument regarding the role of the UES in the beginning of the insurrection. Given that many other sources have identified other universities and high schools as places where people were mobilized into the FMLN, the actual percentage of women who were mobilized through a student network of some sort would be higher than the 25 percent identified by Vázquez and her colleagues. In my study, 40 percent of the women who were active in the revolutionary coalition (fourteen out of thirty-five) said that they had previously participated in student protest activities before they became revolutionary activists.

The finding by Vázquez and her colleagues that the data from the demobilization of the FMLN underestimated the number of urban participants in the FMLN because members of urban commando squads could not officially demobilize, suggests caution in our reading of that data. Nonetheless, the demobilization data is probably more reliable than sources such as journalistic accounts or claims by high-prestige revolutionaries about mid- or low-prestige revolutionaries. My point is not to dismiss any of these sources, but instead to recommend that we draw on a multiplicity of sources, including demobilization data, emphasizing interviews with mid- and low-prestige revolutionaries whenever possible.

An excellent study that provides some data on the social background of the women of the FMLN was conducted by the January 16th Foundation (Fundación 16 de Enero), based on a random sample of eleven hundred women who had been formally demobilized by the United Nations.[10] As one would expect from a multitude of other studies of guerrillas, the majority of the women in this study were quite young.[11] Most of those women lived in rural areas at the time of the study (Fundación 16 de Enero 1993, 8), typically in the municipalities where support for one of the five parties of the FMLN had been strong.[12] That data suggest that the FMLN might been composed mainly of peasants. At the very least (assuming that men were at least as likely to be from the countryside as women), the data seem to confirm that the FMLN had a

10. Of the women selected, 97.5 percent were surveyed, giving the study a level of confidence of 95 percent and a margin of error of 1.1 percent (Fundación 16 de Enero 1993, 2–3, 5).

11. Of those women, 66.3 percent were younger than thirty years old, 86.4 percent were between the ages of ten and forty, and only 4.5 percent were between the ages of fifty and sixty-four, with another 1.1 percent over the age of sixty-five (Fundación 16 de Enero 1993, 6). Their youth is particularly striking when one considers that this study was conducted in the year following the end of the war.

12. The following is a breakdown of the municipalities or regions in which the former guerrillas resided at the time of the study: San Salvador, 20.4 percent; Morazán, 18.4 percent; Usulután, 16.7 percent; Cuscatlán, 12.1 percent; Cabañas, 11.1 percent; Chalatenango, 8.3 percent; San Vicente, 5.7 percent; San Miguel, 4.1 percent; La Libertad, 2.1 percent; La Unión, .4 percent; other, .7 percent (Fundación 16 de Enero 1993, 5). The women were more likely to live in the rural parts of those municipalities than in the regional capitals, with the exception of those who lived in the municipality of San Salvador, who typically lived in the city (1993, 12).

stronger base in the countryside (and a proportionately weaker one in the city) than did the FSLN of Nicaragua.

But were those women peasants? Most did not identify themselves as such. When asked what they had done before joining the FMLN, only 7.5 percent said they had "worked the land," and 56.5 percent said they had "worked in the house" (Fundación 16 de Enero 1993, 56). Housework might have involved unpaid support work for a peasant husband, work that could reasonably be called peasant labor, though there is no way to know what the other people in their household did for a living, or even if they were rural or city dwellers. Another complication is that working in the house does not necessarily indicate that the respondent was a full-time housewife, for that answer might refer to informal-sector labor performed at home, such as washing the clothing of others, selling goods out of her living room, or producing food for sale outside the home.

Fairly small percentages of women identified the other job categories, with the exception of the category of student.[13] Before joining the FMLN, 6.8 percent had worked and studied, while 18.7 percent only studied. Combining these categories, one finds that 25.5 percent of the respondents were students when they decided to join the FMLN (1993, 56). This fact suggests that we would do well to revise our stereotypes of the FMLN as a guerrilla army made up largely of illiterate peasants.

Also, if more than a quarter of women were students upon joining the FMLN, then student organizations probably played an important role in mobilizing some of the women who became midprestige and possibly low-prestige members of the revolutionary coalition, as in fact I found through my interviews with former revolutionary activists, including some from poor rural backgrounds.

A comparison of data from the studies conducted by Carlos Vilas and the January 16th Foundation, gives the impression that slightly more than a quarter of the members of both the Nicaraguan FSLN and the Salvadoran FMLN were students when they joined the guerrillas. This finding is a tentative one, though, since that conclusion is based on studies with significant differences. Vilas found that 29 percent had been students, based on a sample of men and women who were killed in the guerrilla struggle, while the January 16th Foundation found that 25.5 percent had been students, on the basis of a sample of women who lived to see

---

13. Of these women, 1.2 percent had worked in a factory, 2.2 percent had worked as a maid *(empleada)*, .7 percent worked in an office, 1.2 percent worked as a professional, and .6 percent did not respond (Fundación 16 de Enero 1993, 56).

the end of the guerrilla war. Unfortunately, perfectly comparable samples may not be attainable. Since the FSLN won the guerrilla war, it had no need to demobilize its surviving members, and it only collected data on those who had died so it could pay pensions. In contrast, because the FMLN did not win the war and had no way to pay pensions to survivors, it did not collect detailed data on those who had died.

COMPARING MALE AND FEMALE GUERRILLAS

All these studies are helpful in locating my particular study in the context of what we know about the FSLN and FMLN as a whole; however, there is a limit to their usefulness, except for those very few studies that were specifically focused on female guerrillas. For it is quite likely that men and women did not come from identical backgrounds, and most studies combined data on men and women without breaking these data down by sex. Given that joining the guerrilla coalitions was a more radical step for women than for men, as action that was consistent with men's traditional gender roles but inconsistent with women's, it is reasonable to assume that only particular sorts of women were available for mobilization, whereas many more men would be available. In the same family, girls were more likely to be carefully watched than were their brothers, making it easier for boys to become guerrillas (and in fact the majority in the revolutionary coalitions were always men).

Similarly, men with children were far more likely than women with children to leave to join the guerrillas. Of course some women did this too, but it was socially far more difficult for them to do so, and so it was less frequent. Greater constraints on women's mobility meant that a woman would be available to join the guerrillas only in particular circumstances. It helped greatly if she was young with few children or other responsibilities, and if she had the opportunity to organize freely (an opportunity that was enhanced by living in a city and belonging to preexisting networks). In contrast, young men with children or from rural areas could easily join the guerrillas without coming into conflict with their gender and family roles. If anything, joining the revolutionary coalition might enhance their masculinity.

Sonia Aguinada, a high-prestige leader of the ERP party of the FMLN, suggested that it was easier for women to join the FMLN during the 1970s, before the guerrillas united in the FMLN coalition, and before the struggle moved from the cities to the countryside, than in the 1980s. In the early years, "there was no distinction between men and women [although] the majority of the leaders in San Salvador were men. . . . As long as the struggle was concentrated in the cities women had more options. In the countryside women generally stayed at home and it was the men who went out to get organized" (interview, July 15, 1996). She estimated that in the early 1980s, 95 percent of the combatants in the countryside were men, but that over the course of the 1980s, things changed somewhat. "Whole families started to join and that gave women some opportunities to begin participating." By the end of the decade, perhaps 90 percent of the combatants in the countryside were men, in her estimation. At the same time, there was always a much larger percentage of women in the city. "I think that [in the city] a lot of leeway was given to the university women, in that case there certainly was space" (interview, July 15, 1996).

If Aguinada's estimate was at all accurate, then the social backgrounds of the men of the FMLN and of the women differed dramatically.[14] If it is true that only 10 percent of rural combatants were women, while nationally about 30 percent of all the FMLN's combatants were women (Vázquez, Ibáñez, and Murguialday 1996, 21), then female combatants were far more likely than male combatants to be of urban origin. That hypothesis is certainly consistent with my findings, in which women from the countryside often only began their political activism once they had moved to the relative freedom of a city.

Sonia Aguinada also touched on the issue of educational differences between male and female revolutionaries; she felt that there were many more organizational opportunities for women within the universities than in other settings. While I have never seen data that break down the educational backgrounds of the Central American revolutionaries by sex, studies of guerrillas in Cuba and Peru suggest that the average woman who joined the guerrillas had gone to school longer than had the average man who joined.

Since I addressed the question of the social origin of the Cuban guerrillas in some detail in the concluding chapter, I will not revisit that question here, except to note that while the 26th of July guerrillas successfully mobilized male combatants from the rural poor (especially rural proletarians), from the ranks of urban workers, and from the ranks of the urban

14. Admittedly, her estimate shares some of the problems of analyses of the class background of the rank and file made by other high-prestige guerrillas, although sex is much less debated than class (only in rare cases is there disagreement over whether a person is male or female, while categorizing a person by class is often controversial).

student movement, few or perhaps none, of the women who participated in combat in Cuba were members of the rural poor.[15] Instead, these women traced their roots to the student movement, and included among them were professionals who held law and engineering degrees. Put another way, it seems that among the guerrillas there were many men but few women from poor rural backgrounds, while there were men and women from middle- or upper-class urban backgrounds.

Data from Peru also suggest that the social backgrounds of the men and women who participated in guerrilla movements were not identical. Maruja Barrig reports findings from Denis Chávez de Paz's study of prisoners in Lima who had been convicted for crimes related to Shining Path (Sendero Luminoso). As in the case of other guerrilla movements, the convicted members of Shining Path were young (nearly 60 percent were eighteen to twenty-five years old) and the vast majority had migrated to Lima. "One out of every four was a college student, and there was a high presence of blue collar workers and small informal vendors. Of those condemned persons, 86 percent lived with an income below the minimum legal wage. Although their income and their occupation placed them in the popular sector, this contrasted with their high educational level: 36 percent had a college education" (Barrig 1998, 113). Many more of the women than the men fell into the most highly educated group: "57 percent of the women had a college degree against only 31 percent of the men. And of these women, 10 percent had a professional degree or had completed postgraduate studies, something only 4 percent of the men had done" (Barrig 1998, 113).

That the women who had been recruited by Sendero were far more likely to be college students when recruited than were their male counterparts, is not surprising in the light of the findings in this book. Given that girls lead more restricted lives than boys, and that joining a guerrilla organization violates traditional feminine roles while it is consistent with traditional masculine roles, it is logical that female guerrillas do not all come from the same social backgrounds as male guerrillas. Student organizations are one of the few spaces where girls, like boys, are fairly free to act without parental supervision. So it is not surprising that female guerrillas would be more likely than male guerrillas to trace their political roots to student movements.

15. In his comprehensive study, Timothy Wickham-Crowley noted that he never found "a single case of a female peasant joining as an arms-bearing guerrilla" (1992, 21), during what he called the guerrilla movements of the first wave, a group of movements that includes the Cuban guerrillas.

A final note from Peru speaks to the question of education and peasants. An unfortunate tendency in the literature on the Central American guerrillas is for writers to portray guerrillas as having been either students or of peasant background, but never both, a tendency that I have suggested we should reexamine. In the decades that preceded the formation of the three guerrilla groups I have studied, along with Shining Path, there was a massive expansion of university enrollments across Latin America, including at universities—like the University of El Salvador, or the University of San Cristóbal de Huamanga in Peru—that would play critical roles in the formation of the FMLN of El Salvador, and the Shining Path of Peru (Wickham-Crowley 1992, 220).

Those students were not all drawn from the elite, but instead included large numbers of individuals from peasant backgrounds and from poor urban families that themselves had often recently migrated from the countryside. As Barrig noted, the University of San Cristóbal de Huamanga "became the gateway through which the expectations of the young daughters and sons of peasants and small tradespeople and of their families were filtered" (1998, 112). Many of those students, raised in poverty, would find that as college students, they finally could act upon their grievances, for better or worse, through student networks and eventually through the guerrilla movements.

Bibliography

Acevedo, Angela Rosa, et al. 1996. *Los derechos de las mujeres en Nicaragua: Un análisis de género.* Managua: Imprimatur Artes Gráficas.

Acevedo García, Marina. 1995. "Margaritas: Una experiencia de frontera." In Diana Guillén, ed., *Chiapas: Una modernidad inconclusa,* 148–92. Mexico City: Instituto Mora.

Adam, Barry. 1993. "In Nicaragua: Homosexuality Without a Gay World." *Journal of Homosexuality* 24, nos. 3/4:171–81.

Afary, Janet. 1996. "Steering Between Scylla and Charybdis: Shifting Gender Roles in Twentieth-Century Iran." *NWSA Journal* 8, no. 1 (Spring): 28–49.

———. 1997. "The War Against Feminism in the Name of the Almighty: Making Sense of Gender and Muslim Fundamentalism." *New Left Review,* no. 224 (July/August): 89–110.

Afshar, Haleh. 1985. "Women, State, and Ideology in Iran." *Third World Quarterly* 7, no. 2 (April): 256–78.

Alfonso, Pablo. 1985. *Cuba, Castro y los Católicos (del humanismo revolucionario al marxismo totalitario).* Miami: Ediciones Hispamerican Books.

Alvarez, Sonia. 1990. *Engendering Democracy in Brazil: Women's Movements in Transition Politics.* Princeton: Princeton University Press.

———. 1998. "Latin American Feminisms 'Go Global': Trends of the 1990s and Challenges for the New Millennium." In Sonia Alvarez, Evelina Dagnino, and Arturo Escobar, eds., *Cultures of Politics, Politics of Cultures: Re-Visioning Latin American Social Movements,* 293–324. Boulder, Colo.: Westview Press.

Alvarez, Sonia, Evelina Dagnino, and Arturo Escobar, eds. 1998. *Cultures of Politics, Politics of Cultures: Re-Visioning Latin American Social Movements.* Boulder, Colo.: Westview Press.

AMES (Asociación de Mujeres Salvadoreñas). 1981. "Participación de la mujer latinoamericana en las organizaciones sociales y políticas: Reflexiones de las mujeres salvadoreñas." Paper presented at the conference "Primer Seminario Latinoamericano de Investigación Sobre la Mujer," San José, Costa Rica, November 8–14. Available from the Women's International Resource Exchange Service (WIRE), 2700 Broadway, New York, NY 10025.

AMNLAE (Asociación de Mujeres Nicaragüenses Luisa Amanda Espinoza).

1990. "Propuesta de AMNLAE a la Constitución." Reprinted in Clara Murguialday, *Nicaragua, revolución y feminismo (1977–89)*. Madrid: Editorial Revolución.

Anderson, Thomas P. 1971. *Matanza: El Salvador's Communist Revolt of 1932*. Lincoln: University of Nebraska Press.

ANIPA (Asamblea Nacional Indígena Plural por la Autonomía). N.d. *Proyecto de Iniciativa para la Creación de las Regiones Autónomas*. Booklet. N.p.

Arana, Mario. 1997. "General Economic Policy." In Thomas Walker, ed., *Nicaragua Without Illusions: Regime, Transition, and Structural Adjustment in the 1990s*, 81–96. Wilmington, Del.: Scholarly Resources.

Arjomand, Said Amir. 1986. "Iran's Islamic Revolution in Comparative Perspective." *World Politics* 38, no. 3 (April): 383–414.

Asamblea Nacional. 1992. "Ley no. 150: Ley de Reformas al Código Penal." (July 8). Unpublished booklet.

Asociación de Madres Demandantes por la Cuota Alimenticia, IMU, Dignas, and MAM. 1996. Paid advertisement. *La Prensa Gráfica*, June 27.

Aubrey, Andrés, and Angélica Inda. 1997. "Quienes son los 'paramilitares'?" *La Jornada*, December 23. Available: http://www.jornada.unam.mx/index.html

———. 1998. "Who Are the Paramilitaries in Chiapas?" *Report on the Americas* (NACLA [North American Congress on Latin America]) 31, no. 5 (March/April): 8–9.

Babb, Florence. 2001. *After the Revolution: Mapping Gender and Cultural Politics in Neoliberal Nicaragua*. Austin: University of Texas Press.

Barnes, William. 1998. "Incomplete Democracy in Central America: Polarization and Voter Turnout in Nicaragua and El Salvador." *Journal of Interamerican Studies and World Affairs* 40, no. 3 (Fall): 63–101.

Barrig, Maruja. 1998. "Female Leadership, Violence, and Citizenship in Peru." In Jane Jaquette and Sharon Wolchik, eds., *Women and Democracy: Latin America and Central and Eastern Europe*, 104–24. Baltimore: Johns Hopkins University Press.

Barrios Ruiz, Walda, and Leticia Pons Bonals. 1995. *Sexualidad y religión en los altos de Chiapas*. Tuxtla Gutiérrez: Universidad Autónoma de Chiapas.

Barton, Christopher P. 1988. "The Paradox of a Revolutionary Constitution: A Reading of the Nicaraguan Constitution." *Hastings International and Comparative Review* 12, no. 1 (Fall): 49–101.

Becarril, Andrea. 2000. "Fallido intento para desconocer el triunfo de Salazar." *La Jornada*, August 21.

Becerra, Ricardo, Pedro Salazar, and José Woldenburg. 1997. *La reforma electoral de 1996: Una descripción general*. Mexico City: Colección Popular, Fondo de Cultura Económica.

Belli, Gioconda. 1998. "En el escándulo NO está el pecado: Continuación de entrevista a Zoilamérica Narváez." *El Nuevo Diario*, September 22, C1–C2.

Bellinghausen, Hermann. 1997. "Buscarán ONG nuevas vías para la paz en Chiapas: Hace Hugo Trujillo, de Conpaz, un balance autocrítico de esa organización." *La Jornada*, November 26.

Bendaña, Alejandro. 1991. *Una trajedia campesina: Testimonios de la resistencia.* Managua: COMPANIC.

Bengelsdorf, Carollee. 1994. *The Problem of Democracy in Cuba: Between Vision and Reality.* New York: Oxford University Press.

Benjamin, Thomas. 1996. *A Rich Land, a Poor People: Politics and Society in Modern Chiapas.* Albuquerque: University of New Mexico Press.

Berkin, Carol R., and Clara M. Lovett, eds. 1980. *Women, War, and Revolution.* New York: Holmes and Meier.

Blachman, Morris, and Kenneth Sharpe. 1992. "The Transition to 'Electoral' and Democratic Politics in Central America: Assessing the Role of Political Parties." In Louis Goodman et al., *Political Parties and Democracy in Central America.* Boulder, Colo.: Westview Press.

Blandón, María Teresa, ed. 1994. *Memorias: VI encuentro feminista latinoamericano y del caribe, El Salvador 1993.* Managua: Imprenta UCA.

———. 2001. "The Coalición Nacional de Mujeres: An Alliance of Left-Wing Women, Right-Wing Women, and Radical Feminists in Nicaragua." In Victoria González and Karen Kampwirth, eds., *Radical Women in Latin America: Right and Left.* University Park: Penn State University Press.

Boff, Leonardo. 1985. *Church: Charism and Power, Liberation Theology and the Institutional Church.* New York: Crossroad.

Bolt, Mary. 1996. *Sencillamente diferentes: La autoestima de las mujeres lesbianas en los sectores urbanos de Nicaragua.* Managua: Centro Editorial de la Mujer (CEM).

Booth, John. 1985. *The End and the Beginning: The Nicaraguan Revolution.* Boulder, Colo.: Westview Press.

Booth, John, and Thomas W. Walker. 1989. *Understanding Central America.* Boulder, Colo.: Westview Press

Borge, Tomás. 1984. *Carlos, the Dawn is No Longer Beyond Our Reach.* Vancouver: New Star Books.

Bossert, Thomas John. 1985. "Health Policy: The Dilemma of Success." In Thomas Walker, ed., *Nicaragua: The First Five Years.* New York: Praeger.

Brandt, Deborah. 1985. "Popular Education." In Thomas Walker, ed., *Nicaragua: The First Five Years.* New York: Praeger.

Braslavsky, Cecilia. 1992. "Educational Legitimation of Women's Economic Subordination in Brazil." In Nelly Stomquist, ed., *Women and Education in Latin America: Knowledge, Power, and Change.* Boulder, Colo.: Lynne Rienner.

Brysk, Alison. 2000. *From Tribal Village to Global Village: Indian Rights and International Relations in Latin America.* Stanford: Stanford University Press.

Buckley, Mary. 1989. "The 'Woman Question' in the Contemporary Soviet Union." In Sonia Kruks, Rayna Rapp, and Marilyn B. Young, eds., *Promissory Notes: Women in the Transition to Socialism,* 251–81. New York: Monthly Review Press.

Bunster-Burotto, Ximena. 1986. "Surviving Beyond Fear: Women and Torture in Latin America." In June Nash and Helen Safa, eds., *Women and Change in Latin America,* 297–325. South Hadley, Mass.: Bergin and Garvey Press.

Burbach, Roger. 1986. "The Conflict at Home and Abroad: U.S. Imperialism vs. the New Revolutionary Societies." In Richard Fagen, Carmen Diana Deere, and José Luis Carragio, eds., *Transition and Development: Problems of Third World Socialism.* New York: Monthly Review Press.

Burdick, John. 1992. "Rethinking the Study of Social Movements: The Case of Christian Base Communities in Urban Brazil." In Arturo Escobar and Sonia Alvarez, eds., *The Making of Social Movements in Latin America: Identity, Strategy, and Democracy,* 171–84. Boulder, Colo.: Westview Press.

Burguete Cal y Mayor, Aracely. 1999. "Empoderamiento indígena tendencias autonómicas en la región altos de Chiapas." In Aracely Burguete Cal y Mayor, ed., *México: Experiencias de autonomía indígena.* Copenhagen: Grupo Internacional de Trabajo Sobre Asuntos Indígenas (IWGIA).

———, ed. 1999. *México: Experiencias de autonomía indígena.* Copenhagen: Grupo Internacional de Trabajo Sobre Asuntos Indígenas (IWGIA).

Byrne, Hugh. 1996. *El Salvador's Civil War: A Study of Revolution.* Boulder, Colo.: Lynne Rienner.

Cabezas, Omar. 1985. *Fire from the Mountain: The Making of a Sandinista.* New York: Plume.

Castañeda, Jorge G. 1994. *Utopia Unarmed: The Latin American Left After the Cold War.* New York: Vintage.

———. 1995. *The Mexican Shock.* New York: New Press.

Castro, Daniel. 1999a. "The Iron Legions." In Daniel Castro, ed., *Revolution and Revolutionaries: Guerrilla Movements in Latin America,* 191–99. Wilmington, Del.: Scholarly Resources.

———, ed. 1999b. *Revolution and Revolutionaries: Guerrilla Movements in Latin America.* Wilmington, Del.: Scholarly Resources.

Castro, Yolanda, and Nellys Palomo. 1995. "Roban la tienda de artesanías de la organización J'Pas Joloviletik." Letter to the editor. *La Jornada,* December 1, 71.

Castro Apreza, Inés. 1999. "Quitarle el agua al pez: La guerra de baja intensidad en Chiapas (1994–1998)." In Neus Espreste, ed., *Chiapas 8,* 123–41. Mexico City: Ediciones Era.

CCRI (Comité Clandestino Revolucionario Indígena). 1995a. "Da a conocer propuestas del EZLN: Explica el EZLN por qué se requiere otra constitución y un gobierno de transición." In Mario B. Monroy and Carlos Zarco, eds., *Los hombres sin rostro II,* 107–10. Mexico City: Impretei. (Original dated July 27, 1994).

———. 1995b. "EZLN: 'No' a la propuesta de firmar los acuerdos." In Mario B. Monroy and Carlos Zarco, eds., *Los hombres sin rostro II,* 78–82. Mexico City: Impretei. (Original dated June 10, 1994).

———. 1996. "Llama el EZLN a crear un frente político nacional." *La Jornada,* January 2.

Ceceña, Ana Esther, José Zaragoza, and Equipo Chiapas. 1995. "Cronología del conflicto: 1 enero–1 diciembre 1994." In Neus Espresate, ed., *Chiapas 1,* 149–79. Mexico City: Ediciones Era.

CEMUJER. (Centro de Estudios de la Mujer "Norma Virginia Guirola de Her-

rera"). 1992. *Norma: Vida insurgente y feminista.* San Salvador: Talleres Gráficos UCA.

Centro de Investigación y Estudios Municipales (CIEM). 1989. "Encuestas al
sector comerciantes y al sector juvenil en la III región (resultados, referi-
dos a la población femenina)." Unpublished document, Managua(?).

Chamorro, Edgar. 1987. *Packaging the Contras: A Case of CIA Disinformation.* New
York: Institute for Media Analysis. Monograph Series, no. 2.

Chinchilla, Norma. 1990. "Revolutionary Popular Feminism in Nicaragua: Ar-
ticulating Class, Gender, and National Sovereignty." *Gender and Society* 4,
no. 3 (September): 370–97.

———. 1993. "Women's Movements in the Americas: Feminism's Second
Wave." *Report on the Americas* (NACLA [North American Congress on
Latin America]) 27, no. 1 (July/August): 17–23.

———. 1994. "Feminism, Revolution, and Democratic Transitions in
Nicaragua." In Jane Jaquette, ed., *The Women's Movement in Latin America.*
Boulder, Colo.: Westview Press.

———. 1997. "Nationalism, Feminism, and Revolution in Central America." In
Lois West, ed., *Feminist Nationalism,* 201–19. New York: Routledge.

CIACH (Centro de Información y Analisis de Chiapas). 1997a. "The Attempt on
the Life of Bishop Samuel Ruiz and the Effects of Polarization in Chiapas." CIACH Bulletin, no. 80:1–5.

———. 1997b. "The Covert War Waged by Gunmen, White Guards, and Paramilitary Forces." *La Opinion,* bulletin no. 79 (November 11): 1–6. Unpublished document, received by E-mail.

CIACH (Centro de Información y Analisis de Chiapas), CONPAZ (Coordinación
de Organismos No Gubermentales por la Paz), and SIPRO (Servicios In-
formativos Procesados). 1997. *Para entender Chiapas: Chiapas en cifras.*
Mexico City: Impretei.

Cochran, Augustus B., and Catherine V. Scott. 1992. "Class, State, and Popular
Organizations in Mozambique and Nicaragua." *Latin American Perspectives,*
issue 73, vol. 19, no. 2 (Spring): 105–24.

Cock, Jacklyn. 1994. "Women and the Military: Implications for Demilitarization in the 1990s in South Africa." *Gender and Society* 8, no. 2 (June):
152–69.

Cocopa/Ejecutivo. 1997. "Balance comparativo entre la propuesta de reformas
constitucionales presentada por la Cocopa y las observaciones del ejecutivo." In Neus Espresate, ed., *Chiapas 4,* 201–8. Mexico City: Ediciones
Era.

Codina, Teresa. 1992. "Lesbos en el Nuevo Mundo." *Pensamiento Propio* 10:2–4.

Colburn, Forrest. 1994. *The Vogue of Revolution in Poor Countries.* Princeton:
Princeton University Press.

Collier, George. 1994. *Basta! Land and the Zapatista Rebellion in Chiapas.* San Francisco: Food First Books.

———. 2000. "Zapatismo Resurgent: Land and Autonomy in Chiapas." *Report
on the Americas* (NACLA [North American Congress on Latin America])
33, no. 5 (March/April): 20–25, 47.

Collinson, Helen, ed. 1990. *Women and Revolution in Nicaragua*. New Jersey: Zed Books.

Comisaría de la Mujer y la Niñez. N.d. "Mujer: Niña: Niño: Vos tenés derecho al respeto." Unpublished document, Managua.

Comité Nacional Feminista. 1994. "Aquelarre." Unpublished manuscript, Managua, March.

Concha, Miguel. 1996. "El derecho a defender." *La Jornada*, December 14.

CONPAZ (Coordinación de Organismos No Gubermentales por la Paz). 1994. *La Guacamaya*, no. 1 (February).

Conroy, Michael. 1986. "U.S. Economic Policy as Economic Aggression." In Peter Rosset and John Vandermeer, eds., *Nicaragua: Unfinished Revolution, the New Nicaragua Reader*. New York: Grove Press.

Constitución Política. 1987. *La Gaceta* (Managua), January 9.

COOPIBO-Nicaragua. 1995. "Seminario, 'Fortalecimiento de la organizacion de mujeres rurales' memorias." Managua: Imprenta Universitaria (UCA).

Crahan, Margaret. 1987. "Religion and Revolution: Cuba and Nicaragua." Working Paper no. 174, Latin American Program, Wilson Center, Washington, D.C..

Creatividad Feminista. 2000. "Prohibe AID a las ONG hablar o promover el tema del aborto a cambio de financiamiento." (May 19). Available: http://www.creatividadfeminista.org/noticias/usaid.htm

Criquillón, Ana. N.d. (1988?) "Acabamos con el mito del sexo debil: La historia del Programa de Mujeres en la ATC." In Programa de Mujeres del Consejo Internacional de Educación de Adultos y la Asociación de Trabajadores del Campo, *La luna también tiene su propia luz: La lucha por el desarrollo de la conciencia de las mujeres entre las trabajadores rurales nicaragüenses*. Managua(?): n.p.

————. 1995. "The Nicaraguan Women's Movement: Feminist Reflections from Within." In Minor Sinclair, ed., *The New Politics of Survival: Grassroots Movements in Central America*, 209–37. New York: Monthly Review Press.

Cruz, Angelse. 1997. "Desnutrido en algún grado, 43% de niños indígenas: encuesta del INN." *La Jornada*, June 28, 41.

Cuadra, Scarlet. 1996. "Accusations from All Sides." *Barricada Internacional* 16, no. 402 (November): 16–17.

Cuadra, Scarlet, Guillermo Fernández, and Francis Lurys Ubeda.. 1992. "Seeking Unity in Diversity: Nicaraguan Women's Conference." *Barricada Internacional* 12, no. 347 (March): 22–31.

Cuéllar, Mireya, and Alonso Urrutia. 2000. "Fox, presidente electo con 43.43% de los votos: IFE, Labastida obtuvo 36.88 por ciento y Cárdenas 17." *La Jornada*, July 7.

Danner, Mark. 1993. "The Truth of El Mozote." *New Yorker*, December 6.

De Palma, Anthony. 1994. "Mexican State Gets 2 Chiefs; One Official, One Itinerant." *New York Times*, December 9.

Del Valle, Sonia. 1998. Las muertas vivas de Chiapas: Testimonio de una justicia pendiente." *Doble Jornada* (supplement to *La Jornada*), January 5.

Dickey, Christopher. 1985. *With the Contras: A Reporter in the Wilds of Nicaragua*. New York: Simon and Schuster.

Diebold de Cruz, Paula, and Mayra Pasos de Rappacioli. 1975. "Report on the Role of Women in the Economic Development of Nicaragua." Paper prepared for United States Agency for International Development (USAID), Office of Planning and Development, Managua.

DIGNAS (Mujeres por la Dignidad y la Vida). 1993. *Hacer política desde las mujeres: Una propuesta feminista para la participación política de las mujeres salvadoreñas.* San Salvador: Doble G Impresores.

———. 1996. *Montañas con recuerdos de mujer: Una mirada feminista a la participación de las mujeres en los conflictos armados en Centroamérica y Chiapas, memorias del Foro Regional, San Salvador, Diciembre 1995.* San Salvador: Algier's Impresores.

DIGNAS, MAM, IMU, MSM, and Asociación de Mujeres Demandantes de la Cuota Alimenticia. 1996. "Comunicado de Prensa." Unpublished document. San Salvador.

Dillon, Sam. 2000. "In Mexican Campaign, Money Still Buys Votes." *New York Times,* June 19, A1.

Dodson, Michael, and Laura Nuzzi O'Shaugnessy. 1985. "Religion and Politics." In Thomas Walker, ed., *Nicaragua: The First Five Years.* New York: Praeger.

Dunkerley, James. 1982. *The Long War: Dictatorship and Revolution in El Salvador.* London: Junction Books.

Eber, Christine. 1995. *Women and Alcohol in a Highland Maya Town: Water of Hope, Water of Sorrow.* Austin: University of Texas Press.

Eber, Christine, and Brenda Rosenbaum. 1993. "'That We May Serve Beneath Your Hands and Feet': Women Weavers in Highland Chiapas, Mexico." In June Nash, ed., *Crafts in the World Market: The Impact of Global Exchange on Middle-American Artesans.* Albany: State University of New York Press.

Engels, Frederick. 1975. *The Origin of the Family, Private Property, and the State.* New York: International Publishers.

Enloe, Cynthia. 1990. *Bananas, Beaches, and Bases: Making Feminist Sense of International Politics.* Berkeley and Los Angeles: University of California Press.

Enríquez, Laura J. 1991. *Harvesting Change: Labor and Agrarian Reform in Nicaragua, 1979–1990.* Chapel Hill: University of North Carolina Press.

———. 1997. *Agrarian Reform and Class Consciousness in Nicaragua.* Gainesville: University of Florida Press.

Escalante Gonzalbo, María de la Paloma. 1995. "Cambio y políticas modernizadoras en Chiapas." In Diana Guillén, ed., *Chiapas: una modernidad inconclusa,* 11–41. Mexico City: Instituto Mora.

Escobar Morales, César. N.d.. *Aprendemos a convivir: Civica, moral, y urbanidad, sexto grado.* Lima: Editorial Labrusa.

Everingham, Mark. 1996. *Revolution and the Multiclass Coalition in Nicaragua.* Pittsburgh: University of Pittsburgh Press.

Ewen, Alexander. 1994. "Mexico: The Crisis of Identity." *Akwe:kon A Journal of Indigenous Issues* 11, no. 2 (Summer): 28–40.

EZLN. 1995. "Llamado del EZLN al diálogo nacional." In Rosa Rojas, ed., *Chiapas ¿Y las mujeres que?* Vol. 2, 67–70. Mexico City: La Correa Feminista.

———. 1996. *Crónicas intergalácticas EZLN: Primer Encuentro Intercontinental por la Humanidad y Contra el Neoliberalismo.* Mexico City: Prensa Salinillas.

163

EZLN/Gobierno Federal. 1996. "Acuerdos sobre derechos y cultura indígena" (San Andrés Accords). In Neus Espresate, ed., *Chiapas 2*, 133–71. Mexico City: Ediciones Era.

Fagen, Richard R. 1969. *The Transformation of Political Culture in Cuba.* Stanford: Stanford University Press.

———. 1986. "The Politics of Transition." In Richard R. Fagen, Carmen Diana Deere, and José Luis Coraggio, eds., *Transition and Development: Problems of Third World Socialism.* New York: Monthly Review Press.

Fagen, Richard, Carmen Diana Deere, and José Luis Carragio, eds. 1986. *Transition and Development: Problems of Third World Socialism.* New York: Monthly Review Press.

Falquet, France. 1995. "La violencia cultural del sistema educativo: Las mujeres indígenas víctimas de la Escuela." Instituto de Asesoría Antropológica para la Región Maya, documento 044-V-95. San Cristóbal de las Casas.

Farhi, Farideh. 1990. *States and Urban-Based Revolutions: Iran and Nicaragua.* Urbana: University of Illinois Press.

Fauné, María Angélica. 1995. *Mujeres y familias centroamericanas: Principales problemas y tendencias.* Vol. 3. San José, Costa Rica: Litografía e Imprenta LIL.

FDR/FMLN. 1986. "Proposal for a Provisional Government." In M. Gettleman et al., eds., *El Salvador: Central America in the New Cold War.* New York: Grove Press.

Ferguson, Ann. 1993. "Women's Studies Conference, University of Havana, March 15–17, 1993." *NWSA Journal* 5. no. 3 (Fall): 343–48.

Fernández, Manuel. 1984. *Religión y revolución en Cuba (veinticinco años de lucha ateista).* Miami: Saeta Ediciones.

Fernández Ampié, Guillermo. 1990. "Muddy Waters: 'Final Provisional Results' Announced." *Barricada Internacional,* no. 402 (November): 7–8.

Fernández Poncela, Anna. 1996. "The Disruptions of Adjustment: Women in Nicaragua." *Latin American Perspectives,* issue 88, vol. 23, no. 1 (Winter): 49–66.

Figueroa, Martha. 1996. "Las mujeres en Chiapas y el conflicto armado." Unpublished manuscript, May 8, 1–7.

Fink, Marcy. 1992. "Women and Popular Education in Latin America." In Nelly Stromquist, ed., *Women and Education in Latin America: Knowledge, Power, and Change.* Boulder, Colo.: Lynne Rienner.

FIPI and CADDIAC. 1994. *Garantías individuales: Los derechos humanos en la constitución, campaña nacional de alfabetización en derechos humanos.* Mexico City: Talleres de Editorial Praxis.

Fitzsimmons, Tracy. 2000. "A Monstrous Regiment of Women? State, Regime, and Women's Political Organizing in Latin America." *Latin American Research Review* 35, no. 2:216–29.

Flood, Merielle. 1994. "Changing Gender Relations in Zinacantán, Mexico." *Research in Economic Anthropology* 15:145–73.

Flynn, Patricia. 1983. "Women Challenge the Myth." In Stanford Central American Network, ed., *Revolution in Central America.* Boulder, Colo.: Westview Press.

Foran, John. 1992. "A Theory of Third World Social Revolutions: Iran, Nicaragua, and El Salvador Compared." *Critical Sociology* 19, no. 2:3–27.

———. 1993. "Theories of Revolution Revisited: Toward a Fourth Generation?" *Sociological Theory* 11 (March): 1–17.

———. 1994. "The Iranian Revolution of 1977–79: A Challenge for Social Theory." In John Foran, ed., *A Century of Revolution: Social Movements in Iran*, 160–88. Minneapolis: University of Minnesota Press.

———. 1997a. "The Comparative-Historical Sociology of Third World Social Revolutions: Why a Few Succeed, Why Most Fail." In John Foran, ed., *Theorizing Revolutions*, 227–67. New York: Routledge.

———. 1997b. "Discourses and Social Forces: The Role of Culture and Cultural Studies in Understanding Revolutions." In John Foran, ed., *Theorizing Revolutions*, 203–26. New York: Routledge.

Foran, John, Linda Klouzal, and Jean-Pierre Rivera. 1997. "Who Makes Revolutions? Class, Gender, and Race in the Mexican, Cuban, and Nicaraguan Revolutions." *Research in Social Movements, Conflict, and Change* 20:1–60.

Forbis, Melissa. 2000. "Hacia la Autonomía: Zapatista Women and the Development of a New World." Unpublished manuscript, April.

Fox, Jonathan. 1994a. "The Challenge of Democracy: Rebellion as Catalyst." *Akwe:kon: A Journal of Indigenous Issues* 11, no. 2 (Summer): 13–19.

———. 1994b. "The Difficult Transition from Clientelism to Citizenship: Lessons from Mexico." *World Politics* 46 (January): 151–84.

Foweraker, Joe. 1993. *Popular Mobilization in Mexico: The Teachers' Movement, 1977–1987*. Cambridge: Cambridge University Press.

Freeman, Jo. 1975. *The Politics of Women's Liberation*. New York: David McKay.

Freyermuth Enciso, Graciela, and Mariana Fernández Guerrero. 1995. "Migration, Organization, and Identity: The Case of a Women's Group from San Cristóbal de las Casas." *Signs: Journal of Women in Culture and Society* 20, no. 4 (Summer): 970–95.

FSLN (Frente Sandinista de Liberación Nacional). 1986. "The Historic Program of the FSLN." In Peter Rosset and John Vandermeer, eds., *Nicaragua: Unfinished Revolution*. New York: Grove Press.

Fundación 16 de Enero. 1993. "Diagnostico de la situación actual de la mujer ex combatiente." Unpublished manuscript, San Salvador.

Funk, Nanette, and Magda Mueller, eds. 1993. *Gender Politics and Post-Communism: Reflections from Eastern Europe and the Former Soviet Union*. New York: Routledge.

Gallegos, Elena. 1997. "El gobierno está en favor del diálogo, dice Zedillo en Chiapas: La justica social es posible cuando trabajamos juntos, indica." *La Jornada*, June 30, 3.

Garaizábal, Cristina. 1996. "Presentación." In Norma Vázquez, Cristina Ibáñez, and Clara Murguialday. *Mujeres-montaña: Vivencias de guerrilleras y colaboradoras del FMLN*, 13–19. Madrid: Editorial horas y HORAS.

García, Ana Isabel, and Enrique Gomáriz. 1989. *Mujeres centroamericanas*. San José, Costa Rica: FLACSO.

García Oliveras, Julio A. 1979. *José Antonio Echeverría: La lucha estudiantil contra Batista*. Havana: Editora Política.

García Torres, Ana Esther, Esmeralda López Armenta, and Alma Nava Martínez. 1999. "Municipio Autónomo de Polhó." In Neus Espreste, ed., *Chiapas 8,* 211–15. Mexico City: Ediciones Era.

Garfield, Richard M., and Eugenio Taboada. 1986. "Health Services Reforms in Revolutionary Nicaragua." In Peter Rosset and John Vandermeer, eds., *Nicaragua: Unfinished Revolution, the New Nicaragua Reader.* New York: Grove Press.

Gargallo, Francesca. 1987. "La relación entre participación política y conciencia feminista en las militantes salvadoreñas." *Cuadernos Americanos Nueva Epoca,* año 1, vol. 2 (March–April): 58–76.

Garza Caligaris, Anna María. 1991. "Sobre mujeres indígenas y su historia." *Anuario CEI III.* San Cristóbal de las Casas: Universidad Autónoma de Chiapas, 31–42.

Garza Caligaris, Anna María, and Bárbara Cadenas Gordillo. 1994. "Derechos reproductivos en los altos de Chiapas." In Instituto de Estudios Indígenas, *Anuario IEI IV.* San Cristóbal de las Casas: Universidad Autónoma de Chiapas.

Garza Caligaris, Anna María, María Fernanda Paz Salinas, Juana María Ruiz Ortiz, and Angelino Calvo Sánchez. 1993. *Sk'op Antzetik: Una historia de mujeres in la selva de Chiapas.* Tuxtla Gutiérrez: Universidad Autónoma de Chiapas.

Gil Olmos, José. 1997. "Formal integración del FZLN; campaña nacional por la paz, primera tarea." *La Jornada,* September 17.

———. 1998. "El gobierno, sin voluntad para solucionar el caso chiapaneco." *La Jornada,* August 19.

Gil Olmos, José, and Rosa Rojas. 1996. "Irá Marcos a la clausura del foro en San Cristóbal." *La Jornada,* January 7.

Golden, Tim. 1994a. "Mexican Rebel Leader Sees No Quick Settlement." *New York Times,* February 20.

———. 1994b. "Mexico's 2 Faces: Is Political Change Top Priority?" *New York Times,* February 24.

———. 1994c. "Rebels Battle for Hearts of Mexicans." *New York Times,* February 26.

Goldman, Wendy Z. 1993. *Women, the State, and Revolution: Soviet Family Policy and Social Life, 1917–1936.* New York: Cambridge University Press.

Goldstone, Jack A., Ted Robert Gurr, and Farrokh Moshiri, eds. 1991. *Revolutions of the Late Twentieth Century.* Boulder, Colo.: Westview Press.

Gómez Treto, Raúl. 1988. *The Church and Socialism in Cuba.* Maryknoll, N.Y: Orbis Books.

González, Victoria. 1995. "La historia del feminismo en Nicaragua: 1837–1956." *La Boletina* (published by Puntos de Encuentro, Managua), no. 22:7–15.

———. 1996. "Mujeres somocistas: 'La pechuga' y el corazón de la dictadura nicaragüense (1936–1979)" Paper presented at the Tercer Congreso Centroamericano de Historia. Universidad de Costa Rica. San José, Costa Rica, July 15–18.

———. 2001. "Somocista Women, Right-Wing Politics, and Feminism in

Nicaragua, 1936–1979." In Victoria González and Karen Kampwirth, eds., *Radical Women in Latin America: Left and Right.* Penn State University Press.

González, Victoria, and Karen Kampwirth. 2001. Introduction to Victoria González and Karen Kampwirth, eds., *Radical Women in Latin America: Left and Right.* Penn State University Press.

González Hernández, Miguel, and Elvia Quintanar Quintanar. 1999. "La construcción de la región autónoma norte y el ejercicio del gobierno municipal." In Aracely Burguete Cal y Mayor, ed., *México: Experiencias de autonomía indígena,* 210–33. Copenhagen: Grupo Internacional de Trabajo Sobre Asuntos Indígenas (IWGIA).

González Suarez, Enrique, and Fabio González Suarez. 1986 "La mobilización popular frente a la crisis alimentaria." Unpublished document, INIES, Managua..

Goodwin, Jeff. 1997. "State-Centered Approaches to Revolution." In John Foran, ed., *Theorizing Revolution.* London: Routledge.

———. 2001. "Is the Age of Revolutions Over?" In Mark Katz, ed., *Revolution: International Dimensions,* 272–83. Washington, D.C.: Congressional Quarterly Press.

Goven, Joanna. 1993. "The Gendered Foundations of Hungarian Socialism: State, Society, and the Anti-Politics of Anti-Feminism, 1948–1990." Ph.D diss., University of California, Berkeley.

Greenberg-Lake. 1989. "Press release: Nicaragua national election survey." (December 13).

———. 1990. "Results of a poll conducted for Hemisphere Initiatives." (January).

Grenier, Yvon. 1999. *The Emergence of Insurgency in El Salvador: Ideology and Political Will.* Pittsburgh: University of Pittsburgh Press.

Grupo de Mujeres de San Cristóbal, Organización de Médicos Indígenas del Estado de Chiapas, Comisión de Mujeres de CONPAZ. 1994. "Memorias del encuentro-taller: 'Los Derechos de las Mujeres en Nuestras Costumbres y Tradiciones.'" May 19 and 20.

Guerra, Luz Grant. 1993. "The Salvadoran Women's Movement: An Autonomous Movement for Social and Structural Change." Master's thesis, University of Texas, Austin.

Guillén, Diana. 1995. "Del paraíso al infierno terrenal: La Iglesia como canal de participación política." In Diana Guillén, ed., *Chiapas: una modernidad inconclusa,* 42–71. Mexico City: Instituto Mora.

———. 1997. "Mediaciones y rupturas: El orden político en Chiapas." Paper presented at the conference of the Latin American Studies Association (LASA), Guadalajara, Mexico, April 17–19.

Gutiérrez, Margarita, and Nellys Palomo. 1999. "Autonomía con Mirada de Mujer." In Aracely Burguete Cal y Mayor, ed., *México: Experiencias de autonomía indígena,* 54–86. Copenhagen: Grupo Internacional de Trabajo Sobre Asuntos Indígenas (IWGIA).

Hartmann, Betsy. 1987. *Reproductive Rights and Wrongs: The Global Politics of Population Control and Contraceptive Choice.* New York: Harper and Row.

Harvey, Neil. 1994. *Rebellion in Chiapas: Rural Reforms, Campesino Radicalism, and the Limits to Salinismo.* Transformation of Rural Mexico Series, no. 5. San Diego: Center for U.S.-Mexican Studies.

———. 1998. *The Chiapas Rebellion: The Struggle for Land and Liberty.* Durham: Duke University Press.

Hauser, Ewa, Barbara Heyns, and Jane Mansbridge. 1993. "Feminism in the Interstices of Politics and Culture: Poland in Transition." In Nanette Funk and Magda Mueller, eds., *Gender Politics and Post-Communism: Reflections From Eastern Europe and the Former Soviet Union,* 257–73. New York: Routledge.

Hayes, Kathleen. 1996. *Women on the Threshold: Voices of Salvadoran Baptist Women.* Macon: Smyth and Helwys.

Hellman, Judith Adler. 1994a. *Mexican Lives.* New York: New Press.

———. 1994b. "Mexican Popular Movements: Clientelism and the Process of Democratization." *Latin American Perspectives* 21 (Spring): 124–41.

Hemisphere Initiatives/Washington Office on Latin America. 1997. *Democracy Weakened? A Report on the October 20, 1996, Nicaraguan Elections.* N.p.

Hernández Castillo, Rosalva Aída. 1994. "La 'fuerza extraña' es mujer." *Ojarasca* (Mexico City), no. 30 (March): 36–37.

———. 1995. "De la Comunidad a la Convención Estatal de Mujeres: Las campesinas chiapanecas y sus demandas de género." In Grupo Internacional de Trabajo Sobre Asuntos Indígenas, ed., *La explosión de comunidades en Chiapas.* Copenhagen, n.p.

———, ed. 1998. *La otra palabra: Mujeres y violencia en Chiapas, antes y después de Acteal.* Mexico City: CIESAS, COLEM, CIAM.

Hernández Cruz, Antonio. 1999. "Autonomía Tojolab'al: Genesis de un proceso." In Aracely Burguete Cal y Mayor, ed., *México: Experiencias de autonomía indígena,* 171–91. Copenhagen: Grupo Internacional de Trabajo Sobre Asuntos Indígenas (IWGIA).

Hérnandez López, Julio. 1998. "Astillero." *La Jornada,* January 8.

Hernández Navarro, Luis. 1997. "Entre la memoria y el olvido: Guerrillas, movimiento indígena y reformas legales en la hora del EZLN." In Neus Espreste, ed., *Chiapas 4,* 69–92. Mexico City: Ediciones Era.

———. 1998. "The Escalation of the War in Chiapas." *Report on the Americas* (NACLA [North American Congress on Latin America]) 31, no. 5 (March/April): 7–10.

Henríquez, Elio. 1996. "Amenazas de muerte contra 28 integrantes de la Conpaz." *La Jornada,* November 7.

Henríquez, Elio, and Rosa Rojas. 1995. "Asegura Aedpch que 40 de sus militantes han sido asesinados en este año y 860 luchadores sociales han sido encarcelados." *La Jornada,* November 14.

Heyck, Denis Lynn Daly. 1990. *Life Stories of the Nicaraguan Revolution.* New York: Routledge.

Hidalgo, Onécimo, and Mario B. Monroy. 1994. "El estado de Chiapas en cifras." In Mario B. Monroy, ed., *Pensar Chiapas, repensar Mexico: Reflexiones de las ONGs mexicanas sobre el conflicto.* Mexico: Impretei.

Hipsher, Patricia. 2001. "Right- and Left-Wing Women in Post-Revolutionary El

Salvador: Feminist Autonomy and Cross-Political Alliance Building for Gender Equality." In Victoria González and Karen Kampwirth, eds., *Radical Women in Latin America: Left and Right.* University Park: Penn State University Press.

Hiriart, Berta. 1995. "Las cubanas y sus milagros: Bajo el Lema 'Comunicar es Unir' Cubanas Organizan Encuentro Mujer y Comunicación." *Fempress* 164:9.

Hirshon, Sheryl. 1983. *And Also Teach Them to Read.* Westport, Conn.: Lawrence Hill.

Horton, Lynn. 1998. *Peasants in Arms: War and Peace in the Mountains of Nicaragua, 1979–1994.* Athens: Ohio University Press.

Huerta, Juan Ramón. 1998. *El silencio del patriarca: La linea es no hablar de esto.* Managua: Talleres Gráficos de Litografía El Renacimiento.

Hughes, Donna. 1998. "Khatami and the Status of Women in Iran." *Z Magazine*, October, 22–24.

Hunt, Lynn. 1992. *The Family Romance of the French Revolution.* Berkeley and Los Angeles: University of California Press.

Huntington, Samuel. 1968. *Political Order in Changing Societies.* New Haven: Yale University Press.

INEGRI (Instituto Nacional de Estadística Geografía e Informática). 1992. *Estados Unidos Mexicanos: Perfil sociodemografico, XI censo general de población y vivienda, 1990.* Aguascalientes, Ags.: INEGRI.

Instituto de Historia del Movimiento Comunista y de la Revolución Socialista de Cuba. 1985. *Historia del movimiento obrero cubano, 1865–1958* Havana: Editora Política.

Instituto Nacional de Estadísticas y Censos (INEC). 1989a. *Encuesta socio-demográfica nicaragüense, tabulaciones básicas.* Vol. 1: *Características generales de la población.* Managua: Talleres Gráficos de INEC.

———. 1989b. *Encuesta socio-demográfica nicaragüense, tabulaciones básicas.* Vol. 2: *Características demográficas de la población.* Managua: Talleres Gráficos de INEC.

———. 1989c. *Encuesta socio-demográfica nicaragüense, tabulaciones básicas.* Vol. 3: *Características económicos de la población de 10 años y más.* Managua: Talleres Gráficos de INEC.

———. 1989d. *Encuesta socio-demográfica nicaragüense, tabulaciones básicas.* Vol. 4: *Características de la vivienda y del hogar.* Managua: Talleres Gráficos de INEC.

———. 1990. *Nicaragua: Diez años en cifras.* Managua: Talleres Gráficos de INEC.

Instituto Nicaragüense de Seguridad Social. (INSS). 1981. "Analysis comparativo entre la ley anterior y la nueva ley organica de seguridad social." Unpublished document, Managua, May.

Instituto Nicaragüense de Seguridad Social y Bienestar (INSSBI), Dirección de Orientación y Protección Familiar. 1986. "Acciones en el area juridico social familiar en nicaragua." Unpublished document, Managua, November.

———. 1990. "Bienestar social en 10 años de revolución." *El Nuevo Diario*, February 16.

Jaimes Guerrero, M. A. 1995. "An Indigenous American Intifada." In Elaine Katzenberger, ed., *First World, Ha Ha Ha: The Zapatista Challenge*. San Francisco: City Lights Books.

Jaquette, Jane S. 1973. "Women in Revolutionary Movements in Latin America." *Journal of Marriage and the Family* 35 (May): 344–54.

———, ed., 1989. *The Women's Movement in Latin America: Feminism and the Transition to Democracy*. Boston: Unwin Hyman.

Jaquette, Jane S., and Sharon Wolchik, eds. 1998. *Women and Democracy: Latin America and Central and Eastern Europe*. Baltimore: Johns Hopkins University Press.

Jonas, Susanne, and Nancy Stein. 1989. "Elections and Transitions: The Guatemalan and Nicaraguan Cases." In John A. Booth and Mitchell A. Seligson, eds., *Elections and Democracy in Central America*. Chapel Hill: University of North Carolina Press.

———. 1990. "The Construction of Democracy in Nicaragua." In Susanne Jonas and Nancy Stein, eds., *Democracy in Latin America: Visions and Realities*. New York: Bergin and Garvey.

Junta de Gobierno. 1981. *Decretos-Leyes para gobierno de un pais*. Vol. 5, segundo semestre. Managua.N.p.

———. 1984. *Evaluación del decenio de las naciones unidas para la mujer: Igualdad, desarrollo y paz, 1976–1985*. Managua: Oficina de la Mujer.

Kaltefleiter, Caroline. 1995. "Revolution girl style now: trebld reflexivity and the Riot Grrrl Network." Ph.D. diss., Ohio University.

Kampwirth, Karen. 1993. "Democratizing the Nicaraguan Family: Struggles over the State, Households, and Civil Society." Ph.D diss., University of California, Berkeley.

———. 1994. "'The Movement Came to Fill an Emptiness:' Lesbian Feminists Talk About Life in Post-Sandinista Nicaragua." *Sojourner: The Women's Forum*, December, 16–17.

———. 1996a. "Confronting Adversity with Experience: The Emergence of Feminism in Nicaragua." *Social Politics* 3 (Summer/Fall).

———. 1996b. "Creating Space in Chiapas: An Analysis of the Strategies of the Zapatista Army and the Rebel Government in Transition." *Bulletin of Latin American Research* 15, no. 2 (May): 261–67.

———. 1996c. "Gender Inequality and the Zapatista Rebellion: Women's Organizing in Chiapas, Mexico." Paper presented at the annual conference of the American Political Science Association (APSA), San Francisco, August 29 to September 1.

———. 1996d. "The Mother of the Nicaraguans: Doña Violeta and the UNO's Gender Agenda." *Latin American Perspectives*, issue 88, vol. 23, no. 1 (Winter): 67–86.

———. 1997. "Social Policy." In Thomas Walker, ed., *Nicaragua Without Illusions: Regime Transition and Structural Adjustment in the 1990s*, 115–29. Wilmington, Del.: Scholarly Resources.

———. 1998a. "Feminism, Antifeminism, and Electoral Politics in Postwar Nicaragua and El Salvador." *Political Science Quarterly* 113, no. 2 (Summer): 259–79.

———. 1998b. "Legislating Personal Politics in Sandinista Nicaragua, 1979–1992." *Women's Studies International Forum* 21, no. 1:53–64.

———. 1998c. "Peace Talks, but No Peace." *Report on the Americas* (NACLA [North American Congress on Latin America]) 31, no. 5 (March/April): 15–19.

———. 2001. "Women in the Armed Struggles in Nicaragua: Sandinistas and Contras Compared." In Victoria González and Karen Kampwirth, eds., *Radical Women in Latin America: Left and Right*. University Park: Penn State University Press.

———. In progress. "Feminism and other Revolutionary Legacies: Politics in Nicaragua, El Salvador, and Chiapas."

Kanoussi, Dora, ed. 1998. *El Zapatismo y la política*. Mexico City: Plaza y Valdés Editores.

Keane, John. 1988. *Democracy and Civil Society*. London: Verso.

Keddie, Nikki, ed. 1995. *Debating Revolutions*. New York: New York University Press.

Kenez, Peter. 1986. *The Birth of the Propaganda State: Soviet Methods of Mass Mobilization, 1917–1929*. Cambridge: Cambridge University Press.

Kirk, Robin. 1997. *The Monkey's Paw: New Chronicles from Peru*. Amherst: University of Massachusetts Press.

Kruks, Sonia, Rayna Rapp, and Marilyn B. Young, eds. 1989. *Promissory Notes: Women in the Transition to Socialism*. New York: Monthly Review Press.

Kruks, Sonia, and Ben Wisner. 1989. "Ambiguous Transformations: Women, Politics, and Production in Mozambique." In Sonia Kruks, Rayna Rapp, and Marilyn B. Young, eds., *Promissory Notes: Women in the Transition to Socialism*, 148–71. New York: Monthly Review Press.

Laclau, Ernesto, and Chantal Mouffe. 1985. *Hegemony and Socialist Strategy: Towards a Radical Democratic Politics*. New York: Verso.

Lancaster, Roger N. 1988. *Thanks to God and the Revolution: Popular Religion and Class Consciousness in the New Nicaragua*. New York: Columbia University Press.

———. 1992. *Life Is Hard: Machismo, Danger, and the Intimacy of Power in Nicaragua*. Berkeley and Los Angeles: University of California Press.

Lapidus, Gail Warshofsky. 1978. *Women in Soviet Society: Equality, Development, and Social Change*. Berkeley and Los Angeles: University of California Press.

Larios, Roberto. 1991. "Gobierno cede a chantaje EU: Confirman proyecto para renunciar a indemnización de 17 mil millones, pretenden derogar ley que obliga a continuar juicio de La Haya." *Barricada*, April 5.

LASA (Latin American Studies Association). 1985. "Epilogue: The 1984 Elections." In Thomas W. Walker, ed., *Nicaragua: The First Five Years*. New York: Praeger.

Lázaro, Juan. 1990. "Women and Political Violence in Contemporary Peru." *Dialectical Anthropology* 15:233–47.

Legorreta Díaz, María del Carmen. 1998. *Religión, Política y Guerrilla en Las Cañadas de la Selva Lacandona*. Mexico City: Cal y Arena.

Leiner, Marvin. 1994. *Sexual Politics in Cuba: Machismo, Homosexuality, and AIDS*. Boulder, Colo.: Westview Press.

León, Irene. 1993. "VI Encuentro Feminista de América Latina y el Caribe: Una Utopia para todos." In María Teresa Blandóno, ed., *Memorias del VI Encuentro Feminista Latinoamericana y del Caribe.* Managua: Imprenta UCA.

Leyva Solano, Xochitl. 1998. "The New Zapatista Movement: Political Levels, Actors, and Political Discourse in Contemporary Mexico." In Valentina Napolitano and Xochitl Leyva Solano, eds., *Encuentros Antropológicos: Power, Identity, and Mobility in Mexican Society,* 35–55. London: Institute of Latin American Studies.

Leyva Solano, Xochitl, and Gabriel Ascencio Franco. 1996. *Lacandonia al filo del agua.* Mexico City: Centro de Investigaciones y Estudios Superiores en Antropología Social.

Lind, Amy. 1992. "Power, Gender, and Development." In Arturo Escobar and Sonia Alvarez, eds., *The Making of Social Movements in Latin America.* Boulder, Colo.: Westview Press.

Lloyd, Jane-Dale, and Laura Pérez Rosales, eds. 1995. *Paisajes rebeldes: Una larga noche de rebelión indígena.* Mexico City: Universidad Iberoamericano.

Lobao, Linda M. 1990. "Women in Revolutionary Movements: Changing Patterns of Latin American Revolutionary Struggle." *Dialectical Anthropology* 15:211–32.

Lomelí González, Arturo. 1999. "Pueblos indios y autonomías Zapatistas." In Aracely Burguete Cal y Mayor, ed., *México: Experiencias de autonomía indígena,* 234–60. Copenhagen: Grupo Internacional de Trabajo Sobre Asuntos Indígenas (IWGIA).

Long, Kristi. 1996. *We All Fought for Freedom: Women in Poland's Solidarity Movement.* Boulder, Colo.: Westview Press.

López, Juan J. 1999. "The Nontransition in Cuba: Problems and Prospects for Change." Paper presented at the annual meeting of the American Political Science Association (APSA), Atlanta, Ga., September 2–5.

López, Yolanda, Juan Balboa, and Elio Henríquez. 1995. "Bloque Aedpch las carreteras de accesso a Oaxaca, Tabasco y Veracruz; 20 municipios afectados." *La Jornada,* November 21.

Loveman, Brian, and Thomas M. Davies, Jr. 1997a. "Guerrilla Warfare, Revolutionary Theory, and Revolutionary Movements in Latin America." Introduction to Che Guevara, *Guerrilla Warfare.* Wilmington, Del.: Scholarly Resources Press.

———. 1997b. *The Politics of Antipolitics: The Military in Latin America.* Wilmington, Del.: Scholarly Resources Press.

Luciak, Ilja. 1995. "Women in the Transition: The Case of the Female FMLN Combatants in El Salvador." Paper presented at the conference of the Latin American Studies Association (LASA), Washington, D.C., September 28–30.

———. 1998. "Gender Equality and Electoral Politics on the Left: A Comparison of El Salvador and Nicaragua." *Journal of Interamerican Studies and World Affairs* 40 (Spring): 39–66.

———. 2000. "Gender Equality and Democratization in Central America: The

Case of the Revolutionary Left." Paper presented at the conference of the Latin American Studies Association (LASA) in Miami, Fla., March 16–18.

———. 2001. "Gender Equality, Democratization, and the Revolutionary Left in Central America: Guatemala in Comparative Perspective." In Victoria González and Karen Kampwirth, eds., *Radical Women in Latin America: Right and Left.* University Park: Penn State University Press.

Lumsden, Ian. 1996. *Machos, Maricones, and Gays: Cuba and Homosexuality.* Philadelphia: Temple University Press.

Lungo, Mario. 1989. *La lucha de las masas en El Salvador.* San Salvador: UCA Editores.

Lupiáñez Reinlein, José. 1985. *El movimiento estudiantil en Santiago de Cuba, 1952–53.* Havana: Editorial de Ciencias Sociales.

Lutjens, Sheryl. 1995. "Reading Between the Lines: Women, the State, and Rectification in Cuba." *Latin American Perspectives,* issue 85, vol. 22, no. 2 (Spring): 100–124.

———. 1997. "The Politics of Revolution in Latin America: Feminist Perspectives on Theory and Practice." Paper presented at the conference of the Latin American Studies Association (LASA), Guadalajara, Mexico, April 17–19.

Luzón, José Luis. 1987. *Economía, población, y territorio en Cuba (1899–1983).* Madrid: Ediciones Cultura Hispánica.

McAdam, Doug. 1982. *Political Process and the Development of Black Insurgency 1930–1970.* Chicago: University of Chicago Press.

McClintock, Cynthia. 1992. "Theories of Revolution and the Case of Peru." In David Scott Palmer, ed., *Shining Path of Peru.* New York: St. Martin's Press.

———. 1998. *Revolutionary Movements in Latin America: El Salvador's FMLN and Peru's Shining Path.* Washington, D.C.: United States Institute of Peace Press.

Macías, Anna. 1982. *Against All Odds: The Feminist Movement in Mexico to 1940.* Westport, Conn.: Greenwood Press.

Maloof, Judy. 1999. *Voices of Resistance: Testimonies of Cuban and Chilean Women.* Lexington: University of Kentucky Press.

Marcos. 1994. "The First Zapatista Uprising: An Extract of a Letter from Subcommander Marcos." *Akwe:kon: A Journal of Indigenous Issues* 11, no. 2 (Summer): 69.

———. 1995a. "Memo to the Asamblea Estatal Democrática del Pueblo Chiapaneco." *La Jornada,* May 20.

———. 1995b. *Shadows of Tender Fury: The Letters and Communiqués of Subcomandante Marcos and the Zapatista Army of National Liberation.* New York: Monthly Review Press.

———. 1995c. "To the Men and Women Who, in Different Languages and by Different Paths, Believe in a More Human Future and Struggle to Achieve It Today." Unpublished manuscript, March 17.

———. 1996a. "The Future Must Be Made by and for Women: Marcos." *Libertad* (National Commission for Democracy in Mexico), no. 2 (March).

————. 1996b. "Llama el EZLN a un encuentro intercontinental antiliberalismo." *La Jornada,* January 30.

————1997. "No desaparecerá por decreto la rebeldía indigena: Marcos al CNI." *La Jornada,* October 13.

Marel García, Gladys. 1996. *Memoria e identidad: Un estudio específico (1952–1958)* Havana: Editorial de Ciencias Sociales.

Mariscal, Angeles. 1997a. "Detenidos por la matanza declaran su filiación priísta; Otros se dijeron miembros del Partido Cardenista, indica la PGR; delinquen las personas, no las instituciones, señala Palacios Alcocer; rindió declaración el secretario de Gobierno, acusado de negligencia; rifles AK-47, entre las armas utilizadas." *La Jornada,* December 26.

————. 1997b. "En 3 años 11 mil 443 desplazados; en 1997, 500 muertes violentas." *La Jornada,* December 31.

Martinez-Alier, Verena. 1989. *Marriage, Class, and Colour in Nineteenth-Century Cuba: A Study of Racial Attitudes and Sexual Values in a Slave Society.* Ann Arbor: University of Michigan Press.

Mason, David S. 1992. *Revolution in East-Central Europe.* Boulder, Colo.: Westview Press.

Mason, T. David. 1992. "Women's Participation in Central American Revolutions." *Comparative Political Studies* 25, no. 1 (April): 63–89.

Massell, Gregory. 1974. *The Surrogate Proletariat: Moslem Women and Revolutionary Strategies in Soviet Central Asia, 1919–1929.* Princeton: Princeton University Press.

Maxfield, Sylvia, and Richard Stahler-Sholk. 1985. "External Constraints." In Thomas Walker, ed., *Nicaragua: The First Five Years.* New York: Praeger.

MED (Ministerio de Educación). 1984. *Cinco años de educación en la Revolución: 1979–1984.* Managua: MED.

————. 1988. "Evolución del financimiento educativo (1978–1988)." Unpublished document, Managua.

————. 1990a. *Lineamientos del Ministerio de Educación en el Nuevo Gobierno de Salvación Nacional.* Managua: MED.

————. 1990b. "Principales indicadores del sistema educativo, años 1979–1990." [Includes data for 1978]. Unpublished document, Managua.

Mendoza Ramírez, Martha Patricia. 1995. "La intervención política en la Selva Lacandona." In Diana Guillén, ed., *Chiapas: Una modernidad inconclusam,* 114–47. Mexico City: Instituto Mora.

Midlarsky, Manus, and Kenneth Roberts. 1985. "Class, State, and Revolution in Central America: Nicaragua and El Salvador Compared." *Journal of Conflict Resolution* 29, no. 2 (June): 163–93.

Miller, Francesca. 1991. *Latin American Women and the Search for Social Justice.* Hanover: University Press of New England.

MINSA (Ministerio de Salud). 1991. *Plan maestro de salud, 1991–1996.* Managua: MINSA.

————. 1993a. *Política nacional de salud.* Managua: Ediciones Internacionales.

————. 1993b. *Política nacional de salud: Sesión extraordinaria* Managua: n.p.

Mintz, Sidney. 1964. Foreword to Ramiro Guerra y Sánchez, *Sugar and Society in the Caribbean: An Economic History of Cuban Agriculture.* New Haven: Yale University Press.

Mintz, Steven, and Susan Kellogg. 1988. *Domestic Revolutions: A Social History of American Family Life.* New York: Free Press.

Moghadam, Valentine. 1994. "Islamic Populism, Class, and Gender in Postrevolutionary Iran." In John Foran, ed., *A Century of Revolution: Social Movements in Iran*, 189–222. Minneapolis: University of Minnesota Press.

———. 1997. "Gender and Revolutions." In John Foran, ed., *Theorizing Revolutions*, 137–67. London: Routledge.

———. 1999. "Revolution, Religion, and Gender Politics: Iran and Afghanistan Compared." *Journal of Women's History* 10, no. 4 (Winter): 172–95.

Moghissi, Haideh. 1996. *Populism and Feminism in Iran: Women's Struggle in a Male-Defined Revolutionary Movement.* New York: St. Martin's Press.

Molyneux, Maxine. 1984. "Women in Socialist Societies: Problems of Theory and Practice." In Kate Young, Carol Wolkowitz, and Roslyn McCullagh, eds., *Of Marriage and the Market: Women's Subordination Internationally and Its Lessons*, 55–90. London: Routledge & Kegan Paul.

———. 1986. "Mobilization Without Emancipation?" In Richard Fagen et al., eds., *Transition and Development: Problems of Third World Socialism.* New York: Monthly Review Press.

———. 1988. "The Politics of Abortion in Nicaragua: Revolutionary Pragmatism—or Feminism in the Realm of Necessity?" *Feminist Review* no. 29 (May): 114–32.

———. 2000. "Gender, State, and Institutional Change: The Federación de Mujeres Cubanas." In Elizabeth Dore and Maxine Molyneux, eds., *Hidden Histories of Gender and the State in Latin America*, 291–321. Durham: Duke University Press.

Montenegro, Sofía, ed. 1997. *Movimiento de mujeres en Centroamérica.* Managua: Programa Regional La Corriente.

Montgomery, Tommie Sue. 1983. "Liberation and Revolution: Christianity as a Subversive Activity in Central America." In Martin Diskin, ed., *Trouble in Our Backyard: Central America and the United States in the Eighties.* New York: Pantheon Books.

———. 1995. *Revolution in El Salvador: From Civil Strife to Civil Peace.* Boulder, Colo.: Westview Press.

Morales Carazo, Jaime. 1989. *La Contra.* Mexico City: Imprimatur Artes Gráficas.

Morales Henríquez, Viktor. 1980. *De Mrs. Hanna a La Dinorah: Principio y fin de la dictadura somocista, historia de medio siglo de corrupción.* Managua(?): n.p.

Morena, Elsa. 1997. *Mujeres y política en El Salvador.* San José, Costa Rica: FLACSO.

Morquecho, Gaspar. 1994. "Sin paz ni democracia." In Silvia Soriano Hernández, ed., *A propósito de la insurgencia en Chiapas*, 145–55. Mexico City: Asociación para el Desarrollo de la Investigación Científica y Humanística de Chiapas.

———. 1995a. "Comenzó la Cuarta Asamblea Nacional Indígena Plural: Se reúnen en San Cristóbal delegaciones de 12 estados y del extranjero." *La Jornada*, December 9, 16.

———. 1995b. "Encuentro en San Cristóbal de las Casas: Piden mujeres que su sentir se refleje en un proyecto de ley, 'Estamos aquí porque queremos ser escuchadas,' dijeron." *La Jornada,* December 8, 25.

———. 1995c. "Las mujeres en la Asamblea Democrática Estatal del Pueblo Chiapaneco." In Rosa Rojas, ed., *Chiapas ¿Y las mujeres que?* Mexico City: Ediciones La Correa Feminista.

Mujeres 94. 1993a. "Plataforma de las mujeres salvadoreñas." Unpublished document, August 31.

———. 1993b. "Plataforma de las mujeres salvadoreñas: Edición popular." Unpublished document, August.

———. 1994. "Compromisos de los candidatos(as) con el movimiento de mujeres de El Salvador." Unpublished document, March 8.

Mujeres por la dignidad y la vida. 1993. *Hacer política desde las mujeres.* San Salvador: Doble G Impresores.

Murguialday, Clara. 1990. *Nicaragua, revolución y feminismo (1977–1989).* Madrid: Editorial Revolución.

———. 1996. "Mujeres, transición democrática y elecciones: El Salvador en tiempos de posguerra." *Nueva Sociedad* (Caracas, Venezuela), no. 141 (January–February): 34–42.

Murillo, Rosario. 1991. "Mónica Boltodano: Las mujeres Sandinistas" *Ventana* (supplement to *Barricada*), no. 472 (June 3).

Nash, June. 1993. "Maya Household Production in the World Market: The Potters of Amatenango del Valle, Chiapas, Mexico." In June Nash, ed., *Crafts in the World Market: The Impact of Global Exchange on Middle-American Artesans.* Albany: State University of New York Press.

Nashat, Guity, ed. 1993. *Women and Revolution in Iran.* Boulder, Colo.: Westview Press.

National Commission for Democracy in Mexico. 1996a. "Ramona Recovering!" *Libertad* no. 7 (November–December): 1.

———. 1996b. ". . . Y la Comandante Ramona rompió el cerco militar." *Libertad,* no. 7 (November–December): 5.

———. 1997a. "Commandante Ramona inaugura Convención Nacional de Mujeres." *Libertad,* no. 10 (September–October): 3.

———. 1997b. "Ik' otik: We Are the Wind." *Libertad,* no. 11 (October–November): 1.

Navas, María Candelaria. 1985. "Los movimientos femeninos en Centroamerica: 1970–1983." In Daniel Camacho and Rafael Menjívar, eds., *Movimientos populares en Centroamérica.* San José, Costa Rica: EDUCA, FLACSO, UNU, IISUNAM.

———. 1987. "Las organizaciones de mujeres en El Salvador: 1975–1985." Master's thesis, Universidad Nacional Autonoma de Mexico,

Nazzari, Muriel. 1983. "The 'Woman Question' in Cuba: An Analysis of Material Constraints on Its Solution." *Signs* 9, no. 2 (Winter): 51–72.

Novak, Monica. 1999. "A Period of Transition and Redefinition: Post-Communist Polish Female Identity Through the Lens of the Private/Public Distinction." Honor's thesis, Knox College, May 20.

Nuñez Tellez, Carlos. 1981. "El problema fundamental de la mujer: Participar en las transformaciones revolucionarias." Transcript of speech given at the fourth Anniversary of AMNLAE, Managua, September 29.

———. 1986. "La Revolución es también transformadora de las relaciones personales y organización de las nuevas formas de vida." Unpublished document.

Núñez, Orlando, Gloria Cardenal, Amanda Lorío, Sonia Agurto, Juan Morales, Javier Pasquier, Javier Matus, and Rubén Pasos. 1998. *La guerra y el campesinado en Nicaragua*. Managua: Editorial Ciencias Sociales.

Oficina de la Mujer/AMNLAE. 1988. *Aportes al análisis del maltrato en la relación de pareja*. Managua: Libros Especiales (DILESA).

Olivera, Mercedes. 1994. "Aguascalientes y el movimiento social de las mujeres Chiapanecas." In Silvia Soriano Hernández, ed., *A propósito de la insurgencia en Chiapas,* 57–80. Mexico City: Asociación para el Desarrollo de la Investigación Científica y Humanística de Chiapas.

———. 1995. "Practica feminista en el Movimiento Zapatista de Liberación Nacional." In Rosa Rojas, ed., *Chiapas ¿Y las mujeres que?* Vol. 2, 168–84. Mexico City: Editorial La Correa Feminista.

———. 1996. "El Ejército Zapatista y la emancipación de las mujeres chiapanecas." In Mujeres por la Dignidad y la Vida (DIGNAS), eds., *Montañas con recuerdos de mujer: Una mirada feminista a la participación de las mujeres en los conflictos armados en Centroamérica y Chiapas,* 47–57. San Salvador: Algier's Impresores.

Oquist, Paul. 1992. "The Sociopolitical Dynamics of the 1990 Nicaraguan Elections." In Vanessa Castro and Gary Prevost, eds., *The 1990 Elections in Nicaragua and Their Aftermath,* 1–40. Lanham, Md.: Rowman and Littlefield.

Organización de Mujeres Guatemaltecas Refugiadas en México "Mamá Maquín." 1999. *Nuestra experiencia ante los retos del futuro*. San Cristóbal de las Casas: Editorial Fray Bartolomé de las Casas.

Padilla, Martha Luz, Clara Murguialday, and Ana Criquillón. 1987. "Impact of the Sandinista Agrarian Reform on Rural Women's Subordination." In Carmen Diana Deere and Magdalena León, eds., *Rural Women and State Policy,* 124–41. Boulder, Colo.: Westview Press.

Paige, Jeffery M. 1975. *Agrarian Revolution*. New York: Free Press.

———. 1997. *Coffee and Power: Revolution and the Rise of Democracy in Central America*. Cambridge: Harvard University Press.

Pardo-Maurer, R. 1990. *The Contras, 1980–1989: A Special Kind of Politics*. New York: Praeger.

Parsa, Misagh. 2000. *States, Ideologies, and Social Revolutions: A Comparative Analysis of Iran, Nicaragua, and the Philippines*. Cambridge: Cambridge University Press.

Payne, Leigh. 2000. *Uncivil Movements: The Armed Right and Democracy in Latin America*. Baltimore: Johns Hopkins University Press.

Pearce, Jenny. 1986. *Promised Land: Peasant Rebellion in Chalatenango, El Salvador*. London: Latin American Bureau.

Peterson, Anna L. 1997. *Martyrdom and the Politics of Religion: Progressive Catholicism in El Salvador's Civil War*. Albany: State University of New York Press.

Pérez Rojas, Niurka. 1979. *Características sociodemográficas de la familia cubana, 1953–1970.* Havana: Editorial de Ciencias Sociales.

Pérez U., Matilde, and Elio Henriquez. 1995. "Denuncia Aedpch la violencia contra indígenas ante la Procuraduría Estatal." *La Jornada,* October 6.

Pérez-Alemán, Paola. 1990. *Organización, identidad y cambio: Las campesinas en Nicaragua.* Managua: Centro de Investigación y Acción para la Promoción de los Derechos de la Mujer (CIAM).

———. 1992. "Economic Crisis and Women in Nicaragua." In Lourdes Benería and Shelley Feldman, eds., *Unequal Burden: Economic Crises, Persistent Poverty, and Women's Work.* Boulder, Colo.: Westview Press.

Pérez-Stable, Marifeli. 1987. "Cuban Women and the Struggle for 'Conciencia.'" *Cuban Studies* 17.

———. 1993. *The Cuban Revolution: Origins, Course, and Legacy.* New York: Oxford Press.

Petrich, Blanche. 1996. "Crece en México la violencia hacia mujeres indígenas y activistas: AI." *La Jornada,* March 10.

Pizarro Leongómez, Eduardo. 1996. *Insurgencia sin revolución: La guerrilla en Colombia en una perspectiva comparada.* Bogotá: Tercer Mundo Editores

Presidencia de la Republica. 1997. "Ley de organización, competencias y procedimientos del poder ejecutivo." Unpublished document, Managua.

Preston, Julia. 1996. "Zapatista Tour Offers Mud, Sweat, and Radical Chic: La Realidad Journal." *New York Times,* August 13, A5.

———. 1997. "Indian Rebels Draw Throng to a Rally in Mexico City." *New York Times,* September 14.

———. 1998a. "Feuding Indian Villages Bringing Mexican Region to Brink of War." *New York Times,* February 2, A1, A6.

———. 1998b. "Mexico Accuses Policeman of Helping Arm Mass Killers." *New York Times,* January 13, A6.

———. 1998c. "News (and State) Anchor Weighs His: Mexico City Journal." *New York Times,* January 20, A3.

Raleigh, Morrella S. 1994. "Riot grrls and revolution." Master's thesis, Bowling Green State University.

Ramírez Cuevas, Jesús. 1997. "Jamás atendió la policía estatal los llamados de auxilio: Testigos." *La Jornada,* December 30.

Randall, Margaret. 1981. *Sandino's Daughters: Testimonies of Nicaraguan Women in Struggle.* Vancouver: New Star Books.

———. 1992. *Gathering Rage: The Failure of Twentieth Century Revolutions to Develop a Feminist Agenda.* New York: Monthly Review Press.

———. 1993. "To Change Our Own Reality and the World: A Conversation with Lesbians in Nicaragua." *Signs: Journal of Women in Culture and Society* 18:907–24.

———. 1994. *Sandino's Daughter's Revisited.* New Brunswick: Rutgers University Press.

Ready, Kelley. 2001. "A Feminist Reconstruction of Fatherhood Within Neoliberal Constraints: La Asociación de Madres Demandantes in El Salvador." In Victoria González and Karen Kampwirth, eds., *Radical Women in Latin America: Right and Left.* University Park: Penn State University Press.

Reca Moreira, Inés, et al. 1990. *Análisis de las investigaciones sobre la familia cubana, 1970–1987.* Havana: Editorial de las Ciencias Sociales.

Reif, Linda L. 1986. "Women in Latin American Guerrilla Movements: A Comparative Perspective." *Comparative Politics* 18, no. 2 (January): 147–69.

Renard, María Cristina. 1997. "Movimiento campesino y organizaciones políticas: Simojovel-Huitiupán (1974–1990)." In Neus Espresate, ed., *Chiapas 4*, 93–110. Mexico City: Ediciones Era.

Reséndez Fuentes, Andrés. 1995. "Background Women: *Soldaderas* and Female Soldiers in the Mexican Revolution." *Americas* 51, no. 4 (April): 525–53.

Richards, Gareth. 1996. "A Plan of Action: The Women's Coalition." *Barricada Internacional*, no. 402 (November): 29.

Rodríguez, Candelaria. 1994. "Se repenaliza en Chiapas el aborto." In Rosa Rojas, ed., *Chiapas ¿Y las mujeres que?* 135–38. Mexico City: Ediciones la Correa Feminista.

Rodríguez, Ileana. 1996a. "Amor y patria: Desarmando el estado nacional." In DIGNAS, eds., *Montañas con recuerdos de mujer: Una mirada feminista a la participación de las mujeres en los conflictos armados en Centroamérica y Chiapas, memorias del Foro Regional, San Salvador, Diciembre 1995.* San Salvador: Algier's Impresores.

———. 1996b. *Women, Guerrillas, and Love: Understanding War in Central America.* Minneapolis: University of Minnesota Press.

Rodríguez Araujo, Octavio. 1995. "Tiempo y olvido." *La Jornada*, June 8.

Roiz Murillo, William. 1995. "Alfabetizadores rechazan afirmaciones de Chamorro, Tünnerman: Doña Violeta sabe que no fue asi." *Barricada*, April 27.

Rojas, Rosa. 1995a. "De la primera Convención Nacional de Mujeres a la Consulta Nacional del EZLN (cronología de los principales sucesos relacionados con las mujeres en torno al conflicto chiapaneco)." In Rosa Rojas, ed., *Chiapas ¿Y las mujeres que?* 3–70. Mexico City: Ediciones La Correa Feminista.

———. 1995b. Introduction to Rosa Rojas, ed., *Chiapas ¿Y las mujeres que?* Vol. 2, V–XII. Mexico City: Ediciones La Correa Feminista.

———. 1995c. "Negociaciones gobierno federal-EZLN: Primera fase de la mesa 1, grupo 4, sintesis indicativa, situación, derechos y cultura de la mujer indígena." In Rosa Rojas, ed., *Chiapas ¿Y las mujeres que?* 232–37. Mexico City: Ediciones La Correa Feminista.

———. 1995d. "Segunda fase de la Mesa de Larrainzar: Retroseso en los consensos del grupo de mujeres." In Rosa Rojas, ed., *Chiapas ¿Y las mujeres que?* 238–87. Mexico City: Ediciones La Correa Feminista.

———, ed. 1994. *Chiapas ¿Y las mujeres que?* Mexico City: Ediciones La Correa Feminista.

Rojas, Rosa, and José Gil. 1996a. "Pide una profunda reforma del estado." *La Jornada*, January 8.

———. 1996b. "Se prorroga el Foro Nacional." *La Jornada*, January 9.

Rojas, Rosa, and Elio Henriquez. 1995. "Acuerdos de Larráinzar sobre reconocimiento constitucional del sistema juridico indigena y sobre varios rubros de derechos de la mujer indigena." *La Jornada*, November 17.

Rojas Requena, Iliana, Mariana Ravenet Ramírez, and Jorge Hernández Martínez. 1985. *Sociología y desarrollo rural en Cuba.* Havana: Editorial de Ciencias Sociales.

Rosenbaum, Brenda. 1993. *With Our Heads Bowed: The Dynamics of Gender in a Mayan Community.* Albany: Institute for Mesoamerican Studies.

Rosemberg, Fulvia. 1992. "Education, Democratization, and Inequality in Brazil." In Nelly Stromquist, ed., *Women and Education in Latin America: Knowledge, Power, and Change.* Boulder, Colo.: Lynne Rienner.

Ross, John. 1995. *Rebellion from the Roots: Indian Uprising in Chiapas.* Monroe, Maine: Common Courage Press.

Rosset, Peter, and John Vandermeer, eds. 1986. *Nicaragua: Unfinished Revolution, the New Nicaragua Reader.* New York: Grove Press.

Rovira, Guiomar. 1995. "Mujeres indígenas: Protagonistas de la historia." *La Guillotina* 31 (August–September): 14–20.

———. 1997. *Mujeres de maíz.* Mexico City: Ediciones Era.

Ruchwarger, Gary 1985 "Las organizaciones de masas Sandinistas y el proceso revolucionario." In Richard Harris and Carlos Vilas, eds., *La revolución en Nicaragua: Liberación nacional, democracia popular y transformación económica* Mexico City: Ediciones Era.

Ruiz Hernández, Margarito. 1999. "La Asamblea Nacional Indígena Plural por la Autonomía (ANIPA)." In Aracely Burguete Cal y Mayor, ed., *México: Experiencias de autonomía indígena,* 21–53. Copenhagen: Grupo Internacional de Trabajo Sobre Asuntos Indígenas (IWGIA).

Ruiz Hernández, Margarito, and Aracely Burguete Cal y Mayor. 1998. "Chiapas: Organización y lucha indígena al final del milenio (1974–1998). *Asuntos Indígenas,* no. 3:27–33.

Ruiz Ortiz, Juana María. 1991. "El mandato de la mujer." *Anuario CEI II, 1989–1990,* 65–71. Tuxtla Gutiérrez: Universidad Autonoma de Chiapas.

Rus, Jan. 1995. "Local Adaptation to Global Change: The Reordering of Native Society in Highland Chiapas, Mexico, 1974–1994." *European Review of Latin American and Caribbean Studies* 58 (June): 71–89.

Russo, Tim. 2000. "A Day in a Zapatista Autonomous Community." *Report on the Americas* (NACLA [North American Congress on Latin America]) 33, no. 5 (March/April): 23.

Rust, Paula. 1995. *Bisexuality and the Challenge to Lesbian Politics: Sex, Loyalty, and Revolution.* New York: New York University Press.

Saadatmand, Yassaman. 1995. "Separate and Unequal Women in Islamic Republic of Iran." *Journal of South Asian and Middle Eastern Studies* 18, no. 4 (Summer): 1–24.

Salas, Elizabeth. 1990. *Soldaderas in the Mexican Military: Myth and History.* Austin: University of Texas Press.

Sanasarian, Eliz. 1983. "An Analysis of Fida'i and Mujahadin Positions on Women's Rights." In Guity Nashat, ed., *Women and Revolution in Iran,* 97–108. Boulder, Colo.: Westview Press.

Sargent, Lydia, ed. 1981. *Women and Revolution: A Discussion of the Unhappy Marriage of Marxism and Feminism.* Boston: South End Press.

Schirmer, Jennifer. 1993. "The Seeking of Truth and the Gendering of Consciousness." In Sarah Radcliffe and Sallie Westwood, eds., *Viva: Women and Popular Protest in Latin America*. New York: Routledge.

Schroeder, Susan. 1982. *Cuba: A Handbook of Historical Statistics*. Boston: G. K. Hall.

Schultz, Barry, and Robert Slater, eds. 1990. *Revolution and Political Change in the Third World*. Boulder, Colo.: Lynne Rienner.

Schwab, Theodore, and Harold Sims. 1985. "Relations with the Communist States." In Thomas Walker, ed., *Nicaragua: The First Five Years*. New York: Praeger.

Scott, Catherine V. 1994. "'Men in Our Country Behave Like Chiefs': Women and the Angolan Revolution." In Mary Ann Tétreault, ed., *Women and Revolution in Africa, Asia, and the New World*, 89–108. Columbia: University of South Carolina Press.

SEDEPAC (Servicio, Desarrollo y Paz, A.C.). 1996. *Propuestas e las mujeres indígenas al Congreso Nacional Indígena*. Mexico City: Benjamín Alvarez Ch.

Selbin, Eric. 1997. "Revolution in the Real World: Bringing Agency Back In." In John Foran, ed., *Theorizing Revolutions*. London: Routledge.

———. 1999. *Modern Latin American Revolutions*. 2d ed. Boulder, Colo.: Westview Press.

———. 2001. "Same as It Ever Was: The Future of Revolution at the End of the Century." In Mark Katz, ed., *Revolution: International Dimensions*, 284–97. Washington, D.C.: Congressional Quarterly Press.

Sheldon, Kathleen. 1994. "Women and Revolution in Mozambique: A Luta Continua." In Mary Ann Tétreault, ed., *Women and Revolution in Africa, Asia, and the New World*, 33–61. Columbia: University of South Carolina Press.

Shnookal, Deborah. 1991. *Cuban Women Confront the Future: Vilma Espín*. Melbourne: Ocean Press.

Siemienska, Renata. 1998. "Consequences of Economic and Political Changes for Women in Poland." In Jane Jaquette and Sharon Wolchik, eds., *Women and Democracy: Latin America and Central and Eastern Europe*, 125–52. Baltimore: Johns Hopkins University Press.

SIPAZ. 2000. *Informe de SIPAZ* 5, no. 4 (November). Available: http://www.sipaz.org/vol5no4/index.htm

Skocpol, Theda. 1979. *States and Social Revolutions*. Cambridge: Cambridge University Press.

———. 1994. *Social Revolutions in the Modern World*. Cambridge: Cambridge University Press.

Slater, David. 1994. "Power and Social Movements in the Other Occident: Latin America in an International Context." *Latin American Perspectives* 21 (Spring).

Smith, Christian. 1997. *Resisting Reagan: The U.S. Central America Peace Movement* Chicago: University of Chicago Press.

———. 1991. *The Emergence of Liberation Theology: Religion and Social Movement Theory*. Chicago: University of Chicago Press.

Smith, Lois, and Alfred Padula. 1996. *Sex and Revolution: Women in Socialist Cuba*. New York: Oxford Press.

Smith, Steven Kent. 1997. "Renovation and Orthodoxy: Debate and Transition Within the Sandinista National Liberation Front." *Latin American Perspectives*, issue 93, vol. 24, no. 2 (March): 102–16.

Soriano Hernández, Silvia. 1994. "Del Ejército de la Virgen al Ejército Zapatista." In Silvia Soriano Hernández, ed., *A propósito de la insurgencia en Chiapas*, 17–41. Mexico City: Asociación para el Desarrollo de la Investigación Científica y Humanística de Chiapas.

Soro. Julio. 1992. "Revolución en la Revolución: Las mujeres salvadoreñas y la construcción de la democracia." Unpublished manuscript.

Soro, Julio, et al. 1994. *Como los partidos políticos incluyen a las mujeres en sus plataformas políticas*. San Salvador: Red por la Unidad y el Desarollo de las Mujeres Salvadoreñas.

Spence, Jack, et al. 1994. *El Salvador: Elections of the Century, Results, Recommendations, Analysis*. Cambridge, Mass.: Hemisphere Initiatives.

Stacey, Judith. 1983. *Patriarchy and Socialist Revolution in China*. Berkeley and Los Angeles: University of California Press.

Stahler-Sholk, Richard. 1998. "The Lessons of Acteal." *Report on the Americas* (NACLA [North American Congress on Latin America]) 31, no. 5 (March/April): 11–14.

Stanley, William. 1996. *The Protection Racket State: Elite Politics, Military Extortion, and Civil War in El Salvador*. Philadelphia: Temple University Press.

Stavenhagen, Rodolfo. 1999. "Prólogo: Hacia el derecho de autonomía en México." In Aracely Burguete Cal y Mayor, ed., *México: Experiencias de autonomía indígena*, 7–20. Copenhagen: Grupo Internacional de Trabajo Sobre Asuntos Indígenas (IWGIA).

Stephen, Lynn. 1994a. "Convención Estatal de Mujeres Chiapanecas." Unpublished document, November 11.

———. 1994b. "Democratic Convention in Chiapas." *Peacework* (October): 6.

———. 1994c. "Eyewitness Report on the National Democratic Convention, Chiapas, Mexico." *Reporter on Latin America and the Caribbean* (November–December): 5.

———. 1994d. *Hear My Testimony: María Teresa Tula, Human Rights Activist of El Salvador*. Boston: South End Press.

———. 1995. "The Zapatista Army of National Liberation and the National Democratic Convention." *Latin American Perspectives*, issue 87, vol. 22, no. 4 (Fall): 88–99.

———. 1997. *Women and Social Movements in Latin America: Power from Below*. Austin: University of Texas Press.

Stephens, Beth. 1988. "Changes in the Laws Governing the Parent-Child Relationship in Post-Revolutionary Nicaragua." *Hastings International and Comparative Law Review* 12, no. 1 (Fall): 137–71.

Sternbach, Nancy Sporta, Marysa Navarro-Aranguren, Patricia Chuchryk, and Sonia Alvarez. 1992. "Feminisms in Latin America: From Bogotá to San Bernardo." In Arturo Escobar and Sonia Alvarez, eds., *The Making of Social Movements in Latin America: Identity, Strategy, and Democracy*, 207–39. Boulder, Colo.: Westview Press.

Stoll, David. 1990. *Is Latin America Turning Protestant? The Politics of Evangelical Growth*. Berkeley and Los Angeles: University of California Press.

Stoner, K. Lynn. 1991. *From the House to the Streets: The Cuban Women's Movement for Legal Reform, 1898–1940*. Durham: Duke University Press.

Stromquist, Nelly P., ed. 1992. *Women and Education in Latin America: Knowledge, Power, and Change*. Boulder, Colo.: Lynne Rienner.

Suchlicki, Jaime. 1969. *University Students and Revolution in Cuba, 1920–1968*. Coral Gables: University of Miami Press.

Sulloway, Frank J. 1996. *Born to Rebel: Birth Order, Family Dynamics, and Creative Lives*. New York: Pantheon Books.

Tejera Gaona, Héctor. 1996. "Las causas del conflicto en Chiapas." In Hubert C. De Grammont and Héctor Tejera Gaona, eds., *La sociedad rural frente al nuevo milenio*. Vol. 4: *Los nuevos actores sociales y procesos políticos en el campo*. Mexico City: Plaza y Valdés.

Tétreault, Mary Ann, ed. 1994. *Women and Revolution in Africa, Asia, and the New World*. Columbia: University of South Carolina Press.

Toledo Tello, Sonia. 1986. "El papel de la cultura en el proceso de subordinación de las mujeres indígenas de Chiapas." *Anuario* (San Cristóbal de las Casas: Universidad Autonoma de Chiapas), 1:73–87.

Townsend, Janet, Ursula Arrevillaga Matías, Socorro Cancino Córdova, Silvana Pachecho Bonfíl, and Elia Pérez Nasser. 1994. *Voces femeninas de las selvas*. Mexico City: Colegio de Postgraduados, Centro de Estudios del Desarollo Rural.

UNICEF (United Nations International Children's Emergency Fund). 1988. *Analysis de la situación de la mujer en El Salvador*. N.p.: San Salvador.

Univisión. 1989. "News Release." [Regarding Nicaraguan preelectoral poll]. (November 14).

Urrutia, Alonso, and Candelaria Rodríguez. 1995a. "Eduardo Robledo Solicitó licensia; pidió a Samuel Ruiz y Avendaño que renuncien." *La Jornada*, February 15.

———. 1995b. "Robledo se fue cuando estaba más fortalecido que nunca: Ganaderos." *La Jornada*, February 16.

U.S.–El Salvador Institute for Democratic Development. 1994. "Platform of the Women of El Salvador." Unpublished document

Valdés, Teresa, and Enrique Gomáriz. 1995. *Mujeres latinoamericanas en cifras*. Santiago de Chile: Ministerio de Asuntos Sociales de España/FLACSO Chile.

Vázquez, Norma, Cristina Ibáñez, and Clara Murguialday. 1996. *Mujeres-montaña: Vivencias de guerrilleras y colaboradoras del FMLN*. Madrid: Editorial horas y HORAS.

Venegas, Juan Manuel. 1997. "Madrazo: En Acteal, conflicto intercomunitario." *La Jornada*, December 27.

Venagas, Juan Manuel, and Angeles Mariscal. 1998. "Albores Guillén sustituye a Ruiz Ferro; riesgo de choques: EZLN." *La Jornada*, January 8.

Verdery, Katherine. 1994. "From Parent-State to Family Patriarchs: Gender and Nation in Contemporary Eastern Europe." *Eastern European Politics and Societies* 8, no. 2 (Spring): 225–55.

Vilas, Carlos. 1986. *The Sandinista Revolution: National Liberation and Social Trans-formation in Central America.* New York: Monthly Review Press.

———. 1995. *Between Earthquakes and Volcanoes: Market, State, and the Revolutions in Central America.* New York: Monthly Review Press.

Villafuerte Solís, Daniel, and María del Carmen García Aguilar. 1994. "Los altos de Chiapas en el contexto del neoliberalismo: Causas y razones del conflicto indígena." In Silvia Soriano Hernández, ed., *A propósito de la insurgencia en Chiapas,* 83–119. Mexico City: Asociación para el Desarrollo de la Investigación Científica y Humanística en Chiapas.

Walker, Thomas. 1981. *Nicaragua, the Land of Sandino.* Boulder, Colo.: Westview Press.

———, ed. 1985. *Nicaragua: The First Five Years.* New York: Praeger.

———, ed. 1987. *Reagan Versus the Sandinistas: The Undeclared War on Nicaragua.* Boulder, Colo.: Westview Press.

Waylen, Georgina. 1994. "Women and Democratization: Conceptualizing Gender Relations in Transition Politics." *World Politics* 46 (April): 327–54.

———. 1998. "Gender, Feminism, and the State: An Overview." In Vicky Randall and Georgina Waylen, eds., *Gender, Politics, and the State.* London: Routledge.

Wickham-Crowley, Timothy P. 1992. *Guerrillas and Revolution in Latin America: A Comparative Study of Insurgents and Regimes Since 1956.* Princeton: Princeton University Press.

———. 1997. "Structural Theories of Revolution." In John Foran, ed., *Theorizing Revolutions.* London: Routledge.

Williams, Philip. 1989. *The Catholic Church and Politics in Nicaragua and Costa Rica.* Pittsburg: University of Pittsburgh Press.

Williams, Philip, and Knut Walter. 1997. *Militarization and Demilitarization in El Salvador's Transition to Democracy.* Pittsburgh: University of Pittsburgh Press.

Wolf, Eric R. 1969. *Peasant Wars of the Twentieth Century.* New York: Harper and Row.

Womack, John. 1999. *Rebellion in Chiapas: An Historical Reader.* New York: New Press.

Wright, Robin. 2000. *The Last Great Revolution: Turmoil and Transformation in Iran.* New York: Alfred A. Knopf.

Zeitlin, Maurice. 1967. *Revolutionary Politics and the Cuban Working Class.* Princeton: Princeton University Press.

Zwerling, Philip, and Connie Martin. 1985. *Nicaragua: A New Kind of Revolution.* Chicago: Lawrence Hill Books.

PERIODICAL ISSUES AND ANONYMOUS ARTICLES

Barricada. 1992. "Más cambio para Managua: Agua potable, alcantarillado, pupitres." Paid advertisement. October 21, 2B.

———. 1995. "La señora Chamorro debe una disculpa." April 26.

Barricada Internacional. 1990. "Results of the Feb. 25, 1990 Elections." (March 10).

———. 1996a. "Finding Common Ground to Build On: National Women's Coalition." Vol. 16, no. 394 (March): 19–20.

———. 1996b. "Sharing Out the Spoils: Alemán Names His Cabinet." Vol. 16, no. 403 (December): 6–7

La Boletina: Un aporte de Puntos de Encuentro a la comunicación entre mujeres. 1992. No. 5 (March–April).

———. 1993. No. 10 (January).

———. 1996a. No. 25 (March).

———. 1996b. No 28 (October, November, December).

———. 1997a. "Los puntos en agenda del 'Ministro de la Familia'" (published by "Puntos de Encuentro," Managua). No. 30 (April, May, June): 12–19.

———. 1997b. "Ministerio de la Familia: No todo lo que brilla es oro!" No. 31 (July, August): 20–30.

———. 1998. "Con mujeres salvadoreñas: Para que inventar la pólvora si ya existe *La Boletina!*" No. 35 (May, June, July): 71–72.

———. 1999. Letter to the Editor from Bárbara Rojas Echeverría (Holguin, Cuba). No. 39. (April–June): 89.

———. 2000. "Comisarías de la mujer en peligro de extinción" (published by "Puntos de Encuentro," Managua). No. 41 (January): 36–39.

Envío. 1996–97a. "A New Period For the Nation: The 33 Days That Shook Nicaragua." Vol. 15, no. 185–86 (December–January).

———. 1996–97b. "The Roots of the Electoral Crisis: The 33 Days that Shook Nicaragua." Vol. 15, no. 185–86. (December–January).

———. 1998a. "A Test in Ethics for a Society in Crisis." Vol. 17, no. 200 (March): 3–9.

———. 1998b. "Cuban Women's History—Jottings and Voices." Vol. 17. no. 208 (November): 27–43.

Gente (supplement to *Barricada*). 1991. "El feminismo a La Nica." *Barricada* (Managua), March 8, 10.

La Jornada. 1996a. "Quien se esfuerza por la paz? El gobierno: 21.9%; el EZLN, 75.6%" (September 10).

———. 1996b. "Alianza Cívica: el gobierno, obligado a un viraje en el diálago en Chiapas." (September 11).

———. 1997. "Mas de 200 muertes desde 1995, saldo de acciones paramilitares: Datos de grupos defensores de derechos humanos: Datos de grupos defensores de derechos humanos." (December 28).

———. 1998. "Chiapas: Recambios en el Vacio." (January 8).

New York Times. 2000. "A Portrait of Mexican Voters." July 4, A6.

La Prensa. 1991. "Honores en Washington a Chamorro," April 15.

Prensa Gráfica. 1996. "Piden despenalizar el aborto," June 21, 3.

Index